Freedom to Offend

FREEDOM TO OFFEND

How New York Remade Movie Culture

RAYMOND J. HABERSKI JR.

THE UNIVERSITY PRESS OF KENTUCKY

Publication of this volume was made possible in part by a grant
from the National Endowment for the Humanities.

Scholarly publisher for the Commonwealth,
serving Bellarmine University, Berea College, Centre College of Kentucky,
Eastern Kentucky University, The Filson Historical Society, Georgetown
College, Kentucky Historical Society, Kentucky State University, Morehead
State University, Murray State University, Northern Kentucky University,
Transylvania University, University of Kentucky, University of Louisville,
and Western Kentucky University.

Editorial and Sales Offices: The University Press of Kentucky
663 South Limestone Street, Lexington, Kentucky 40508-4008
www.kentuckypress.com

11 10 09 08 07   5 4 3 2 1

Library of Congress Cataloging-in-Publication Data

Haberski, Raymond J., 1968-
  Freedom to offend : how New York remade movie culture / Raymond J.
Haberski, Jr.
    p. cm.
  Includes bibliographical references and index.
  ISBN-13: 978-0-8131-2429-2 (hardcover : alk. paper)
  ISBN-10: 0-8131-2429-8 (hardcover : alk. paper) 1. Motion pictures—
Censorship—New York (State)—New York—History. 2. Film criticism—
New York (State)—New York—History. 3. Motion pictures—New York
(State)—New York—History. I. Title.
PN1995.64.N495 2007
363.3109747'1—dc22   2006039696

 Member of the Association of
American University Presses

This book is dedicated to the memory of
Raymond E. Haberski (1916–2004)

Contents

Acknowledgments   ix

Introduction: Cinema Naïveté   1

1. The Web of Control   13

2. *The Miracle* and Bosley Crowther   39

3. *Baby Doll* and *Commonweal* Criticism   61

4. Amos Vogel and Confrontational Cinema   90

5. The "Flaming" Freedom of Jonas Mekas   119

6. The End of New York Movie Culture   152

7. Did *Bonnie and Clyde* Kill Bosley Crowther?   177

8. The Failure of Porno Chic   202

Conclusion:
The Irrelevance of Controversial Culture   224

Notes   231

Bibliography   251

Index   259

Acknowledgments

MY FIRST DEBT OF GRATITUDE goes to Jonas Mekas and the folks who help him operate Anthology Film Archives in New York City. Mekas and his staff gave me access to material that covered a significant period in the history of New York's avant-garde cinema and a formative period in Mekas's life. They did so with an openness characteristic of Mekas's approach to his work and his love of film. While my argument might seem critical of some of the decisions Mekas made during the mid-1960s, I continue to be a great admirer of the legacy that Mekas has forged almost in spite of the great odds that have always worked against him and the cinema he champions.

I was assisted in the archives of Lincoln Center for the Performing Arts by Judith Johnson and her very able staff. They made room for me amid the boxes of their small office as well as within their very busy schedules. I thank them for their consideration and help. Likewise, Charles Silver and Ronald Magliozzi at the Museum of Modern Art's Film Study Center helped me navigate through their various clippings collections during a period of renovation that forced the whole museum and all its departments to move to Queens. Their office was cramped, inadequate, and wholly unbecoming the kind of work they do, and yet these two film scholars have carried on a tradition of accommodation that has consistently been nothing less than heroic. I am also grateful to the New York State Archives for awarding me a Larry J. Hackman Research Residency grant to conduct research in the state's censorship files.

I have also had the good fortune to test a few of the arguments included in this book before diverse audiences. I thank the scholars of Copenhagen Business School who invited me to speak at a conference on popular culture in the Americas, especially Birgitte Madelung, Niels Bjerre-Poulsen, Dale Carter, and executive assistant Merete Borch. Graduate students of Ohio University's Department of History and Contemporary History Institute asked me to address them as one who had made it to the other side of graduate school and lived to tell the story. Lastly, Charles Van Eaton and his colleagues at Bryan College, especially Michael Palmer, gave me a wonderful opportunity to meet their excellent students and address their evangelical Christian community.

At Marian College, my friends and colleagues have helped me in ways too numerous to list. I have benefited from attentive listeners and engaging intellectuals, especially Dave Shumate, Carolyn Johnston, Patrick Kiley, Pierre Atlas, Bill Mirola, and Dave Benson. My work-study assistant Megan Hunter helped me amass many of the articles and essays in the bibliography, I thank her for her diligent work. The library staff at Marian was quick to respond to my requests and patient with my late books. I appreciate all the support that the Marian community in general has consistently shown me.

While writing can be a lonely pursuit, I have benefited from the encouragement of an intellectual community that included Laura Wittern-Keller, Robert Brent Toplin, Ralph Leck, Alonzo Hamby, Peter Rollins, Ray Carney, Louis Menand, Dana Polan, and good friends and fellow historians Marc Selverstone and Jeff Coker. George Cotkin provided me with his editorial and historical expertise at a number of stages during the process of writing and reviewing this manuscript, and I am grateful for his gentle but always persuasive suggestions. Charley Alexander and Dave Steigerwald willingly gave an earlier version of this manuscript a careful and thoughtful reading. Their advice improved what remains, though I absolve them and George of responsibility for lingering weaknesses.

Those who provided shelter and conversation during my New York sojourns include historian Steve Remy and his wife, Beth Kilgore; Christian Thiim and his wife, Sumana; and close family friends Pilar Cragan and Bob and Claudia Klein. They made research in New York a treat and have humbled me with their affection.

To my family I owe my deepest thanks. My uncles, aunts, and cousins were generous in their interest—especially Brian Shields and Michael Manley—and even more generous with their love. My in-laws, Ellyn and Gene Kroupa, have welcomed me into their family with unqualified acceptance and affection; I thank them for making Madison a second home for me. My sisters and their mates are both my dearest friends and most faithful supporters. I can still fail, but never in their eyes. For my parents, my career as a historian is a triumph, and for that I am eternally grateful to them. During the writing of this book I made two enormous leaps: I got married and my wife gave birth to our baby girl. Suddenly going to the movies didn't seem like such a big deal anymore. In other words, I am enchanted with my girls.

This book is dedicated to the memory of the grandfather after whom my dad and I take our first names, Raymond E. Haberski. He was the type of person who earned the easy admiration of others. I wish the world were populated with more like him.

Introduction

Cinema Naïveté

WE LIVE ALONG a cultural fault line that constantly threatens the vitality of the arts in America. On one side of this fault is the commonplace complaint that there is too much sex, violence, and offensive material in art and media. On the other side is an equally strong force that defends speech and expression in absolute terms, that resists anything that smells of censorship, and that elevates art of all kinds to an irreproachable level. Occupying but often lost in the cultural space between these two positions is a delicate ironic stance. This is an irony that contextualizes the concerns of both sides but remains independent enough to resist the Manichean terms of the debate. Without such irony we get riots over cartoons, churches boycotting movies with gay characters, and museum curators staunchly defending urine-soaked crucifixes.

It was the absence of such irony that made a recent documentary so noteworthy to me. In 2005, Brian Grazer, a producer of Hollywood hits and a recipient of Academy Awards, released a documentary about the notorious 1972 pornographic film *Deep Throat*. The result, *Inside Deep Throat*, characterized the most successful porn movie ever made as a kind of cultural landmark—a symbol of resistance against forces of repression and censorship. In the summer of 1972, New York City police officers, acting as part of a citywide crackdown on pornography, confiscated prints of *Deep Throat* from the Manhattan theater at which it premiered. And while few claimed either in 1972 or in 2005 that *Deep Throat* was a great film, many suggested that the public had a right to see it because we live in a democracy.[1]

Thus, *Inside Deep Throat* created the impression that all cultural

1

expressions have inherent legitimacy, and that even one as dubious as *Deep Throat* is worthy of defense. But a defense based on what? Sheila Nevins of HBO Documentary, the distributor of *Inside Deep Throat*, offered a classic rationale. She related how Grazer had convinced her that *Deep Throat* was "much more than a silly comic romp that featured fellatio as its centerpiece." Indeed, she came to view the legal storm surrounding it as an "emblem of repressive forces attempting to halt a certain kind of expression." Nevins recounted: "Brian was incredibly convincing when he talked about how, in some ways, 1972 and 2005 aren't so very different in terms of repressive forces and that maybe America hasn't changed so much in three decades." It is true that since the early 1970s, Americans have come to accept a strange hypocrisy: they express moral indignation when faced with modest displays of nudity (as was recently illustrated by the outrage elicited by Janet Jackson's exposed breast) but continue to spend hundreds of millions of dollars a year on pornography. Yet in her defense of *Deep Throat*, Nevins identified the source of this hypocrisy without necessarily understanding the implications of it. She noted that while *Deep Throat* was not a great movie, "it has a right to exist in a democracy." Why? Because it was a "political movie . . . almost a First Amendment movie in a strange way." Fair enough, but what does that defense suggest about culture? Isn't it a bit naive to see porn as progress?[2]

The *New Yorker's* film critic Anthony Lane thought so. He skeptically observed that the makers of *Inside Deep Throat* imagined with a kind of wistful nostalgia a bygone era brimming "with Ambrosian innocence." Indeed, the documentary rehashed an old argument that when *Deep Throat* entered the mainstream, American culture had reached the apex of a pluralistic age in which all artistic expressions could at last compete in a kind of paradise of audience choice. Thus, *Deep Throat* represented an intellectual and artistic vanguard—a moment that coupled filmic liberation with sexual liberation.[3]

However, that argument perpetuated a strange kind of intellectual misconception: that in a democratic culture, in order for anything to be created, everything must have cultural worth. This is a misconception that has many well-meaning supporters. For example, the very able film historian Jon Lewis (one of the on-screen defenders of *Deep Throat*) goes so far as to suggest in his book *Hollywood v. Hardcore* that the mainstreaming of porn was not an unintelligent fad but rather something that "spoke . . . to and for a number of late-sixties/early-seventies phenomena ranging from the sexual revolution to women's lib and the civil rights movement." An attack on porn represented, according to Lewis and evidently the makers of *Inside Deep Throat*, nothing less than an attack on democracy. The implicit lesson of the film was that the only alternative to defending *Deep Throat* was censoring *Deep Throat*. Of course, the subtext of almost any discussion of a controversial piece of culture is that to reject it or refuse to defend it leads in one direction—repression.[4]

Thus, *Inside Deep Throat* illustrated a common conundrum in evaluating controversial culture—one that typically pits the free speech folks against the moral code folks. Both groups take popular culture very seriously, so seriously that they are usually willing to resort to abstractions and extremes in order to defend their positions. Free speech absolutists protect every cultural expression as if it might be the last—as one libertarian critic put it regarding Oliver Stone's *Natural Born Killers*, "the First Amendment protects bad art as well as good." That might be true, but that defense strikes me as a cop-out; bad art can hide behind a legal abstraction rather than face an aesthetic test. Advocates of a universal moral code find every transgression against their standards to be part of an invidious invasion that if left unchecked will destroy the very edifice on which their belief system rests. Speaking about the Hollywood release *Brokeback Mountain*, one commentator concluded that this single movie had "a pernicious effect on society." Surely the sexuality of gay cowboys is less of a threat to our social health than the cigarettes they smoke. Nonetheless, we are caught between arguments that flow from abstractions. Both make sense to a certain degree. Should not movies and other artistic expressions be protected as free speech? But it also seems sensible, at the least, to address concerns about the accumulation of offensive culture.[5]

These positions, though, actually say more about how we see each other than about what we are watching on movie screens. Even though both sides appeal to the idea of democratic culture, their actions illustrate that they don't trust anybody very much. Free speech absolutists distrust all authority and therefore dismiss any attempt to restrict culture out of fear that something meaningful will be lost; moralists distrust human nature and therefore seek to restrict culture out of fear that something meaningful will be found in culture they dislike. And each side works from the assumption that the world would be a better place if only its vision won out—in a democratic forum, of course. Under such pressure, democratic culture has become a clash of egos—a conflict that reduces discussion about culture to a game of winner takes all.[6]

I see this predicament as a consequence of flawed logic that fails to appreciate the irony of taking movies too seriously. I do not mean that we in the audience can't be offended or that there is no recourse when we are. Yet I am consistently amazed at how easily we are manipulated by controversies seemingly manufactured—and definitely marketed—to get a rise out of us. The titles of movies that do this are almost interchangeable, the themes consistent: sex, violence, religion, and occasionally politics. At the same time, however, it is disheartening to watch how quickly and somewhat mindlessly offensive movies are defended—many are barely worth protecting as bad art, much less as significant speech.

To get a better understanding of the culture that gave rise to a defense of *Deep Throat*, this book investigates debates over controversial films, debates that began almost immediately after the Second World War and flourished primarily in one city, New York. While not the only place where audiences watched controversial movies, New York had critics, media, theaters, audiences, and censors that, taken together, transformed moviegoing into an intellectual and cultural circus. Moreover, debates within New York movie culture illustrated that the public exhibition of a film such as *Deep Throat* was more than merely the sum total of changes to laws. In other words, while the courts gradually outlawed the practice of prior censorship—censoring a film before the public sees it—a conversation took place in New York over the expectations and concerns of a postcensor movie culture. That conversation has had consequences for our own time because it remade the idea of confrontational cinema into a kind of intellectual style. The appearance of outrage has grown more important than engaging what provokes it.[7]

From the beginning of American cinema, New York had been the largest market for every type of film and, as a result, was a place in which moviegoing often became a public act of defiance against cultural authority. New York served as the center of a web of control that had the potential to ensnare any movie shown in the United States. Almost every movie that played in the United States premiered in New

York, but before a distributor was allowed to book a movie in theaters in other parts of the country, it had to receive the approval of the most influential state censorship board in the country, the New York State Motion Picture Division. Moreover, the New York City license commissioner possessed the power to close down any theater that played a movie deemed obscene by his office. New York was also home to millions of Catholics, a fact that helped amplify the influence of the Legion of Decency—an organization established within the Catholic Church to influence moviegoing through widely publicized reviews and, more ominously, the threat of public boycotts against films "condemned" by the Legion. Assisting the Legion in the prevention of "immoral" films was the Production Code Administration (PCA), Hollywood's in-house censorship board. The PCA maintained a New York office that carefully scrutinized movies under a set of standards that had been written at the insistence and with the cooperation of the U.S. Catholic Church. So even though Hollywood was the undisputed filmmaking capital of the country, New York was the place that could make or break a movie.[8]

In the early postwar period, challenges to this regime of control were part of a general intellectual movement that sought to legitimize mass culture while protecting it from censorship. Those who opposed censorship believed that censoring movies not only failed to realize an idealized version of American life but amounted to antidemocratic containment of a legitimate form of speech and art, thus preventing the production of better films. Brooks Atkinson, a cultural critic for the *New York Times* in the 1940s, offered a concise illustration of that argument. From his rather privileged post at the *Times*, Atkinson railed against both censors and the popular disposition that supported censorship because he believed this regime of control was both arbitrary and wholly undemocratic. He seemed especially outraged by a disjunction that he believed was inimical to New York City—although the city was fast becoming the cultural capital of the world, its culture was still under the control of bureaucratic simpletons.[9]

As an example, he pointed to the administrative code of New York City that allowed the city's commissioner of licenses to inspect and close down a variety of establishments, ranging from unclean kitchens to theaters that showed "dirty" movies. "No free society can afford," he declared, "to delegate to any one man or any group of people authority to censor ideas, points of view, morals or manners by any process that evades the courts and remains outside the law. . . . To be fully democratic, such cases should be tried before legally constituted juries of citizens. For it is the citizens of a community who in the last analysis have a right to decide questions of this nature." Atkinson concluded that a collective public conscience would regulate movies much better and more fairly because movies were, in a very real sense, the people's art. He trusted that in a democratic culture, the rational nature and sympathies of the people would ultimately prevail. "Even without court action or censorship," he argued, "the public would never tolerate as accurate a portrayal of everything that happens among human beings in the ordinary course of daily affairs." Was he wrong?[10]

Ultimately, he was, and the lines of people waiting to see an "accurate" portrayal of sex in *Deep Throat* proved that. Yet Atkinson's faith that both movies and audience taste for them would improve with the elimination of censorship, while a bit naive, was understandable. He was responding to a sensibility that was hopelessly limited.

Atkinson defended the movies as free speech to counter the work of stalwarts such as Martin Quigley, who for nearly thirty years, from the 1930s through the early 1960s, was a fixture of the censorial establishment. As a staunch Catholic, Quigley believed in the moral imperative to constrain the power of movies. He was also the publisher of the influential industry journal *Motion Picture Herald,* and as such used his position to become a major force behind the creation of Hollywood's Production Code. This was a commercial arrangement—one that proved to be lucrative for both Quigley and the studios because the studios paid Quigley to ensure the safety, and therefore the financial viability, of their movies. And yet Quigley also offered an intellectual rationale for his stance. In 1958, near the end of his career, Quigley told an interviewer that he did "not believe the concept of 'unnatural behavior' at any time or under any circumstance provides acceptable subject matter for mass entertainment. . . . I see no relation whatsoever between 'out-and-out vulgarity' and a 'work of art.' . . . Art of all kinds has as its primary purpose the ennoblement of man, and however excellent a work of art may be—a *so-called* work of art may be—if its influence is a depraving influence and not an ennobling influence, I do not believe it's entitled to be labeled a work of art." Quigley subscribed to a view of culture that rested on a simplified version of Matthew Arnold's dictum that defined culture as the best that is known and thought in the world. For those like Quigley who supported censorship, the Victorianism of a nineteenth-century British critic made sense because it suggested that social responsibility—the betterment of society—was at the heart of restricting movies. Not surprisingly, Hollywood's moguls found it exceedingly difficult to challenge such an approach without denigrating their industry's image and losing their audience. Moreover, it was an approach that appealed to those civil servants—state and local censors—who were charged with protecting the public from mass entertainment.[11]

Quigley's view undoubtedly had a chilling effect on the ability of the film industry to deal with certain subjects or to show certain scenes. No doubt such constraint was unreasonable because the standards on which it was based showed little faith in the intelligence of filmmakers or moviegoers. However, Quigley's objections also raised a fundamental dilemma for popular art. As popular art, movies have always required a defense that goes beyond a circular argument that whatever can be captured or portrayed on film has inherent worth. Of course, distinguishing good art from bad is a much more vexing problem than deciding what should be censored. In other words, in the absence of censorship, there still needs to be a way to guide public taste.

In the postwar period, two seminal New York critics established the parameters within which the broad discussion of postcensor movie culture would take place. Gilbert Seldes and Susan Sontag, writing from different generations and from different intellectual positions, offered insight that revealed both the great promise and the great problems of freeing an expression as popular as the movies from the effects of a censoring mind-set. Their insight was especially significant because it took shape within New York's movie culture—the crucible of a new popular aesthetic.

With the publication of his first book in 1924, *The Seven Lively Arts*, Gilbert Seldes established himself as the most judicious observer of the popular arts in America. In 1950, Seldes's second book appeared, *The Great Audience*. In the intervening years, Seldes had observed that the popular arts had begun to influence and even replace the traditional arts in significance and relevance to a majority of Americans. That development, he mused, led to a broad revision of taste. Unlike in his first book, though, Seldes was guarded in his celebration of popular culture. The popular arts, he concluded, "create their own audience, making people over; they create the climate of feeling in which we all live. The other arts are private and personal, they influence the lives of those who enjoy them; the effect of the public arts cannot be escaped by turning off the radio or television set, by refusing to go to the movies; neither indifference nor our contempt give us immunity against them." Seldes seemed to suggest that the cumulative effect of millions of people watching hundreds (perhaps thousands) of movies had once and for all altered the calculus of art. A film could be a work of art in its own right and, more important, the culture that surrounded a film—the relationship it had to its audience—made moviegoing almost as significant as the work on the screen. Thus, even though a movie might be dismissed as artistically negligible, the numbers of people flocking to it gave it cultural power. That power translated into money for the producers and a realignment of popular taste.[12]

Seldes feared this great audience because, if left unchecked, its taste in movies threatened to turn American culture into an Orwellian nightmare—the "great audience" as the core of cultural fascism. Popularity, relevance, and taste would merge into a mass of vulgarized entertainment. Here he shared and anticipated the concerns of other critics who issued grave warnings against the pervasive influence of mass culture.[13]

But Seldes found hope in a financial crisis that hit Hollywood during the early postwar period. For decades the American industry had pumped out a product that tended to be generic; it was a system that allowed Hollywood to treat moviegoers with a kind of industrial arrogance. That began to change in the late 1940s, as movie attendance suffered a dramatic decline. "All we can be sure of," Seldes contended, "is that to attract a large audience the movies would be compelled to satisfy many more *kinds* of interest; they would have to become a genuinely democratic, instead of a mass-minority, entertainment; and in a democracy like ours, encouragement of individual interests and satisfaction of many various desires are the surest protection against the constant threat of robotization and the ultimate emergence of the mass man." Seldes hoped that Hollywood, out of commercial necessity and in line with the era's democratic atmosphere, might create a movie culture that accommodated a wide diversity of preferences but avoided the leveling of all cultural expressions. The result would be culture for the masses but not mass culture. And the model for this alternative movie world was New York, because it had sizeable audiences for almost every kind of film available—from the first-run Hollywood productions to avant-garde shorts.[14]

Susan Sontag believed that New York's diverse movie culture had to influence not merely the kinds of movies produced but the style of criticism needed to understand them. By the mid-1960s, Sontag provocatively dismissed the prevailing opinion that mass culture had to meet a standard that would somehow ensure better movies and a more refined audience. In a series of radical essays published in 1966 as a book entitled *Against Interpretation,* Sontag argued that American culture needed a way to transcend the ideal of linking culture to society's moral health. In one of her manifestos, she contended that a "new sensibility" had emerged that rejected the evaluation of art based on content and social purpose. She dismissed older forms of judgment as misguided because they had overlooked the aesthetic pleasure of form. Art didn't need to be intentional or political or social; in her terms, the act of understanding a work of art or even a movie rested on personal, almost instinctual reactions rather than interpretation shaped by an overly cautious—and overtly political—elite.[15]

The problem was, however, that Sontag did not necessarily want to advance the democratization of criticism—not all opinions were equal. She continued to believe in a rigorous notion of taste, but not one based on criteria external to the individual observer. As critic Craig Seligman suggests in a recent book, Sontag relished taking a position that opposed both prevailing authority and the masses. Yet such intellectual gymnastics ultimately trapped her in a cultural conundrum. In "Notes on Camp," her most provocative essay in the book, Sontag set herself up for disappointment. "A sensibility," she coyly began, "is one of the hardest things to talk about; but there are special reasons why Camp, in particular, has never been discussed. It is not a natural mode of sensibility, if there be any such. Indeed the essence of Camp is its love of the unnatural: of artifice and exaggeration. And Camp is esoteric—something of a private code, a badge of identity even, among small urban cliques." Indeed, Sontag had created an interesting dilemma: in celebrating camp for its ability to subvert the stodgiest manifestations of traditional criticism, she had made it possible to discover new cultural avenues without feeling silly or irrelevant. But camp could also be used to champion transgressive culture as an end in itself. A camp sensibility seemed to promote the willful disregard for anyone else's sensibility.[16]

Her criticism promised a curious distinction to those who embraced it—it was ambiguous and yet clever in its promise of power. "To share a sensibility in words, especially one that is alive and powerful," she cautioned, "one must be tentative and nimble." So nimble, it seemed, that even Sontag got caught in the rush to adopt the camp sensibility. Seligman relates that Sontag "cringed at 'the speed at which a bulky essay in *Partisan Review* [became] a hot tip in *Time*'; the ten thousand readers of *Partisan Review*, she once joked to a student audience, 'were all the readers I ever wanted to have—until I was dead, of course.'"[17]

So how did Sontag's work become so hot? She wrote it in New York about a culture that was emerging around her at a moment when that city had become attractive to the rest of country as a symbol of cultural subversion. The force and popularity of her essay on camp, though, burdened Sontag with a dubious legacy—she has been blamed for the decline of criticism by, in Hilton Kramer's words, ennobling the idea of "failed seriousness." Seligman dismisses Kramer's accusation but also acknowledges that it was Sontag who made it intellectually respectable to embrace art as a primarily adversarial act. In Sontag, we can see how cultural experience morphed from Seldes's rather optimistic notion of culture as individual diversity in pursuit of a common goal to Sontag's ultimately cynical notion of criticism as a secret cabal that exists to subvert whatever is mainstream. In short, Seldes hoped New York's movie culture might alter American moviegoing; Sontag suggested the force of New York's influence would simply make traditional moviegoing irrelevant.[18]

Nothing illustrated the troubling implications of Sontag's revolt better than her serious defense of pornography. In 1967, Sontag published "The Pornographic Imagination." Her intention in the essay was not to defend all porn but to advance a discussion about obscenity in art beyond the social effects pornography had on society. Sontag pointed out that it was nearly impossible to measure the effects of any cultural expression on an individual. However, it was possible, she contended, to imagine changing artistic standards to accommodate works of art that were offensive but still significant.

To be fair, Sontag elevated works of literature. And it is hard to argue with her evaluation that in the past many of the greatest works of art had initially been scrutinized solely for their potential to corrupt the public. Yet, in a strange twist of logic, Sontag at once rejected the rationale of censorship but also relied on moral codes that made art controversial. For her vision, an artist acted most strongly when he or she was transgressive. The only way to be transgressive was to violate laws and standards that mattered. She believed that an artist was a "freelance explorer of spiritual dangers . . . making forays into and taking up positions on the frontiers of consciousness." It was a role that allowed an artist more latitude than the rest of society in both what was explored and how it was reported. This was, she explained, the "dialectic of outrage." The artist "seeks to make his work repulsive, obscure, inaccessible; in short, to give what is, or seems to be, *not* wanted. . . . The exemplary modern artist is a broker in madness." Thus, this kind of artist had to be brutal and dangerous in order to be effective—something traditional authorities had wanted to protect society from.[19]

Sontag's vision struck a chord in the late 1960s because it reimagined the heroic artist as something made possible only when the audience joined the heroic project of transgressing boundaries. While the artist offended public norms, the audience was expected to acknowledge the obscenity and, following the new sensibility, to become an accomplice to the cultural crime. She called this the "poetry of transgression." "He who transgresses not only breaks a rule. He goes somewhere that the others are not; and he knows something the others don't know." How intoxicating it was to imagine knowing something that others do not. There are few areas of knowledge more off-limits than pornography. Taken to its logical end, the combination of the new sensibility and the pornographic imagination made defending pornography as art a heroic public act.[20]

To discuss literary pornography in the abstract might seem reasonable, since there must be a place at which the vestiges of humaneness meet the edges of brutality. However, seeing pornographic films as mere abstractions simply provided a rather glossy veneer for a pretty shabby experience. And this was Sontag's unfortunate and probably unintentional contribution to the age that made *Deep Throat* significant. It became intellectually chic to think of pornography as an art form in need of a defense.

We can forgive Sontag for being hopeful, yet we must mourn her naïveté. While she had no illusions that the expansion of culture to include pornography was going to make better citizens of everyone, her type of criticism turned democracy and pluralism on its head. Rather than propose a world where everyone is a critic, the new sensibility and the pornographic imagination, taken to their ultimate conclusion, could thrive only in a world without critical thought. If Sontag had hoped to shift the discussion about American culture from what was good and bad to what was a worthwhile experience, she succeeded. But instead of adding worth to culture, she ensured that the debate would dissolve into one over permissibility rather than suitability.

This was the other side of the looking glass—what had been high culture was denigrated as inauthentic; what had been obscene culture was elevated to new heights of promise. But armed with a new sensibility, all experience could find an aesthetic. In a fine critique of Sontag's argument, cultural critic Rochelle Gurstein noted: "What is at stake here is not only our judgment about which kinds of aesthetic experience are worth having but, more fundamentally, the limits of knowledge and the limits of representation."[21]

Yet how should these limits be set, and who should set them? After all, we don't need a public watchdog or gatekeeper protecting us from our own tastes, do we? I believe we need something more than what we have now. I do not want censors or courts telling us what is good art and what is bad. Rather, I want a culture that encourages us to defend our tastes—our aesthetic decisions. We cannot fall back on legal and moral abstractions when aesthetic concerns are at stake. When we rely on abstractions we lose a necessary irony. Without this irony we become incapable of distinguishing the controversy over *Deep Throat* from one that erupted at the same theater twenty-two and one-half years earlier. This book aims to change that by returning to December 1949.

1

The Web of Control

WHEN *THE BICYCLE THIEF* premiered in 1949 at Manhattan's World Theater, it revealed what was wrong and what was right with American movie culture. The story line of the film had little in common with the typical feel-good picture produced in America. Vitorrio de Sica, the film's director, depicted the pathos of postwar Italian life through the story of a young father's search for his stolen bicycle. Film historian Gregory Black suggests: "Had Hollywood gotten its hands on the script Antonio [the father] would likely have recovered his bicycle, and the last scene would have shown him riding off to work with his proud wife and son waving from the doorway." Instead, the film ends with the father broken and crying, walking down a crowded Italian street in shame, holding his little boy's hand. And yet the picture grossed more at the World in the first five weeks of its run than any foreign film had previously. It was popular because it was so different than the typical Hollywood film, but it was given a chance to be popular because it opened in New York.[1]

The weekend before the film's premier, the *New York Times Magazine* helped create a buzz by running a two-page photo spread profiling the two stars, Enzo Staiola, who played Bruno, the little boy, and Lamberto Maggiorani, his screen father. The *Times* made special mention that neither had any previous acting experience, which contributed to their performances' being "remarkable and moving." Likewise, *Commonweal*, a Catholic weekly written by laypeople, ran a review the week after the movie's New York premier, claiming that the plot was as "realistically simple (and complicated) as life." Reviewers in a number of American publications lauded the perceptive camera work that

laid bare the desperation of postwar Italy. *Commonweal* had particular
praise for the "realistic portrayal of emotions." The reviewer concluded: "'The Bicycle Thief' is a well-rounded slice of life and as a movie it
is a gem of understanding." John Mason Brown, writing in the popular
Saturday Review, expressed his respect for the director's delicate balance of sorrow and humor. Foreign films, Brown noted, had been doing this with great skill since the end of the war. It seemed to him that
because the film's realism appeared so "unposed and uncontrived," the
understated tone of the picture achieved its "power by making everything exceptional in it appear to be average." Such vision eluded American filmmakers. "Hollywood, even in its most courageous moments,"
Brown argued, approached "our very real, though dissimilar, problems
in terms of make-believe. Instead of showing things as they are, it puts
on a show." As America's "Dream Factory," the movie industry had
made itself wealthy by eschewing reality, yet it was still realistic enough
to respond to changes in audience tastes.[2]

The success of *The Bicycle Thief* in New York City attracted the
attention of Warner Bros., one of Hollywood's movie conglomerates,
which hoped to book the film for its theaters in other cities. That was
exactly what Joseph Burstyn, the film's New York–based distributor,
hoped would happen. The film had opened at a small art theater, the
type that catered to a particular segment of the mass audience for movies. Burstyn had made a name for himself by importing a string of foreign films—many in the emerging genre of Italian neorealism—that
had enjoyed modest commercial but exceptional critical success in the
relatively small exhibition market. Like other Italian films, such as *Pai-
san* and *Open City*, *The Bicycle Thief* fell into a pattern of distribution
that Burstyn had honed to a commercial art—a small but devoted New
York City audience loved it, and critics writing for the city's newspapers and journals lauded it. Burstyn had imported a winner, and if he
could score big in the nation's single largest movie market—New York
City—he had a shot at a wide national distribution.

Responding to Warner Bros.' request, Burstyn mailed a print to
Hollywood's in-house review board, the Production Code Administration. On 31 January 1950, the head of the PCA, Joseph Breen, wrote
to Burstyn after screening the film. Speaking for the PCA, Breen asked
for revisions to the final cut, demanding the excision of two scenes: one
that showed the young boy relieving himself against a wall and another

of a very brief and quite innocent look inside a brothel. Why require such cuts? As Leonard Leff and Jerold Simmons explain in their history of the PCA, Breen "simply believed . . . that if he ever allowed even the most innocent of toilet gags, unscrupulous producers would flood the screen with them." Differentiating between crass commercialism and art was not something Breen, or almost any other authority in movie culture, considered part of his job.[3]

On his end, Burstyn followed his instincts and Vittorio de Sica's orders and refused to make cuts to the finished film. Appreciating what a little controversy might mean to the success of the movie, Burstyn attempted to get as much mileage out of Breen's decision as he could. Throughout 1950, while a contest of wills thrust the small Italian film into the spotlight, Burstyn ran ads in New York City papers highlighting the PCA's attempts to "cut" the film. In one layout advertising the film in theaters all over the five boroughs of New York City, Westchester, Long Island, and northern New Jersey, an oversized cartoon depicted Bruno in his controversial pose: with his back to readers, he declares, "I'm the kid they tried to cut out of Bicycle Thief . . . But couldn't!" Under the film's title were the series of awards it had won, including Best Foreign Film of the Year from the New York Film Critics Circle and the National Board of Review's top prize as the Best Film of the Year. Elsewhere, ads for the World Theater presented Bruno in one of his tragic scenes, seeming to look up at a statement that read "Please don't let them cut me out of . . . *Bicycle Thief*" (with the title in full movie announcement type). This was, the World announced, "the prize picture they want to censor!" But people who came to the World would see the "Uncensored Version!" of the movie playing for its "6th Month!" For anyone living in New York City or anywhere close to it, it would have been hard to avoid awareness of de Sica's relatively small film.[4]

Compounding the controversy caused by *The Bicycle Thief* was the fact that both state and city censors had allowed its exhibition. The New York State Board of Censorship licensed the film on 8 December 1949 after the elimination of two lines of dialogue—both referring to the brothel scene. Without such a license, Burstyn would have been in violation of state law if he had attempted to screen the film. Furthermore, the review board of the Catholic Church, the Legion of Decency, based in New York, gave the film a B rating, meaning that it was "objectionable in part" but not bad enough to condemn outright. The Knights of Columbus did, though, picket a few New York City theaters that showed it because the group believed it glorified crime. But, again, Burstyn and the owner of the World were fortunate in that the most effective unofficial censorship body had "passed" the film.[5]

Even politicians typically hostile to the movies came out in favor of it. Colorado senator Edwin C. Johnson had caused a stir in Hollywood when he introduced a bill in March of 1950 proposing to require a federal licensing process for most people involved in making movies. Johnson argued for a "practical method whereby the mad dogs of the industry may be put on a leash to protect public morals." Breen might have agreed with the rationale, even if he couldn't agree to the bill without supporting the elimination of his job. But Johnson's opinion of *The Bicycle Thief* was that it was "the most fascinating and engrossing picture I had ever seen." To Breen's chagrin, he stood alone as seemingly the only authority figure to reject the picture.[6]

Burstyn challenged Breen's ruling by appealing to the Motion Picture Association of America (MPAA)—the parent organization that governed Hollywood from New York, the industry's financial capital. It was a bold attempt to circumvent the PCA and Hollywood tradition, for if it had proved successful it could have spelled the end of Breen's reign. Forces on both sides built their cases: Burstyn had defenders such as Bosley Crowther at the *New York Times* and Elmer Rice, a playwright who wrote to MPAA president Eric Johnston on behalf of the American Civil Liberties Union. Breen appealed directly to the men who had hired him in the first place, the officials of the MPAA. With the bottom line firmly in view, the association sided with their man and declined to make a somber Italian film a test case for new movie morals. The last thing the MPAA wanted was a controversy sparked by a small-time distributor over a film that wasn't even American, even if audiences in the city around them clearly loved the picture. The MPAA and Hollywood could still resist the cultural influence of New York.

Burstyn and de Sica had run up against a sensibility that had shaped American movie culture almost since the inception of filmmaking. Breen's response to *The Bicycle Thief* was not only consistent with that sensibility, it was part of a system of obstructions—a web of control—designed to preserve the nation's movie culture as clean, traditional, and mostly American entertainment. De Sica's film grated against such principles by being realistic, modern, and foreign—and, because it was also popular, action by traditional authorities became even more necessary.

Thus, while Breen could take solace in the fact that his adversary had been a relatively minor figure in a city on the other coast, what disturbed him was that the type of movie promoted by Burstyn had hit a chord with audiences and bigger, more traditional distributors. Hollywood's chief censor sensed a dangerous development brewing in his motion picture world. An associate of Breen reinforced those suspicions: "*The Bicycle Thief* is a trial balloon rather than a case in its own right," Fred Niblo believed. "Evidently it has the backing or blessing of some people in the studios who have lent themselves, consciously or stupidly, to the role of boring from within. It may well be that this is only the first round of a bigger fight."[7]

The controversy surrounding *The Bicycle Thief* had begun not within Hollywood but in New York City. Breen and the PCA continued to maintain a check on the assumptions that governed the mainstream film industry. What he and others did not have control over were the forces beginning to emerge in America's alternative movie capital, New York. Breen's fight with Burstyn had revealed that Hollywood was changing, but not from within.

Through most of the postwar period, the vast majority of movies released in America had to contend with the rules and regulations of municipal and state censorship boards, the whims of the Production Code Administration, and the dictates of the Catholic Church, not to mention evaluations from critics and the fickle purchasing power of the moviegoing audience. The success of such a system relied on the uncontested authority of formal and informal censorship organizations. This is not to say that as a result of censorship American movies were simply poor substitutes of what they could have been. In fact, film historians widely regard the years when the stiffest control was exerted over movies as the golden age of the American film industry. The productivity and style of Hollywood filmmaking grew to maturity under the influence of studio bosses and the PCA. In a sense, it was because movies emerged out of struggle with competing forces that the system had, as historian Thomas Schatz contends, "a special genius."[8]

The position of traditional authorities in the immediate postwar era, despite the "trial balloon" theory applied to *The Bicycle Thief*, seemed incontestable. The revenue of the big studios had hit an all-time high in 1946 of $1.69 billion in admissions, which accounted for a little less than 82 percent of the total money spent by Americans on amusements—the sixteenth year in a row that Hollywood had accounted for over 80 percent of that budget. The system clearly worked, both financially and culturally, because it was built as much on the assumptions of widespread acceptance by almost every sector of movie culture, from the producers to the audience, as on codes and laws.[9]

Since the 1920s, America's motion picture industry had been dominated by five large, mature oligopolies—Warner Bros., Loews Inc. (which owned MGM), Paramount, RKO, and Twentieth Century–Fox. The Big Five, as they were known, produced, distributed, and exhibited most of the big-budget, money-making pictures produced in the United States. Aligned with these companies were the Little Three: Universal, Columbia, and United Artists; with smaller production and distribution capacities, they furnished the larger companies with less expensive pictures and distribution deals. While the total output of these eight companies accounted for an estimated 60 percent of the yearly market, their dominance rested on the control over almost all A-list Hollywood movies made and almost all first-run theaters in which they were seen. Movies made money in their first run, when ticket prices and sales were high. Subsequent runs meant lower prices and fewer tickets sold. First-run theaters in big cities accounted for 70 percent of the ticket revenue in the nation; controlling the production, distribution, and exhibition of pictures that played in those theaters translated into enormous profits.

The Big Five and the Little Three also controlled talent—the army of people from actors to directors to technicians who made the movies. Studio contracts obligated the talent to remain faithful to a studio. The chief way around such an arrangement was to have a studio loan its talent to another, usually on a mutually beneficial basis. Independent producers and distributors were effectively frozen out of this market—they could not tap into the top tier of moviemaking and distribution. Historian Tino Balio explains that "in order to secure financing from banking institutions, independents had to guarantee national distribution and access to better-class theaters. Only then could their pictures stand a chance of making a profit." Without bank loans, movies did not get made. Therefore, the United States had a very small market for independent films. With eight companies controlling how movies were made, who would be in those movies, when those movies would enter the market, and how long they would stay, Hollywood's power was pretty much uncontested. Moreover, the PCA seal was directly linked to Hollywood's control—no seal, no distribution.[10]

From 1921 to 1966, Hollywood operated under the guidance of an in-house review board, or censors, initially called the Hays office but later known officially as the Production Code Administration. Before the major revisions to the code were enacted in the late 1960s, studios submitted scripts and films to PCA officials for approval. Why did Hollywood adopt such a policy? Industry titans hoped this practice would protect their product from excessive scrutiny outside their control. For the movie moguls, the bottom line was always easy to see: avoid bad publicity because that translated into poor ticket sales.

Such logic allowed two very different views of censorship to coexist: censorship was either essential to the preservation of the film industry because it protected both the industry and ostensibly the public, or it was ultimately disastrous for both filmmakers and moviegoers because it constrained the creative development of a popular art. Either way, though, advocates on both sides had to admit that movies were made to affect those who watched them. The question that demanded to be answered was how such influence should be treated—in other words, were movies like a social disease that the public needed protection from or were they sources for ideas to which the public should have access?

For most of its history, the Production Code of the Motion Picture Producers and Directors of America, Inc. held to three general principles:

1. No picture shall be produced which will lower the moral standards of those who see it. Hence, sympathy of the audience shall never be thrown to the side of crime, wrong-doing, evil or sin.
2. Correct standards of life, subject only to the requirements of drama and entertainment, shall be presented.

3. Law, natural or human, shall not be ridiculed, nor shall sympathy be created for its violation.

The Production Code included twelve separate sections covering topics from "Crimes against the Law" and "Sex" to "Religion" and "Repellent Subjects." Generally, the PCA ensured that depictions of sex, crime, drugs, and religion were handled in ways that would be inoffensive to audiences operating at a maturity level slightly higher than children. And yet, even though such codes were clearly overprotective, they reflected an understanding that was difficult to dismiss: "The motion pictures, which are the most popular of modern arts for the masses, have their moral quality from the intention of the minds which produce them and from their effects on the moral lives and reactions of their audiences. This," the fathers of the code declared, "gives them a most important morality." Fair enough. Most moviegoers agreed that movies had power and that such power needed to be checked in some way. However, there was a fundamental problem with applying the code: enforcing it required obvious industrywide collusion.[11]

Beginning in 1938, the U.S. Justice Department introduced charges of collusion and monopoly against the movie industry in the case *United States v. Paramount Pictures, Inc., et al.*—the Paramount case. It took another ten years before the Supreme Court finally heard this case. The Court ruled in 1948 that the companies named in the suit (the Big Five and Little Three) had to divest their theater holdings from their production and distribution companies. In an effort to encourage competition in the movie world, the Justice Department and the Supreme Court had, at least in theory, forced studios to operate as if they existed in an open market with exhibitors. It would no longer be possible for the industry to require exhibitors to take movies without seeing them first, a practice known as blind-bidding. Nor could the industry package an A-list movie with a number of B pictures, a practice called block-booking. The cumulative effect of the antitrust rulings was to force studios to sell each film based on its merits.

The Paramount case did little to help the small, independent producers, distributors, and exhibitors it seemed designed to support because the Court's ruling did nothing to the basic calculus of production and distribution—big companies retained the capital to dominate the industry. Yet *New York Times* film critic Bosley Crowther had a different interpretation of the Paramount case. To him, it illustrated that the government could see beyond simply the "commercial aspects. . . [to] a concern [for] the cultural importance of motion pictures." For the first time, the nation's highest court hinted that movies were something more than industrial goods and therefore might be cultural expressions worthy of legal protection in their own right rather than something to protect the public from.[12]

The separation of exhibition from production had a significant effect on Hollywood's approach to making movies. It meant that the monolithic hold Hollywood had on the imagination of moviegoers could no longer be assumed. The industry would be forced to compete not so much for the markets where movies were shown but for the minds of moviegoers in those markets, and in doing so the moviemakers would have to compete among themselves. Theater owners would continue to exhibit studio products, but they could also demand other kinds of movies that the public wanted to see. Such a prospect altered the relationship between the two sides of the screen. The audience would have, really for the first time, some say over what Hollywood produced. I don't mean to suggest that movie culture had suddenly grown democratic and truly popular—it hadn't; audiences did not dictate what Hollywood made—but the industry did have to contend with the idea that audience taste needed to be addressed. That concept would profoundly alter how Hollywood used its Production Code.

In the early postwar period, Hollywood underwent a sort of spiritual crisis. The industry, although not essentially threatened, had to face that it was losing its audience's attention and allegiance, not only because television had cut into its market, but because other types of movies were gaining more interest from audiences. Without a doubt, the market that provided the clearest illustration of this crisis was the nation's largest, New York City. In November 1946, the *New York Times* cosponsored a public forum to discuss the issue, "Have the Movies Failed Us?" Wrapped up in that question was the assumption that movies had some obligation to the audience—an obligation, though, to do what? The forum was heard over WQXR on its radio show *What's on Your Mind?* in front of the Glen Ridge, New Jersey, Women's Club. Five panelists, including Bosley Crowther, concluded that audience tastes could influence what Hollywood produced. They implied in their comments that if the public was dissatisfied with the movies, then the public had the power through the purchasing of tickets to speak its collective mind. Patronize those that are good, the panelists suggested—especially those that are realistic.[13]

Another panel hosted by *Life* magazine echoed such sentiments. Moderator Eric Hodgins attempted to identify what prevented American movies from keeping up with American tastes. "The air is full of threats to the movies—they reverberate from Hollywood itself," he observed. "Everybody loves the movies, but what is everybody going to do about them?" Producer David O. Selznick admitted that the industry faced "a drastically changed audience." But what that meant seemed beyond Selznick's ability to imagine. Hodgins queried every sector of movie culture, from the industry to the audience, and they all seemed to arrive at a common conclusion: American movies were hampered by the series of controls under which they were made and exhibited. "Hollywood is trying to comply with thousands of prohibitions," Hodgins summarized, "and its aim is thus becoming the barren and self-defeating aim of not displeasing anybody." Because of such containment, Hollywood neglected its "active audience," and while it pursued the "universal picture," the movie studios routinely deceived the public with dishonest advertising. But the real crime was the ultimate quality of the movies: "As means of being both more truthful and less standardized," Hodgins suggested, "Hollywood should spend less money on each picture and make more pictures of greater variety."[14]

Letters from frustrated moviegoers printed in the *New York Times* provided a direct illustration of Hodgins's conclusions. In one letter, entitled "Free Advice to Hollywood," a moviegoer suggested, "I think it is a good lesson and potent warning to Hollywood that the critics topped their 1946 ten-best lists with foreign films. Hollywood had been sitting on its laurels for too long, and if it doesn't wake up it will soon find the public clamoring for only English and French films." Sounding a bit desperate, he pleaded: "No more 'significant' pictures in which the hero finds his Shangri-La."[15]

In another long letter printed in the *Times*, a reader sneered that "the movies, with their vulgar and incompetent ways, their sniveling concern with luxury and high-priced entertainment, are drifting further away from human behavior and the true ways of our world." Segments of the audience were growing frustrated with American movies, which compared unfavorably to foreign films. "American motion pictures should pause to 'clean house,'" one writer advised, "offering the public movies devoid of pretentious emotion, implausible situations and annoying heroics." Another wrote in to admit that "I am one of Hollywood's disappointed customers. I like movies and I would go to see them often, except that what happened yesterday made me quite certain I will not go again for a month or two, except to see newsreels." The moviegoer had seen two "incredibly bad" movies—probably B pictures forced on an exhibitor who needed to fill his quota of product in a block-booking contract. Audiences were becoming indignant not because movies were getting worse but because their options were getting broader and better with the influx of foreign films. Imports, moviegoers could be fairly certain, would be worth the price of a ticket—especially since critics helped publicize the best foreign films. A letter writer who agreed with the one above wrote in to say, "I too, including my family, have taken to seeing only the foreign films." Moviegoers had become less willing to waste money on the pat Hollywood tales.[16]

Some moviegoers did write in to defend Hollywood. One man attempted to remind other readers that not all foreign films were superior pictures—a defense that did not exactly bestow a great deal of honor on Hollywood's efforts. His letter elicited a flurry of responses, all contesting his implied support for Hollywood. One writer sarcastically wished the man luck trying to find quality American movies, while another asked, "Why should we be 'tolerant' of an industry that has unparalleled resources in money, technical equipment and talent—and yet produces hardly six pictures a year that are not an insult to half-adult intelligence?" A final letter revealed just how transparent the web of control and the censorsing sensibility had become: "What is wrong [with movies]," the writer declared, "is the asinine restrictions of the Eric Johnston office [MPAA] and the Legion of Decency, which water all adult themes down to the ten-year-old level. The cure is for our producers to ignore these two institutions for unreconstructed prudes and to make pictures for grown-ups."[17]

In a long article for the *Atlantic Monthly*, Gilbert Seldes intimated that perhaps the industry was listening. He reported on a rather candid speech made by Eric Johnston. Johnston told the studio chiefs that Hollywood would have to take into consideration the improving educational level of its audience. "America is growing up," he observed, "and films must catch up with that 'phenomenon.'" To Seldes, the future was clear as well: "The opportunity is exceptional because television will, to an extent, drain off the audience for the average picture, and the West Coast studios will eventually manufacture films cut to the standards of the new medium. They will be free then to make pictures for precisely those in-theater audiences which neither radio-television nor their own average productions have been able to attract." Seldes also noted, somewhat triumphantly, that movie critics for decades had been arguing that movies as an art deserved more respect from both the industry and the censors. After all, he concluded, "respect for one's art is the high road to success."[18]

A rather profound obstacle on that road remained, though. Even if Hollywood embraced movies as art, that would not magically transform movie culture. The industry had played it safe for so long out of fear of retribution—rejection by state or municipal review boards and, perhaps most seriously, a commercial boycott arranged by the Catholic Legion of Decency. The transformation of the industry's Production Code in the early 1930s came in part from the influence exerted by the Catholic Church and its representatives in Hollywood. In November 1933, Catholic officials in the United States held a conference at the Catholic University of America, where discussions took place regarding the damage movies had been doing to American life. Following these discussions, the church's American hierarchy created the Episcopal Committee on Motion Pictures to coordinate Catholic influence over the movie industry. At the center of this initiative was Martin Quigley, a devout Catholic who had grown disenchanted with the laxity with which the Hays Code had been enforced. He and a small committee of four Catholic bishops drafted a three-part plan for the creation of the Catholic Legion of Decency. When censorship failed to contain movies, the Legion would swing into action by mobilizing the Catholic faithful to boycott theaters that showed suspect films, thereby encouraging the industry to practice more stringent self-regulation and conformity with the Production Code. Yet, as ominous as the Legion seemed, it would have been powerless without the support of its parishioners, who were rallied to various causes primarily through church-supported literature (newspapers, magazines, and books) and from the pulpit. The original film czar Will Hays responded to the potential of such collective action by making a move to placate the Catholic hierarchy: the MPAA hired a hard-nosed Catholic from Philadelphia, Joseph Breen, as head of the PCA in December 1933. Breen would serve as chief censor of Hollywood for the next twenty years.[19]

While the PCA had offices in both Hollywood and New York, the national Legion of Decency was, by 1936, based in New York City. Using the offices of Catholic charities, the Legion issued its evaluations of movies by publishing reviews in Catholic newspapers and periodicals. Patrick Cardinal Hayes took responsibility for the Legion in New York and selected Father Edward Robert Moore and Father Joseph Daly to run the Legion's daily operations. Close by, though, was Martin Quigley, who had recently moved his publishing company from Chicago to New York. The actual rating of movies, however, was given not to a priest but to the director of the International Federation of Catholic Alumnae (IFCA), a Catholic women's organization. Mary Looram and the IFCA had been reviewing movies for ten years before the Legion was formed. Initially, the group lost its job to priests at the inception of the Legion, but as historian Gregory Black notes, "the women were back in grace after they agreed to add a 'condemned' category to their reviews."[20]

The reviewers were organized into two groups, one for the East Coast and one for the West. Looram's job was to compile reviewers' comments for publication in papers such as the *Brooklyn Tablet*—a daily Catholic newspaper with a circulation that included the large Catholic population on Long Island as well as Brooklyn. Those comments were also printed in most Catholic publications throughout the country. The most influential aspect of reviewing, though, was the assignment of a classification for each movie. Under the auspices of the Legion, Looram's staff created a four-level rating system: AI indicated unobjectionable, for general patronage; AII unobjectionable, for adults; B objectionable in part; and C condemned. A rating of C could spell financial ruin for a Hollywood movie if theaters refused to book it out of fear of Catholic boycotts.

The key, of course, was getting Catholics in big cities to follow the Legion's guidance. To give the rating system and declarations by the Legion some weight, the church introduced a pledge, written by Bishop McNicholas of Cincinnati, to be taken by all Catholics at one mass every year. The faithful stood, raised their right hands, and pledged to "form a right conscience about pictures that are dangerous to [one's] moral life" and (most frightening to the movie industry) to "stay away altogether from places of amusement which show them as a matter of policy." In the early postwar years, Catholics sought clarification of the pledge. "The pledge is a promise," one priest wrote in the Catholic journal *Sign*, "and its binding force comes from the virtue of fidelity." Another related, without mincing words, "At most, this pledge would seem to be only a promise. . . . However, by reason of the matter promised, the fulfillment of this pledge may be a grave obligation, binding under pain of mortal sin."[21]

The strength of such language was more than likely a result of the fragility of the church's intermediary role in movie culture. Gregory Black explains that the Legion of Decency was "little more than a loose confederation of local organizations." In fact, each diocese appointed a director to oversee Legion affairs, which meant that "the level of enthusiasm for the Legion depended on the commitment of the bishop. For the most part," Black continues, "local directors did little more than maintain contact with local theater owners and managers to keep them informed of Legion concerns, speak to local Catholic organizations and schools about the Legion, distribute Legion literature, answer questions about controversial films, and submit a yearly report."[22]

While this sounds innocuous enough, the effects of such actions on movie culture could appear quite dubious to some, especially to organizations that also had a mission to improve movies. The National Board of Review (NBR) had launched a "Better Films" campaign in the 1920s as a two-pronged effort to encourage the American movie industry to make higher-quality products and to help it counter the forces of censorship that were appearing across the country in many big cities. As early as 1926, the NBR had contacted Mary Looram, at that time only a member of the IFCA, to apply a little friendly persuasion. W. A. Barrett, president of the National Board of Review, wrote that his organization was "opposed to censorship and [was] endeavoring to offer a constructive program of selection and classification of the better films, the broadcasting of information about them and the building up of affiliated groups in various communities through the country, to act with in the support of these films when they appear in the theatres, in order to encourage the production and exhibition of the ever finer type of motion picture." Any hope of rapprochement, though, was dashed once Barrett read a transcript of a radio speech Looram made to inaugurate the Legion's activities. Sent to him by a friend with the message "Here is a more truculent note from Mrs. Looram," the speech, Barrett recognized, showed that the new organization had launched a campaign in direct opposition to the NBR's mission:

> All citizens no matter what creed they profess, *are privileged* to join the Legion just as our Motion Picture Bureau of the International Federation of Catholic Alumnae for twelve years has urged all Americans to follow the slogan of our Bureau, "Let Your Theatre Ticket Be Your Ballot for Better Movies." That slogan contains practically the same message as the Pledge of Decency, namely the necessity of boycotting indecent pictures and patronizing the good ones.
>
> As the Tablet points out, the campaign is not merely destructive. The first object, to be sure, is negative—doing away with sordid and indecent pictures. But the drive is constructive inasmuch as it hopes to increase the number of good pictures. This will mean placing the industry on a better basis and will bring back many who have been driven away.[23]

Eventually, the NBR would turn toward outright opposition to Legion tactics and the obvious alliance between the Legion and the PCA. After World War II, the NBR would help the ACLU campaign against censorship through the National Council on Freedom from Censorship. A press release sent out by the council's chairman, Elmer Rice, in June 1948 made clear where the resistance should be centered: "It is . . . proposed to set up a coordinating council of all interested agencies," he explained. "New York is the logical center for such unity."[24]

Despite opposition to Catholic censorship, the power of the Legion had a significant influence on moviegoing. With Joseph Breen directing the PCA and Martin Quigley assisting the Legion, it was a rare occasion when the PCA and the Legion disagreed on a movie. It was Catholic and Hollywood collusion. But that union also played upon assumptions many moviegoers held regarding the crass nature of the movie industry. Indeed, Jimmie Fidler, a powerful conservative Hollywood columnist, was quoted in the conservative Catholic journal *Ave Maria* defending the Legion for having "never been accused, even by producers whose financial toes were stepped upon, of using its enormous power unfairly. It has never censored a cinema that did not deserve censorship," he declared. "All in all, both the public and the motion pictures have benefited." And when the Production Code came under increasing fire in the first years after the war, the *Sign* editorialized that a world without the code would be one in which chaos and smut reigned. It would be a world, moreover, akin to what existed before the war. "Mass murder, pillage, and war," readers were reminded, "are the inevitable results of numbed individual consciences."[25]

The Legion was also part of a larger social movement within the church known as Catholic Action—a collection of groups that heeded Pope Pius X's charge to "embody in social change the conviction that Catholicism offered solutions to all the problems of the modern world." The two cultural organizations that carried out this charge most conspicuously were the Legion and the National Organization for Decent Literature (NODL). When faced with accusations that their tactics were, at the very least, antidemocratic, these organizations shot back that they had an obligation to voice their displeasure with immoral material such as books and movies and were only making a fruitful contribution to American democracy rather than acting as passive victims of a culture produced—as these many groups accurately pointed out—by an industry. Leaders of these organizations repeatedly defended their work, arguing that they were not censors and did not support censorship. Una M. Cadegan, a historian of Catholic institutions, explains: "Defenders of the Legion and the NODL . . . maintained that their program reflected the values of all 'decent' or 'right-thinking' people. They claimed to be speaking for the majority of their fellow citizens, a cultural majority powerless in the face of amoral, monied conglomerates. Further, they were affirming their own right to define mid-century culture against, as they saw it, both Eastern sophisticates and West Coast moguls."[26]

This did not mean that Catholics spoke with a single voice, though; Catholic periodicals represented different points on the theological and political spectrums. For example, *Commonweal* and *America* were published in New York City and therefore tended to have a bent more tolerant of liberal views; *Ave Maria*, on the other hand, came from Fort Wayne, Indiana, among the most conservative dioceses in the nation. Throughout the postwar years, the ways in which journals such as these addressed the Catholic role in movie censorship would reflect a broadening and ultimately undermining force working within Catholic opinion. The source of such division did not, quite clearly, come from the heartland, but rather from New York. The Legion's effectiveness, after all, rested as much on the cooperation of secular organizations—especially the PCA—as it did on the individual consciences of practicing Catholics. Both relationships hung in the balance after the war.

Ironically, Catholic involvement in the debate over movie culture had implications for the church. A democratizing trend took hold within the church that could be seen in public as well as private debates over movie culture. It might seem facile to speak about the historical trajectory of a religious institution through its position on movies, but unlike theological debates, questions about movies invariably dealt with the relationship between church officials and the Catholic laity. Movie culture was, frankly, a democratic affair that the church hoped to control through its hierarchical authority. Yet something was revealed by the fact that mountains of editorials and articles were published in Catholic journals discussing how to relate to the movies, and scores of letters were written by parishioners and answered by priests regarding the rules of moviegoing. Catholic opinion was not monolithic; many church officials feared what Joe Breig of the conservative journal *Ave Maria* had warned of: "I cannot but conclude, that a great many Catholics are dragging their heels in this matter. I learn this from talking with them; and even if I didn't, I could learn it from observing the quality of movies."[27]

By the late 1940s, Catholic opinion of the Legion was clearly undergoing a reevaluation. In a number of articles in the Catholic press, priests defended the Legion and its work in ways that made it clear that the church's authority over matters such as the movies was being questioned. An editorialist for *Ave Maria* defended the work of the Legion as nothing short of heroic and condemned those who criticized it as utterly irredeemable. "They are so crammed with self-sufficiency," he sneered, "so dilated with pride of opinion, grown so gross in evil by surrenders to devil, world, and flesh, they resent any attempts to build up standards of conduct which express a contrast of reproach to their own undisciplined lives." Slightly more coolheaded arguments depicted a church that "contains within itself the power to regulate aright and to sanctify every new phase of human progress. Accordingly, she is fully able to direct mankind in the use of motion pictures in such wise that they will be beneficial to the attainment of eternal life." This role was to be played in a country that was not even half Catholic. Some members of the Catholic press interpreted questions about the Legion and the yearly pledge of obedience to it taken by all Catholics to be more instructive than ominous. In 1946, a commentator for the liberal Catholic periodical *Commonweal* wrote that the pledge was becoming a mere afterthought in many parishes. "If the faithful find thrust upon them each year promises so sweeping that they would change the habits of a lifetime," he concluded, "they will simply dismiss it."[28]

What could not be quite so easily dismissed were the laws governing the exhibition of movies in New York. Even if the PCA and the Legion failed to restrain movie culture, the laws governing moviegoing in New York would. New York City had been among the first major cities in the nation to enact laws for the protection of its residents. In 1909, at the recommendation of his chief of police, Mayor George B. McClellan closed all of the 550 picture show establishments in the city. This was the first move in a gradual aggrandizement of municipal control over moviegoing in New York. By 1914, the city entrusted a commissioner of licenses "to issue, renew and revoke licenses in relation to theatres." His power applied to the Greater New York Charter and required him and his officials "to investigate the character of exhibitions in these theatres and to report . . . any offense against 'morality, decency or public welfare,' committed in said exhibitions." In language that reflected the underlying obligation officials had, the office of the commissioner "constitute[d] the only protection afforded larger communities from the evils of immoral and vicious exhibitions."[29]

In protecting audiences, however, the state also designated the limits of movie culture. There was little room for conflict over interpreting movies, especially when those movies dealt with sex. In 1917, a New York State Supreme Court whose jurisdiction included Manhattan ruled on a case involving a movie entitled *The Hand That Rocks the Cradle*. Because the film dealt with the subject of birth control, the court decided that the state had an interest in preventing a theater from showing it. The commissioner had deemed it "immoral, indecent, [and] against the public welfare," and because he was the public official appointed by the city to patrol public amusements, his power to determine what New Yorkers could and could not see was law. After all, as the justices saw it, the right to exhibit a movie was "not an absolute one, but in the nature of a privilege granted by the state."[30]

The key state ally in this fight to contain the potential damage of movies was the censorship board of New York. Since 1921, the elected New York State Legislature had helped preserve moral norms by creating the Motion Picture Commission to supervise and censor movies shown throughout the state. In 1927, the state board had become a division of the New York State Education Department, where it stayed until its dissolution in the late 1960s. The Motion Picture Division, as it was renamed, had a director and officers appointed by the New York State Board of Regents, but the candidates for those posts were selected in open civil service exams. According to the charter establishing the commission, the director and his officials could grant films a license, a permit, or neither one. The latter two categories pertained to newsreels and scientific or educational films. "All other motion pictures," commanded the charter, "must be submitted for examination with a required application for a license and fees." The process in theory paid for itself through fees charged to the distributors of the movies. With a license secured, distributors could safely sell movies to exhibitors throughout the state. New York's censors could reject a film if they found it "obscene, indecent, immoral, inhuman, sacrilegious, or . . . of such a character that its exhibition would tend to corrupt morals, or incite to crime." Each decision made by this small board of reviewers created a small paper trail, so that a distributor, producer, or exhibitor could appeal a decision to the board of regents or, if that remedy did not satisfy a plaintiff, to the courts.[31]

This system was a model for other state organizations. Film and legal historian Laura Wittern-Keller contends that the New York board was considered the most influential in the nation, and not surprisingly, challenges to its authority in the court system were closely monitored by censors and judges throughout the country. But what made such boards so powerful was that most, like New York's, were allowed to subject motion pictures to prior restraint. Wittern-Keller explains how different the legal scrutiny of movies was from the regulation of other media. "If Mr. X had a book that was considered dangerously obscene in mid-century America, no governmental body could have kept him from publishing it. . . . However," she continues, "if Mr. X were a movie producer or distributor, his film would never have been seen in most movie theaters if it had been deemed to be unacceptable. It would not become part of the 'marketplace of ideas' and no one would even know much about it. Moreover, X's only recourse would be to bring suit against the censors and prove to a judge (as there were no jury trials) or a series of judges that his film was not objectionable under the terms of the statute of regulation." That kind of control prevailed across the United States, affecting, Wittern-Keller estimates, 60 percent of people living in cities and 40 percent of the general movie audience.[32]

At the core of city, state, and industry codes—the rationale making prior restraint seem sincere—was the assumption that movies had special force among the public, and therefore, the public needed protection from indecent and immoral material, which would certainly pervade movies without strict regulation. The twenty-four-page booklet of New York State's *Law, Rules, and Regulations for Review and Licensing of Motion Pictures* concluded with: "No motion picture will be licensed or a permit granted for its exhibition within the State of New York, which may be classified, or any part thereof, *as obscene, indecent, immoral, inhuman, sacrilegious, or which is of such a character that its exhibition would tend to corrupt morals or incite to crime.*" Application of the code made it possible to reject movies such as *Illegal Wives*, submitted in April 1946 and rejected "in toto" a month later because the reviewers determined that it was "sacrilegious, immoral, tends to incite crime, [and] tends to corrupt morals." The board formally rejected it under other titles as well, including *Polygamy*, *Child Marriage*, and *The Bishop's Daughter*, with the note: "While this picture might be said to be a picture against the evils of polygamy, all the operations of this evil practice are laid bare in the picture, together with forced marriage, murder and arson." Indeed, all the things that make up any soap opera worth its salt today.[33]

A fundamental problem with the state's standards, though, was the failure to account for artistic aspirations. In October 1946, New York's censors looked at a Mexican film entitled *La mulata de Cordoba*. After a somewhat lengthy debate between the reviewers and the distributors, the board rejected the film in June 1947. However, the reviewer who wrote the final report seemed to find the story quite compelling. In a lengthy synopsis of the movie, he explained that the film included miscegenation and "deals with the unhappy life of a beautiful mullato [*sic*] girl who eventually chooses to die saving the life of the man who had been her implacable nemesis from birth to death." That story line, the censor concluded, "would tend to deepen, intensify and extend racial hatreds and in no particular way is any attempt made to point toward a solution." Therefore, the picture was "rejected in toto," for the typical reasons: it was "immoral, tends to corrupt morals, [and] tends to incite crime." One gets the sense that the problem with the film was that it was too good and too powerful. Moreover, there seemed to be a standing rule that if films contained illicit or explicit sex of any kind—even if such themes were vital to telling a compelling and realistic story—the reviewers had to reject them. The real world was not yet allowed to break through the mostly sanitized version seen on the screen.[34]

Hugh M. Flick, New York State's chief censor for most of the postwar period, defended such actions on democratic principles. To him, censors were charged with preserving what he identified as the "moral and spiritual values" of the nation. "Without a general understanding and acceptance of moral and spiritual values," he explained, "not only does freedom have little meaning but also liberty becomes license." He, too, emphasized the importance of citizen action in checking the dangerous freedom of moviemakers. "The agencies of government must bend every effort to furnish citizens through education the means of resilient thinking to meet the needs of transient mores." In common with the Catholic position, Flick believed that censors served a democratic end by helping the people see the nefarious intentions of an industry bent on making money with or without respect for any standards of decency.[35]

To become director of New York State's influential board of censorship, Flick had to score high on the civil service exam. He assumed his new position in April 1949 at the salary of $6,700 a year and with a staff of seven. When asked by a reporter what his position entailed, he responded as he had on his civil service exam: "I believe in it as a public service, but I don't consider it one of censorship in the popular sense of the word. It's more like the pure food laws, the roughest kind of screening to protect the public from actual abuse." Flick's job was to "help ward off the whole impact of today's mass media." However, even New York's chief censor felt conflicted about censorship. He and his staff had the responsibility to review hundreds of movies a year and the power to prevent almost any picture from reaching the screen. While such authority might seem quite impressive, Flick admitted to Otis Guernsey of the *New York Herald Tribune* that he hoped a revision of the censorship process would allow the burden of judgment to be shared with the public.[36]

Thus, for the first half of film history, motion pictures had to traverse an obstacle course justified by the widely accepted notion that they were dangerous. Those who struggled to contain and regulate the movies regarded themselves as heroes—battling the forces of raw capitalism and smut. However, that changed after World War II as a new cultural sensibility took shape. It seems to me that New York movie culture remade American movie culture, subtly but completely. One might say, using a line from complexity theory, that changes in the national movie culture were sensitively dependent on conditions that initially took shape in New York. The pattern of moviegoing changed after 1945, allowing for the relative success of a movie like *The Bicycle Thief*. In the early postwar period, one significant influence on that emerging pattern was Joseph Burstyn.

Burstyn was a lifelong bachelor who lived in a three-room apartment in "an eccentric looking building" on the southwest side of Central Park. He did most of his work from the late afternoon into the early morning hours, sleeping late in the morning. In a profile of Burstyn for the magazine *Park East*, Herbert Mitgang described him as someone who came alive in the evening, with a "quicksilverish expression," "porcelain-blue eyes," and a face crowned by a "flying V of silver hair." He was a Jewish immigrant from Poland who had arrived as a boy with his family in 1921 and bounced around large midwestern cities for almost ten years before settling in New York. By the early 1930s, he had entered the movie business, forming a distribution company with Arthur Mayer, his business partner for almost twenty years. The two immigrants imported and distributed foreign films. Mitgang noted that New York was just about the only market in the country that could support such a livelihood. And within that scene Burstyn was a "legendary figure."[37]

The scrappy distributor became, in a sense, a metaphorical butterfly who by flapping his wings helped to set in motion a typhoon that would eventually rearrange the landscape of moviegoing. Burstyn unfortunately had a relatively short career in New York because he died suddenly and prematurely in 1953. Yet in the early years of the postwar period, Burstyn left his mark on American movie culture. In 1952, Burstyn won a landmark case before the U.S. Supreme Court that helped establish First Amendment protection for movies. *Burstyn v. Wilson* reversed the Court's 1915 decision in *Mutual v. Ohio*, marking the beginning of a string of cases that steadily eroded the legal framework of motion picture censorship. Burstyn fought this legal battle in order to distribute yet another small Italian film, *The Miracle*, and did so almost completely alone, using his own small savings. His work in this case, though, represented more than simply a strike against the web of legal control that surrounded movies. Burstyn also manifested a spirit that became so pervasive it even infected Hollywood. His involvement with films and filmmakers from abroad made him a champion for both the commercial and artistic aspects of movies. He was never above using dubious advertising campaigns to attract patrons—such as featuring sultry women in ads for films that had little to do with sex. But he also developed a sophisticated argument in support of broadening the traditional American understanding of movies. He rejected the labels "art film" and "foreign film," insisting that "there are two kinds, good films and bad films. . . . There are two requirements for pictures—first, they've got to be good; second, audiences must be informed about them properly."[38]

"A few people hold that Burstyn's artistic approach frequently gives way to commercialism," Mitgang admitted. "They say he is . . . not unwilling to extract the last animalistic ounce from an 'art' picture in an advertising campaign." That was a fair observation but an unjust conclusion to draw from it. True, Burstyn liked to generate publicity for his pictures, but the financial payoff was only half the story. His experience with Italian films illustrated that point. Near the end of 1945, Burstyn agreed to buy an Italian film from an American soldier who claimed that he had acquired the print from a man who shared an apartment with him, a young filmmaker named Roberto Rossellini. The film was *Open City*, and Burstyn had to attend two screenings of it before he agreed to a deal. He recounted that at the end of the second screening the audience had reacted strongly, almost violently, to the film. Burstyn remembered thinking, "If it caused enthusiasm and controversy, people want to see it." In February 1946, the film opened at the World Theater. By 1951, Eitel Monaco, president of the Italian movie industry, officially commended Burstyn in a swanky ceremony held in the penthouse of the Museum of Modern Art. "Because of his pioneer work," Monaco declared, "the number of people who see our best films is not fifty thousand but five million." When Burstyn had time to reflect on his role in changing American movie culture, he simply acknowledged, "I like movies." He did indeed. But he liked those movies that brought people to theaters in such numbers that they were willing to stand in lines to see, debate, and scrutinize a film. Burstyn embraced everything that American movie culture had been designed to prevent: controversy, foreignness, seriousness. But his work and his success illustrated that, at least in New York, things were about to change.[39]

From 1946 to 1947, the total revenue earned by foreign films distributed in the United States increased from $5.6 million to $8.01 million. Writing for the *Times*, Thomas Pryor reported, "Distributors who have been handling such movies for years frankly admit that their market is bigger now than ever before." He attributed the surge in interest to the success of films such as Roberto Rossellini's *Open City* and the reception they received in New York City. According to *Variety*, runs in New York City represented 60 percent of the total gross a foreign film could expect. The industry journal also speculated that the success of most foreign pictures was due to advertising them as more racy and explicit than the typical Hollywood movie. "Few foreign films have yet to break into the affiliated circuits," *Variety* noted, "and when they do, it is generally because they have more than critical nods."[40]

The postwar era was a boom time for foreign films, and it took Hollywood close to a generation to catch up to the material and frankness of them. In her book on the rise of art house cinema, Barbara Wilinsky reports that between 1946 and 1949, the number of foreign film importers and distributors increased from twenty-five to sixty-two. Most of the best-run and successful art house cinemas were located in New York City—a total of 40 percent of all such theaters. Charles Skouras, a big-time distributor, owned sixty-two neighborhood theaters in the city and by 1947 had responded to changes in audience taste by running foreign films as a part of double bills with Hollywood pictures. The manager of the Bijou Theater in lower Manhattan actually cancelled his booking of the quite popular *The Best Years of Our Lives* in favor of a French film because he figured that the traditional neighborhood audience expected to see it. Wilinsky adds that distributors and exhibitors were attracted to such fare for more than artistic reasons. They understood that there was money to be made as long as movies were marketed in the right way. "Art films . . . were seen to offer two very different alternatives to Hollywood cinema," Wilinsky explains. "On the one hand, art cinema was seen as 'noncommercial' and artistically motivated, offering an escape from the brash commercialism of Hollywood." This was a sentiment evident in letters to the *New York Times* in support of foreign films. "On the other hand," Wilinsky continues, "critics depicted the art cinema industry as actually more vulgar in its commercialism than Hollywood, willing to take advantage of any sexual angle to attract an audience." Indeed, Arthur Mayer admitted that "the only sensational successes scored by Burstyn and myself in the fifteen years in which we were engaged in business were with foreign pictures whose artistic and ideological merits were aided and abetted at the box office by their frank sex content." While this was undoubtedly the case, it was also true that these movies could "catch and reflect the warmth and vitality of daily life with more candor and realism and less sentimentality and adolescent clichés than are customary in American films."[41]

The audience seemed to demand reality. Foreign films provided it, but so did the geographic center of the alternative movie world. In a very real way, New York City became not simply the biggest market for all types of films, but the city itself—its style and substance—represented an alternative to Hollywood's product and glitter. New York had always been the market where the financial fates of movies rose or fell. But it increasingly became the place where American movie culture was being remade. If American audiences craved—even somewhat ambiguously—something beyond what Hollywood produced and what that city represented, New York provided both.

In an article for the *New York Times Magazine* in August 1947, critic Bosley Crowther mused about New York's role in American movie culture. In a piece entitled "Hollywood versus New York," he discussed Mayor William O'Dwyer's attempts to attract filmmaking back to the city. To Crowther, such a development had "spiritual" as well as financial implications, "for it is reasonably charged that our movies are unimaginative and standardized because the people who make them live concentrated, insular lives." He noted that realism in movies was becoming more important, mostly because it seemed the audience expected it. If that was the case, Crowther suggested, "some decentralization must take place if Hollywood's pictures are not to descend to an even lower level."[42]

Crowther's point hit upon an interesting conundrum facing American movie culture at that time. Men like Joseph Burstyn were becoming not merely relatively successful within their film markets but somewhat respected for their willful opposition to the older order. Censors feared two separate though not mutually exclusive developments: a legal negation of their power and widespread public disregard of the sensibility that informed their power. Burstyn's experience with *The Bicycle Thief* illustrated that the institutions of censorship still commanded official respect. But not for long.

2

The Miracle and Bosley Crowther

FILM CRITICS RECEIVE letters from moviegoers all the time. Most letters, of course, take issue with a negative review of a popular movie. In January 1951, *New York Times* film critic Bosley Crowther received a letter from a man who had something very different to say. He recounted the experience he and his wife had trying to buy a ticket at the Paris Theater for a trio of foreign films entitled *The Ways of Love:* Marcel Pagnol's *Jofroi,* Jean Renoir's *A Day in the Country,* and Roberto Rossellini's *The Miracle.* The man told Crowther that they encountered a picket line that circled in front of the theater and would have turned away except that they were intrigued by the hostility of the crowd — "all husky young men" making a fuss. The couple found the films enjoyable, "although not exactly great," but on the way out were treated to a barrage of remarks: "Why dontcha go to an American movie?" one of the pickets yelled. "No decent man would take a decent woman to that filth!" "How'd yuh like the Paris cesspool, huh?" Booton Herndon and his wife walked into a protest that was fraught with larger implications for American culture. Herndon wrote specifically to Crowther because Crowther had used his *Times* column to defend the right of moviegoers to see the movie that was causing all the excitement — Rossellini's *The Miracle.* Your "quiet words of approval," Herndon wrote to Crowther, were not drowned out by "a bunch of ruffians." Crowther replied, "You wisely reflected an ugly irony in the whole affair. I can't tell you how disagreeable the whole thing has been to me."[1]

It was rare for a film critic to be taken seriously prior to 1950, much less to be seen as someone to look to for moral support. Yet Bosley Crowther became such a critic—singular in the power he had to make or break a picture (especially a foreign film) and even heroic at times in how he chose to exercise that considerable power. Unfortunately, Crowther has not been remembered for such stands. His legacy rests on two reviews he wrote during the same movie season in 1967: in the first, he panned *Bonnie and Clyde* (1967) because he found the movie too violent and pretentious; in the second, he cheered the disastrous *Cleopatra* (1967) for its grand production value. In other words, Crowther became the critic that a younger generation loved to bury. By the late 1960s, as Crowther approached retirement, the only thing that other critics seemed to agree on consistently was Crowther's growing irrelevance.

I aim to revise that perception but not necessarily the evaluation of Crowther as a middling critic. Thus, I will concede up front that Crowther's criticism does not have the timeless quality of writers such as James Agee, Robert Warshow, or Pauline Kael. However, none of the great film critics—those credited with having their own "schools" of criticism—fought as long and hard as Crowther did to free the screen of inordinate restrictions. It is the longevity and constancy of that struggle on which his legacy should be based. While other critics were outspoken about censorship, none wrote about it from the front page of the *New York Times* Arts and Leisure section for twenty-five years, as Crowther did. Over time his column served as a kind of popular forum for debates over what he called the "free screen," providing him and his readers with insight into an evolving cultural paradox. Crowther came to understand, as many critics have since his time, that a free screen is not an end in itself.

Crowther was an important critic in part because he wrote to his audience. But such an approach never made him a leading critic, just a prominent one. He was not agile like James Agee, seeing film as an art form that did not need an audience to affirm its significance. Crowther was not angry like Dwight Macdonald or erudite like Manny Farber or Parker Tyler or daring like Archer Winsten of the *New York Post*, all of whom fought for movies and filmmakers because they regarded cinema as another source for intellectual progress. Crowther operated in another arena, the place where most moviegoers could be found and the place in which, frankly, a contest of wills had to be won before the theoretical musings of other critics could make a difference in the larger movie culture. Crowther dealt with the crisis that immediately affected mainstream movie culture, and he hoped that writing against censorship and in favor of freedom for the screen would help all pictures earn the right to compete in an open cultural marketplace. That was both an honorable and a naive project.

Exactly a year after the premiere of *The Bicycle Thief*, *The Miracle*, a small movie booked at a small theater, had its premiere. During a cold and snowy Christmas season, most New Yorkers did not initially take notice of the opening night of the trilogy of movies that include Rossellini's film—but Bosley Crowther did. As the first-string movie critic for the *New York Times*, he wrote reviews both during the week and for the paper's Sunday edition. At midweek, Crowther crowed: "Judged by the highest standards, on either its parts or the whole, [*The Ways of Love*] emerges as fully the most rewarding foreign language entertainment of the year." Of course, it was *The Miracle*, in particular, that caught his attention. Crowther related the story line to his readers: "[It] tells a violent story of an idiot woman in a raw Italian town who, in a transport of religious emotion, is seduced by a stranger whom she thinks is her special saint. Found pregnant and revealed as a transgressor, this poor, mad woman is ridiculed for harboring the crazy notion that she has conceived immaculately. And thus, cast out by her cruel neighbors, she suffers her time in solitude until she is ready to be delivered of a baby when she crawls alone and bears her child in an empty church." By Sunday, Crowther had begun to prepare his public for the controversy that was at that point brewing. He suggested that the film could be taken in a few ways, including as a mockery of a central Catholic belief—the Immaculate Conception. It was a situation made much worse by the fact that the film opened on the same weekend as the celebration of the Feast Day of the Immaculate Conception. Catholics in the United States pledged their obedience to the Legion of Decency during that mass. And if that was not enough irony, Mary was the patron saint of the United States. Understanding some of this, Crowther acknowledged the film's potential to stir controversy but added, as only a film critic could, "because of [Anna] Magnani's performance, it seems to this reviewer to be just a vastly compassionate comprehension of the suffering and the triumph of birth. Here is an understanding of the feebleness and loneliness of men." Yet Crowther knew well that movies had never been judged solely on their artistic merits. In the weeks that followed the premiere of *The Miracle*, Crowther participated in the hottest debate over a movie since, perhaps, D. W. Griffith's racially charged epic, *The Birth of a Nation*, had prompted the NAACP to picket theaters.[2]

The extent of this "stir" was not apparent to anyone in late 1950, but two years later, *The Miracle* occupied a special place in film and legal history. The controversy sparked by the film's exhibition ultimately led to the U.S. Supreme Court's extending to movies, for the first time, some protection from prior censorship. Before that happened, though, the web of control that had constrained the exhibition of movies in New York and around the country closed in tightly around the minor Italian import. At issue was whether this film or any film had the right to offend any group of moviegoers—in this case Catholics. Defense of the movie occupied two fronts, legal and cultural. Joseph Burstyn again picked a legal fight against the various forces of control. Bosley Crowther fought along the cultural front by making a plea for taste. He championed a "free screen," or the notion that adults should have the power (since they had the ability) to make their own decisions about what to see.

That position might sound mundane in our contemporary world, in which unlimited access to material over the Internet and cable television allows adults (and children) to see anything they want anytime they want it. But Crowther's campaign was a complex appeal to democratic culture. In an era that still had a public culture—where people actually had to decide what they as a community could tolerate rather than what each individual could choose to have in the privacy of home—the controversy engaged by Crowther suggested that moviegoers had a right to see sophisticated stories on the big screen, but in turn, they had an obligation to exercise this right responsibly.[3]

The controversy over *The Miracle* began on 23 December 1950, when Lillian Gerard, the manager of the Paris Theater, received two official letters from the license commissioner of the City of New York telling her that exhibition of this specific film had to stop or he, Edward T. McCaffrey, would revoke the theater's privilege to exhibit movies. No theater had the right, McCaffrey decided, to make a mockery of any religion. Upon hearing of this threat, Joseph Burstyn could not contain his shock. Gerard remembers: "His prematurely white mane of hair stood upright, his doll eyes dazed, innocent, incredulous, and frightened. 'They can't do this to us,' he cried!" They could and they did. McCaffrey's second letter read: "I understand that you did show this film [*The Miracle*] at an evening performance on December 22, 1950. I now take the occasion to inform you that this letter is being delivered by a licensed inspector who is authorized by me to inform you that your license has been suspended and that the suspension is immediately in effect upon any further showing of *The Miracle*." McCaffrey had apparently made an unannounced appearance at the theater the afternoon of 22 December, accompanied by a Catholic priest and one of his inspectors. He left so enraged that he threatened to close any theater in the city that disregarded his prohibition. In a letter to Burstyn, the commissioner advised him "to cooperate by eliminating the film from your booking program with any New York City theater."[4]

News of this situation traveled fast after Richard Parke, a reporter for the *New York Times*, called Gerard. One of his editors had tried to see a matinee that day but found the theater closed. The story of the city's attempt to ban *The Miracle* ironically broke on Christmas Eve and continued into the Christmas Day papers. The second article ran with a picture of Commissioner McCaffrey under the caption "Bans Italian Film." The *Times* also included comments decrying McCaffrey's decision from Joseph Manckiewcz (president of the Screen Directors Guild), King Vidor, producer Milton Sperling, and actor Howard Lindsay, who asked "whether the 8,000,000 citizens of New York City are permitted to see only such pictures as are acceptable personally to Mr. McCaffrey." Many papers picked up the controversy. And while news reporters chronicled the legal battles that began almost immediately after McCaffrey's threats, Crowther waged a different kind of war, primarily from his column in the Sunday edition of the *Times*.[5]

Bosley Crowther had been the top movie critic at the *Times* since 1940. He had left his hometown, Winston-Salem, North Carolina, to attend Princeton University, where he earned a history degree. In 1928, his senior year in high school, he won a national contest for writing the best essay in a college newspaper. The prize was $500 and a job at the *Times* as a "cub" reporter. He initially rejected the post, but came to his senses and took it when he realized that the biggest big-city newspaper in America could pay considerably more than he could earn back home.[6]

Crowther started as a reporter for the city beat and wrote messages carried on the enormous glowing sign that continuously wrapped news reports around the *Times* building. He joined the drama desk in 1933 when the senior writer in that department, Brooks Atkinson, asked Crowther to become his assistant. For the next five years, Crowther covered the theater district and, one would imagine, was influenced by some of Atkinson's decidedly anticensorship views. By 1938, Crowther was also writing movie reviews, and when regular movie critic Frank Nugent moved to Hollywood in 1940, the position of first-string movie critic opened up. Crowther was the top critic for the most influential newspaper in the country for the next twenty-seven years.

The Miracle made Crowther into a fighter. Before that film, he had harshly criticized New York State censors for banning the 1946 film *Scarlet Street* and had been one of many critics to shower acclaim on *The Bicycle Thief*. But the case of *The Miracle* was different because of who condemned the film and because of how Crowther chose to defend it. On 28 December 1950, the New York Film Critics Circle, of which Crowther was vice president, sent a resolution by telegram to New York City mayor Vincent Impelliteri expressing the group's opposition to the move by the license commissioner. The critics were joined by the America Civil Liberties Union in this protest; its New York branch made an official offer "to give aid through our attorneys to any theatre willing to make an appropriate test case."[7]

Early in 1951, the *Miracle* case became a legal fight. Joseph Burstyn challenged Commissioner McCaffrey's decision by appealing it to the New York Supreme Court for New York County. Writing for that court, Justice Aron Steuer declared that the State Education Department, not the commissioner of licenses of New York City, had the power "to determine whether a motion picture [is] indecent, immoral or sacrilegious." He continued that "a local law which purports to give such municipal officer regulatory power as to the content of film is unconstitutional." As Laura Wittern-Keller has observed, the court's decision marked "the first time in thirty-five years that a commissioner's decision to interfere with a film had been reversed."[8]

McCaffrey was relatively powerless—a position he obviously found frustratingly new. His work, though, simply shifted tracks, moving to a more informal, indirect exercise of authority. New York City's municipal offices were largely run by Catholics, including the license commissioner, the fire commissioner, and the mayor. As many city residents knew at the time, the power directing the Catholic presence in New York resided at St. Patrick's Cathedral in the person of Francis Cardinal Spellman. As legal wrangling continued over the exhibition of *The Miracle*, a boycott began at the Paris Theater. It was inspired by a letter from Cardinal Spellman that was read at all New York City masses on 7 January 1951. The letter instructed the faithful—all Catholics in New York City and in the United States—to boycott any theater that dared to exhibit a movie the Legion of Decency condemned as "a sacrilegious and blasphemous mockery of Christian religious truth." Taking up Spellman's call to organize were two powerful Catholic organizations, the Knights of Columbus and the Catholic War Veterans. This last organization had released a statement before the cardinal's appeal declaring that it would back the decision by its former state commander, the city's commissioner of licenses, Edward T. McCaffrey.[9]

The legal snare, though, had not disappeared. On 19 January 1951, the New York State Board of Regents announced that it would hold a hearing on the matter of *The Miracle*. The regents pointed to the many letters they had received in opposition to the movie as evidence that something needed to be done. Wittern-Keller points out that the regents failed to mention the many letters they received in favor of approving the movie for distribution. A hearing was scheduled for 30 January—the first of its kind, because never before had this body been pressed to reevaluate a decision made by its motion picture division. The hearing was a bit of a sham. The regents refused to hear from Burstyn or his lawyer, Ephraim London, or from the eight groups and twenty-four individuals who had "filed statements with the committee and expected to be heard." Moreover, a small group of the regents had attended a screening of the film, after which they declared to reporters that they had found it sacrilegious—before they had heard testimony from any of the parties involved in the dispute. Not surprisingly, on 16 February 1951, the board of regents reversed a previous decision to license *The Miracle* and officially banned it from New York theaters. "*The Miracle* was suppressed in the name of freedom of religion—on religious grounds," Wittern-Keller explains. The lack of legal clarity actually enabled the state to take the action it did. It became increasingly clear that before censorship regimes could be toppled, prevailing opinion about the legitimacy of censorship had to change. And that is where Bosley Crowther came in.[10]

Members of the public began to respond to this string of events, many by writing to Bosley Crowther. One writer called *The Miracle* "Fascist inspired," contending that McCaffrey had every right to ban it because it mocked "the sacred in art in so universal a medium as the screen" and therefore was "a brazen trespass on the sacred rights and feelings of Believers and cannot claim universal privilege." The exhibition of the film was no mere trifling matter to those who believed that movies had that special power to connect—for good or ill—to millions of moviegoers in a diverse movie culture. At the same time, others in the audience believed that "the action of the License Commission in stopping the showing of the 'Miracle' is simply fantastic." Another pleaded: "Please take a strong editorial stand against License Commissioner banning of 'Miracle' at Paris Theatre." A letter from still another reader echoed such sentiments: "The forced withdrawal of the film 'The Miracle' should not be permitted to pass without challenge." One man wrote in to express his outrage against the antidemocratic nature of the censoring: "This is but the latest of a series of such actions by bigoted and ignorant groups and individuals of various extractions and persuasions, and I sincerely hope that you will use your paper's editorial prestige to condemn a practice so foreign to our way of life."[11]

Crowther responded in an article published on Sunday, 14 January 1951. Using the generous amount of space afforded him on the front page of the Arts section, Crowther began an earnest campaign for, as he declared, "A Free Screen." He suggested that controversies sparked by *The Miracle* and the British film *Oliver Twist* (which had outraged Jewish moviegoers because of the depiction of Fagin) "should be compelling occasion for people to give most solemn thought to the question of whether they are in favor of freedom of the screen—and how much." As a critic for a large, mass-circulation daily with a wide readership, Crowther took obvious care to characterize the issue of an offensive screen as something serious that should be handled within some kind of democratic forum. "The basic consideration . . . in the case of any picture which some element or groups may oppose," he wrote, "is whether real freedom of expression on the screen is sincerely desired and whether the cause of this freedom is worth enduring offense to maintain." In the *Miracle* case, Crowther saw all the issues that had prevented American filmmaking from maturing properly. Like many critics by the 1950s, Crowther believed movies were a legitimate—even vital—art, but filmmakers would never realize their medium's full potential until restrictions on what could be made were significantly loosened. He asked rhetorically, "Should we abide by the principle that enlightenment depends upon free thought and that the movies are one of our most potent media of enlightenment? . . . After all," he concluded, "if a certain type of picture is not to the general public's taste it is not—and will not be—expedient for theatres to show that type of film." Here was Crowther at his most democratic and diplomatic: he hoped movie culture would be shaped not by the domineering interests of minority groups but by general taste and popular opinion. He seemed to say, if you don't like a movie, don't see it; but don't prevent others from seeing it and please do not prevent someone from making it.[12]

Predictably, letters poured in to the *Times* responding to the news of McCaffrey's actions, Spellman's condemnation, and Crowther's stance. The *Times* ran six of them; five responded negatively to Crowther's position, one positively—the sole letter in support of Crowther was from a woman in New York City who praised the critic for opposing "self-appointed censors." This number was a fraction of the hundreds of responses that Crowther had received. He wrote back to many letter writers, beginning one with the apology, "Please forgive the tardiness of this reply. I have so many letters on the subject that it is taking me time to answer them." In a letter dated 29 January 1951, Crowther estimated that the ratio of favorable to unfavorable mail was "about 2–3." He provided such specific information in response to a letter writer who believed, based on the letters reprinted in the paper, that the overwhelming reaction was negative. That was not the case, though these letters revealed an interest in debating the nature of censorship and movie culture that surprised even Crowther.[13]

The exchange of letters represented a great outpouring of civic concern for both sides of the screen. Letters opposing McCaffrey's actions (and Spellman's denunciation) argued from a position in support of free speech, the integrity of movies as art, and the right of filmmakers to choose what they create and people to choose what they see. Letters critical of Crowther's stand condemned the corrupting influence of film, championed the right to protect religious beliefs from defamation, and expressed shock that a *Times* columnist would defend an "immoral" picture.

"I was greatly disturbed and surprised at your decision in favor of such trash," Salvatore Cantatore chided Crowther. As pastor of Mt. Carmel Church in Poughkeepsie, New York (about fifty miles north of New York City), Cantatore wanted to remind the *Times* critic that this case was about more than just a movie: "Today, more than ever," he preached, "when civilization is fighting for its survival, man must keep his eyes directed toward his spiritual destiny and use all his faculties to foster the true light and beauty of life and dispel the oncoming clouds of pagan materialism. Anyone working in the opposite direction is far more dangerous to our country than any Fifth Column, and he is the real one responsible for the collapse of civilization."[14]

It wasn't every day that a film critic was considered a subversive Antichrist, or that movies were thought to have the power to destroy Western civilization. Crowther responded to the Poughkeepsie priest respectfully: "I am sorry we do not agree on the merits of this film, and I am particularly sorry there had been so much controversy and bad feeling over it. But it is obvious," Crowther assured him, "that this is a picture which can say anything to different men. And I do not think that one need be irreligious or disrespectful of anyone else's religion in admiring it. I certainly do not regard myself as an evil or vicious man and yet I saw great humility and compassion in this picture. There's nothing more that I can say."[15]

Many of the letters Crowther received were articulate and impassioned arguments that dealt quite directly with the issues at the heart of the larger debate over movies as art, speech, and menace. For example, letters prompted Crowther to deliberate on the critic's relationship to the public. A letter from Patricia Mitchell defending the Catholic Church's position challenged Crowther to be more concrete. "In your column," she asserted, "you do not take the stand that either picture [*The Miracle* or *Oliver Twist*] is good or bad. You raise the question in return, 'Can we permit the exploitation of offensive drama for the sake of commercialism?'" Indeed, what was the point, she suggested, of offending the public? Forcing the issue, she continued: "Your presentation of the problem of freedom of the screen leads me to believe that because you have recognized this as a question to be contended with immediately you have brought it before your public without consider-

ing the matter fully." Crowther's reply ducked the issue. He retreated
to abstraction: "I might remind you that freedom of religion does not
mean freedom to suppress that which the people of a certain religion
find offensive to them." Fair enough; a minority point of view should
not dictate the rules that govern culture for all. However, Crowther's
explanation failed to address the larger issue of the justification for art.
For surely not every offensive work deserved the same treatment.[16]

Another letter raised a similar issue: "It seems that truth to you is
only relative," Marion Malara wrote to Crowther. "It depends not on
an objective standard but on the opinions or fancies of one group or
another. For what has expediency to do with truth?" To that accusation, Crowther shot back, "I disagree with you that the function of the
critic is to determine and enforce the common good. . . . I may express
my opinion on the subject, as you or anyone else may express theirs,
but I do not believe that anyone should have authority to enforce his
opinion in matters of art." In reply to another treatise on the rights and
responsibilities of critics, Crowther offered a homily on democratically
constructed standards: "Responsibility," he explained, "is something
which every man must determine for himself, and if he takes it upon
himself to do something which the majority of people may abhor, it is
up to the people to show that person that he has violated their truths
and their good taste." Yet how would such truths and taste be constructed? Where would optimistic pluralism end and hard-nosed, intrusive
restrictions begin? One thing was clear at this point in Crowther's career—he declared he was unwilling to tolerate "the suppression of the
arts as a means of wiping [evil] out of the world."[17]

Others would not be so generous. The affair concerning the Paris Theater indeed grew ugly and even dangerous. At their peak, the
pickets numbered over a thousand participants. Lillian Gerard remembered that many who marched seemed to be on their way to or coming
back from attending Catholic mass. "All through January, the pickets
maintained a constant vigil," she recalled. "They came every day after
work, and were there all day on weekends, waiting for us to yield."
Near the end of January, groups began to exchange bomb threats. On
Saturday evening, 20 January 1951, the evening manager of the Paris
Theater received such a threat by phone, forcing him to hustle nearly
six hundred people out into the cold New York night. It was a dramatic
scene. As the audience emptied the theater, two hundred more people,

who had been waiting outside to buy tickets to a later show, were pro-
tested by twenty-five pickets from the Catholic War Veterans. After this
episode, the fire department allowed people back into the theater and
issued Gerard and her manager a summons for the thirty-five people
who stood at the back of the theater waiting for the next show—using
the code violation as a subtle form of harassment. The next Saturday,
at 4:00 P.M., Cardinal Spellman received a threat of his own. A letter
arrived, crudely threatening: "Your barbarous church will be bombed
during one of the masses tomorrow. Nobody will know how it will be
delivered." The threat was signed "Mason." Several hours later the Paris Theater received its second bomb threat of the week. Once again,
movie patrons had to be evacuated so that the fire department could
search the building.[18]

Bosley Crowther and other New York film critics also came under
attack—though in their case bombs became barbs and the throwers
were well known. When the New York Film Critics Circle announced
plans to award *The Ways of Love* Best Foreign Language Film of 1950
at Radio City Music Hall, the hall's manager received a call from Martin Quigley, the man behind the Production Code and, in this case,
the axman for New York's Catholic officials. According to G. E. Eys-
sell, the managing director of Rockefeller Center, Quigley had told
him that if the ceremony went forward as planned, "Catholic Church
authorities would be gravely offended by this incident and it would not
be surprising if, on account of such an event, the Church would urge
the Catholic people to avoid attendance at the Music Hall in protest."
The threat worked; the ceremony was moved to a smaller, less con-
spicuous venue. Quigley gloated to a *Times* reporter that he was "glad
his warning had resulted in withdrawal of the award ceremony from
the Music Hall." He added that he "had spoken for no one but himself and had been following no advice or instructions in delivering his
warning." The critics still honored *The Ways of Love* and its distributor,
Joseph Burstyn, but they did so in the Rainbow Room atop Rockefeller
Center, far from the maddened crowd below. During the ceremony
the tempestuous film distributor reflected on the affair that he helped
spark, pausing to apologize if he had "brought some embarrassment"
to his supporters and his city.[19]

There seemed to be little shame on the other side. Two of the
Catholic faithful wrote to Crowther attempting to explain why Cardi-

nal Spellman was "obliged to protect the faith and morals of Catholics by all morally good means at his disposal. In the case of the showing of the 'Miracle' his duty was further necessitated because of the failure of the State Board of Ed. & drama critics such as yourself to comply with their obligations." In response, Crowther acknowledged the right of Cardinal Spellman and the Legion of Decency "to instruct the faithful not to see the film." But, reflecting on what had transpired recently, he shot back: "as one of those New York critics, I feel, however, that 'pressure' which was used to deny us the freedom of making our annual awards at Radio City Music Hall was of a distinctly 'insidious nature' and I feel sure that if you reason this thing out as a democratic American, you will think so too."[20]

In an era in which minority rights were just beginning to emerge as a test of American democratic principles, Crowther's dilemma with his Catholic readers struck an odd chord. His detractors had somehow found that freedom was served when censors cut to placate the wishes of a minority. "Is freedom *really* restricted when blasphemy . . . is not permitted?" one Catholic asked. Another argued with rather strained logic that democracy was advanced by following the judgment of a particular minority. After noting that two million Catholics had risen up "as one . . . to protest something that can be condemned even by the common tenets of decency," the writer declared, "I say continuing this picture is rule by the minority, because where do you have an organized group who approve it that is as large as the group that objects?" A Protestant minister provided an answer: "Let Cardinal Spellman and all the Roman Catholic hierarchy understand," he told Crowther, "that millions of American Christians and millions of America's other religious people have not elected them to decide for us what is damaging to our religious life." Another simply admitted, "Our principal weakness is the silence of great groups of citizenry, which articulate minorities are quick to interpret as consent."[21]

The intensity of the fight over *The Miracle* had warped the seriousness of the issue; it was slowly becoming something other than a dispute over the blasphemous nature of an Italian film. Crowther made that clear in a reply to a Catholic reader: "I am not sure that we are so far in disagreement, as you seem to think. Believe me, I find 'evil and blasphemy' in any guise as distasteful as do you, but I also feel that any endeavor to determine and legislate against either in art is dangerous."

During the course of this controversy, Catholic tactics had revealed an institution in trouble rather than a group fighting for respect against a bigoted world. In a letter to Patrick F. Scanlon, the editor of the powerful and influential Catholic daily newspaper the *Brooklyn Tablet*, Crowther scolded Scanlon for accusing the New York Film Critics Circle of being anti-Catholic. "This strikes me," Crowther admonished him, "as the sort of baseless innuendo which will only provoke unchristian resentment and hate." Indeed, the Catholic Church by 1950 was in a position of unprecedented power—a fact that made it more often a target of criticism than a target of bigotry.[22]

Irrepressible critic Gilbert Seldes asked, "What is any group to do if picketing and protest fail to remove from public attention anything offensive to its moral sense?" To many New York Catholics the answer was to demand a change in the law that governed Catholics and non-Catholics alike—an inversion, Seldes pointed out, of the Jeffersonian principle of minority rights. "Given sufficient organization," Seldes observed, "minorities can paralyze the general will of the people." Movies were the perfect test for this principle because, he reasoned, "they remain the one great popular art which people pay to see and about which, consequently, they would protest if their feelings were sufficiently outraged."[23]

Crowther's most extensive reflection on the controversy over *The Miracle* was published as a lengthy review in the *Atlantic Monthly*—which again generated hundreds of letters in response. Crowther argued that the central legal issue was sacrilege and whether such a definition could apply to a movie in the public sector. But while that question meandered through the courts, Crowther found it "hard to believe that such oppression could occur in this country at this time, especially in a great enlightened city and over a minor piece of motion picture art." He assumed a tone of feigned shock that a small Italian art film could cause such a stir in New York City. That this could have happened, he suggested, indicated that what was really happening was "a calculated showdown test of strength" by the city's reigning powers. Crowther intimated that Catholic opinion, like general opinion, was divided over the issue of blasphemy; thus, that was not really the issue. The problem was that the film had challenged the Catholic Church's ability to marshal both the laity and the state censors to exercise its will. The fact that the film opened in New York had special significance because of the power the church wielded over the rest of the nation from this one city. "The most logical assumption," Crowther offered, "is that *The Miracle* became an issue after it opened in New York, and that the Catholic artillery was assembled in mounting arrays as it was seen that the distributor and the theatre were far from minded to heed the special objections of the Church." In other words, the Legion attacked to save face. And therefore it had to mount boycotts to make its point. Crowther recounted the scene outside the theater for effect: "An ugly and fanatic spirit was often apparent among the marching men as they shouted in the faces of people lined up to buy tickets, 'Don't enter that cesspool!' and 'Don't look at that filth!' A grim sort of jingoism was also confused in their cries, 'This is a Communist picture!' and 'Buy American!'" Even the powerful editor Martin Quigley got desperate during this fight, resorting to threats against the managers of Radio City Music Hall. What were the Catholic Church and Quigley afraid of? "Obviously the emotion that has been roused by the *Miracle* case has only increased the confusion in the public mind about film censorship," Crowther observed. And that was dangerous to authorities with a vested interest in public acceptance of such control.[24]

As before, reactions to Crowther's article were mixed, quite eloquent at times, and surprisingly thorough. Robert Sherrill, future writer for the *Nation* and *Washington Post*, wrote in to encourage Crowther and the editors. "You will, undoubtedly, be mightily condemned by some for unveiling a frighteningly powerful pressure group. But don't knuckle under," he implored them. "The majority of Atlantic readers will support you." He was probably correct that most of the magazine's readers did support its decision to run the piece. However, a fair number of offended readers made their opinions clear as well. "If this story is typical of your editorial policy, you can stop sending me your magazine now," one declared. Though he had not seen the film at issue, he believed it was no better, no more "natural" (a defense Crowther had offered) than a "bowel movement." Another reader put her response more succinctly and less colorfully: "I opened the magazine and read one article, 'The Miracle.' Please cancel my subscription, and refund the balance of $5.50. . . . I'd much rather give the money to some worthy organization than read such trash."[25]

The letters for and against Crowther's position and the editors' decision to run his piece were about fifty-fifty. The sheer volume of mail, though, forced the editors to send back a standard reply to those letters voicing objection or condemnation and demanding a refund of their subscription. It read, in part:

> In the same mail which brought your letter of denunciation came a note from a prominent Protestant in New York canceling her subscription because we had accepted the advertisement of the Knights of Columbus. Tempers are unreasonably short in these days of anxiety.
>
> I ask you to reconsider. It is not the Atlantic's policy to persecute any religious body. We criticize only when we feel that a fundamental American principle is at stake and we defend just as strenuously as we criticize.
>
> I believe it perfectly proper for the Catholic Church to proscribe certain books and films which it believes its members should not see. . . . But I have never heard any Roman Catholic argue that the list should be enforced the country over. This was the freedom which Mr. Crowther was upholding in his article.[26]

Crowther and his stand on a small Italian film had grown into a widespread intellectual public debate over the dimensions of a free society. The effect of Crowther's decision to make that stand reshaped his career as a film critic. While he was not the only critic to comment on the controversy—to be alive and writing in New York City at the time required at least a passing notice of it—he was the only critic who became part of that controversy. Because of his involvement, Crowther transformed the Arts section of the *New York Times* into a forum for discussions on censorship. It made the paper into an actor in the struggle over a "free screen." Moreover, Crowther paid considerable attention to public reactions. His longer pieces on Sundays illustrated that he had read his mail and felt some responsibility to respond to it. He took his job as a public intellectual literally—he wanted to serve the public good by advancing concerns and issues raised by his readers. That sincerity was a product of Crowther's intellectual approach to criticism. He wrote about an art made popular by a mass audience, and he wrote his reviews and his think pieces with those people in mind. While undoubtedly interested in leading his readers in some direction, Crowther also clearly felt obligated to appreciate the somewhat intimate relationship many of his readers believed they had with him. In later years, Crowther's concern for the welfare of his audience could seem patronizing when he worried publicly about the effect movies had on society, and his critics blasted him for considering it possible to determine the limits of public morality. Yet in the era of *The Miracle*, Crowther helped establish the terms of a new kind of debate over the freedom of the screen.

Not all Catholics came out against Crowther. The liberal editors at *Commonweal* also questioned the effect the church's authority had on this ostensibly democratic art. Throughout the controversy over *The Miracle*, the Catholic hierarchy had framed the fight over the film in Manichean terms; officials such as Cardinal Spellman and the priests who parroted his views imagined it to be another battle in the cold war. Yet William P. Clancy, a professor at Notre Dame University and an editor of the *Commonweal*, believed that the rash Catholic response bordered on "a semi-ecclesiastical McCarthyism." He forcefully questioned the rationale used by the Catholic Church to exercise an inordinate amount of influence over a pluralistic society. Clancy had been an informal ally of Crowther throughout the *Miracle* case, among the few prominent Catholic intellectuals to stick his neck out and dissent from the church's position on the movie and on Crowther.[27]

In the more conservative Catholic journal the *Sign*, a letter writer wanted to know if the church had banned all Catholics from seeing *The Miracle*, since "current opinion seems to be that no organization can be so dictatorial." In response, the editors seized the opportunity to condemn what seemed to them the obvious source of such thought. "Since entertainment is either moral or immoral, it is sad that a Catholic takes his cue from Hollywood rather than from the Legion of Decency," the *Sign* declared. "One may as well adopt Bosley Crowther of the *New York Times* as a mentor."[28]

It seems clear from reading William Clancy's work during this controversy and after that he, too, had been reading Crowther but arriving at a very different conclusion. Clancy had the audacity to entitle one of his pieces on the *Miracle* case "The Catholic as Philistine," emphasizing one aspect of Catholic criticism that had troubled many Catholic intellectuals in the postwar period. Reaction to a minor foreign film had illustrated the Catholic proclivity for seeing almost any incident on which the hierarchy focused as a threat to the moral nature of mankind. Such an approach illustrated the too-real connection the church still had to its medieval past. The church was attempting to carve a place for Catholic opinion within a world no longer beholden to any absolute authority. Clancy argued that "surely the last place such judgments can be reached is in the partisan atmosphere of the picket line. It seems obvious that to fail to recognize this is to fail to recognize the reverence due the being, complexity, and integrity of truth." Clancy's position was closer to Crowther's than to Cardinal Spellman's, which was not too surprising since editors at *Commonweal* were not priests and published the journal for readers who were not necessarily Catholic. But for him the crisis at hand was not the potential damage a movie could do but the withering relevance of Catholic opinion. Speaking very much like Crowther, Clancy put some faith in the people who read his work, for, he argued, "the type of educated person, Catholic or non-Catholic . . . who makes a habit of attending outstanding foreign films is usually quite capable of protecting his own intellectual, spiritual, and moral integrity, of using his own judgments."[29]

Perhaps there is no clearer illustration that Clancy attempted to move Catholic opinion toward Crowther than his piece entitled "Freedom of the Screen." Crowther had written a number of articles in the *Times* using such a term to discuss all arguments and legal cases against the prior censorship of films. In Clancy's view, freedom of the screen was a foregone conclusion by the mid-1950s; thus, Catholics had to assess whether or not they wanted to be part of the conversation over the future of moviemaking and moviegoing. But to participate in such a discussion, one had to agree that "prior censorship of motion pictures . . . [was] repugnant to any free society because such censorship is necessarily arbitrary to a high degree." Clancy's argument was a bold appeal to accept a more fluid and pluralistic system of cultural norms. In other words, he became an advocate for democratic culture. "Democracy must, sometimes, be saved from the righteous as well as protected against the wicked," he preached. And he reasoned further that if "the country has survived with freedom of speech and of the press . . . it will probably survive with this new freedom." His chief concern, though, remained "that too frequently it is Catholic voices which are raised most violently in protest and fear whenever a freedom is born."[30]

Clancy would also find common cause with Crowther on a tangen-

tial issue that burned even more intensely than the problem of censorship—anti-Communism. The same year that the *Miracle* case was
resolved, Crowther panned the 1952 film *My Son John* as a simplistic
and heavy-handed anti-Communist tirade. The movie was "so strongly
dedicated to the purpose of the American anti-Communist purge,"
wrote Crowther, "that it seethes with the sort of emotionalism and il-
logic that is characteristic of so much thinking these days. There are
some . . . things about this picture that may cause a thoughtful person
to feel a shudder of apprehension at the militance and dogmatism it
reveals—its snide attitude toward intellectuals, its obvious pitch for religious conformity and its eventual whole-hearted endorsement of its
Legionnaire's stubborn bigotry."[31]

The review provoked a predictable negative response but also
prompted Clancy to send Crowther a letter of appreciation. He gave
Crowther an advance copy of an editorial his journal intended to run
that was critical of the film and even more critical of the positive response to it by many Catholics. Expressing some exasperation, Clancy
wrote: "The majority of the Catholic press seems to have been almost
indecent in its haste to embrace this frightening film." He hoped to
offer "a more sober and responsible Catholic stand on this issue." Clancy even invited Crowther to meet with the editorial staff to discuss "a
number of real problems connected with Catholic film activities."[32]

The meeting of minds between critic and Catholic suggested that
the cultural context in which movies existed was changing. A similar
meeting of the minds between a distributor and the Supreme Court
also suggested the emergence of a new era. Joseph Burstyn used
$60,000 of his own money and lawyers from the ACLU to appeal his
case all the way to the U.S. Supreme Court. Along the way, his mission was stymied at every level by official New York, from the board of
regents—the body that had final authority over the censorship arm of
the state—to the highest state court, the court of appeals. On 26 May
1952, the U.S. Supreme Court overturned them all. In a unanimous
decision, Justice Tom Clark famously asserted: "It cannot be doubted
that motion pictures are a significant medium for the communication
of ideas. They may affect public attitudes and behavior in a variety of
ways, ranging from direct espousal of a political or social doctrine to
the subtle shaping of thought which characterizes all artistic expression. The importance of motion pictures as an organ of public opinion

is not lessened by the fact that they are designed to entertain as well as to inform."[33]

The court had taken a step toward redefining movies—while still commerce, they were also a form of speech. And then the court went a step further, taking on the working definition of movies that had made the censoring sensibility seem sensible. "It is urged," Clark noted, "that motion pictures do not fall within the First Amendment's aegis because their production, distribution, and exhibition is a large-scale business conducted for private profit. We cannot agree. That books, newspapers, and magazines are published and sold for profit does not prevent them from being a form of expression whose liberty is safeguarded by the First Amendment. We fail to see why operation for profit should have any different effect in the case of motion pictures." True, they were manufactured by an industry for commercial profit, but so was most other speech. The court illustrated that society should no longer tolerate treating one kind of commercial speech as if it were toxic waste.[34]

Clark also addressed the underlying fear that had motivated censors across time. "It is further urged that motion pictures possess a greater capacity for evil, particularly among the youth of a community, than other modes of expression. Even if one were to accept this hypothesis, it does not follow that motion pictures should be disqualified from First Amendment protection. If there be capacity for evil it may be relevant in determining the permissible scope of community control, but it does not authorize substantially unbridled censorship such as we have here." The court made it official: movies were entitled to protection even if they were offensive. "For the foregoing reasons," the court concluded, "expression by means of motion pictures is included within the free speech and free press guaranty of the First and Fourteenth Amendments."[35]

The implications of the court's decision were murky at the time and have yet to receive a full investigation. The *Miracle* case did not declare all movie censorship unconstitutional. States could still create laws that prevented the exhibition of movies deemed legally obscene. And Hollywood's Production Code remained alive and well for another sixteen years. But the case did function as a cultural tipping point after which assumptions that supported movie censorship came under increased scrutiny. It was a step toward the world that allowed *Deep Throat*.[36]

Joseph Burstyn died the year after his historic victory. At his funeral, Bosley Crowther delivered a eulogy. Reading from a typewritten page of remarks, Crowther reminded mourners that Burstyn had "approached [the *Miracle* case] with reluctance and apprehension." After all, the man's livelihood was on the line either way he took the case. Crowther noted that Burstyn's heroics were all the more remarkable because he moved forward despite his fears. "His fears and anxieties and apprehensions that crowded upon him in this case were the very fuel that he used to fire his resolution when the challenge appeared." Burstyn did this with his own money and without Hollywood putting its muscle—publicly and unified—behind him. When asked to reflect on his victory, Burstyn spoke pragmatically, like a businessman: "When the swimming pools begin drying up," he mused, "then Hollywood will begin thinking about freedom too. You can't give in to censorship; you must stand up for your self-respect." The industry's fortunes had indeed declined since the mid-1940s, and it had slowly begun to come around to the notion of moviemaking that Crowther had argued for since the end of the war. Realism and mature themes would bring adults into theaters, but only the public, Crowther argued, could persuade Hollywood to brave the wrath of pro-censorship forces. In the midst of Burstyn's case against censorship, Crowther declared in the *Times:* "Unless the screen is free to cultivate this audience, with taste and intelligence, it will be doomed. A great and potential art medium will be forced to theatrical decay—at least, in this great and vital country where it has found its most stimulating soil."[37]

From the days of the *Miracle* case until the end of his career with the *Times* in 1967, Crowther stuck to a liberal faith in the potential of movies. His language emphasized the complexities of moviemaking and the experience of moviegoing. His foes—the PCA and the Legion—worked consistently to contain and reduce the contingencies governing movie culture. To combat them, Crowther worked toward educating the public to appreciate a fuller view of movies as art. Following Crowther's baptism by fire, he did indeed preach a liberal creed of tolerance, responsibility, and, most of all, freedom.[38]

In his column celebrating the Supreme Court decision in the *Miracle* case, Crowther wrote, "The sudden prospect of no censors is a startling and heady thing, containing all sort of intimations of lurid and reckless unrestraint. Such pop-eyed anticipations are not only baseless but absurd. The screen with its new implied freedom, can be no more reckless than the legitimate theatre or the press." Later, in 1954, when the Supreme Court again ruled against the censors of New York State in the case of the French film *La Ronde,* Crowther illustrated his faith in the people: "Private opinion is weak but public opinion is almost omnipotent, someone has said, and that is a rather apt rule to rely upon with respect to films." The critic understood that some people will always go to see pornography but wanted to believe that "the vast majority of the people will exercise judgment and taste according to what they have discovered is pleasing and rewarding to them." "A free screen," Crowther declared, "means not only freedom for those who sell, it means freedom for those who buy. That is implicit in the nature of our democracy."[39]

It seems to me that unlike his fellow critics in literature, theater, and, certainly, high art, Crowther had to consider how the idea of the audience influenced his work. Since the inception of motion pictures, commentators had referred to them as a "democratic art." That notion had thrived because the people who patronized movies were, quite frankly, as significant to the movie culture as those who created the pictures themselves. What comes through from reading Crowther's reviews and the letters he received about them is that his significance as a critic depended almost completely on the relevance of his position on censorship to his audience. Once censors had been beaten, the critic—the great liberal champion of the people's right to see movies—encountered a much tougher foe, an ambiguous world of artistic freedom and individual taste. Crowther helped to disentangle movies from the web of control but was unable to convince other, postcensorship generations that his kind of liberal criticism remained relevant.[40]

Crowther hoped it would be possible "for pictures to be made on any theme, so long as they are made with integrity and offered to the public for what they are. Then it will be up to the public to decide what it wants to see. This is the only arrangement that is feasible for the survival of a true art, and it is only as an artistic medium of consistently strong communication that the theatrical motion picture will survive." Crowther's tragic mistake was to imagine that the public would never be as cynical about human nature and popular taste as censors had been. He came to learn that if the defense of movie art demanded the abolition of censorship, an irrepressible public made it almost necessary to bring it back.[41]

3

Baby Doll **and** *Commonweal* **Criticism**

IT LOOMED ALMOST as large as the Statue of Liberty, and its symbolic significance was, in a certain sense, comparable to that homage to freedom. The *New York Times* described it as a "Red-Blonde Beauty with 75-Foot Legs." What was it? "Why," the *Times* declared, "it's Baby Doll of Times Square!" Throughout most of the fall of 1956, artist Robert Everhart had constructed a billboard for an upcoming steamy Hollywood movie entitled *Baby Doll*. The lead actress and main attraction of the film was a movie starlet named Carroll Baker. Director Elia Kazan had the idea to create an advertising campaign using the signature motif of the movie—a sexily clad Baker lying in an oversized crib sucking her thumb while looking directly out at those looking in. In addition to that photo appearing in front of theaters, atop marquees, and in newspapers, Kazan also had this image projected to monstrous proportions along New York City's Great White Way—Broadway. The billboard covered 15,600 square feet between 45th and 46th streets—in other words, it took up a full block of New York City's Times Square, the flashiest piece of real estate in the country.

Everhart had been building billboards in New York City since 1910 and had done similar giant presentations of Marion Davies, Marilyn Monroe, and, during the Second World War, a GI gritting his teeth while biting a pin from a grenade. Everhart was known as the best in the business, and his "Baby Doll" stretched 135 feet long, which meant that it was only 15 feet shorter than Lady Liberty in New York Harbor. In the fall of 1956, there was little to suggest that the Baby Doll billboard would have much else in common with the nation's clearest symbol of democracy and freedom. And yet a controversy erupted over Kazan's movie, sparked in part by Everhart's billboard, that became a significant turning point in a long-running battle to free movie culture from its old order.[1]

The alluring, gigantic picture of Baby Doll was a short walk from the most powerful Catholic outside Rome, Francis Cardinal Spellman. The cardinal's residence and office were next to St. Patrick's Cathedral, a massive church that sits on its own large piece of prime real estate at 5th Avenue and 50th Street, a few blocks over and up from Times Square. Thus, in the fall and winter of 1956, the city's sexiest newcomer shared a neighborhood with its most revered resident. For Spellman, known as the American pope, the church could not tolerate such a blatant affront to its role as curator of the nation's moral health. Through the Catholic Legion of Decency, the church had consistently warned its faithful of the dangers of placing themselves in close proximity to sin. Like an enormous sun of sinfulness emanating its prurient, sensual heat, the block-long billboard of Baby Doll seemed designed to burn all who looked up at it. Kazan exclaimed in an interview with French film critic Michel Ciment that even he was astonished by the size of the sign: "It was such a big sign! *A whole city block!*" But he also admitted to an ulterior motive: "It was like defying the Legion of Decency. It was a great pleasure to do it."[2]

It is not hard to imagine how the controversy erupted. Cardinal Spellman devoted part of his Christmas season each year to visiting U.S. troops around the world. In the late fall of 1956, he had been to Asia, where the cold war had become considerably hotter following the Chinese Communist revolution in 1949 and the war in Korea from 1950 to 1953. When he returned to New York in preparation for the Christmas celebration, Spellman was disgusted to find that this sacred season was marred yet again by a movie. The man who more than likely reinforced Spellman's outrage was the church's expert on such matters, Martin Quigley, whose office overlooked Times Square. As he had done many times in the past, the magazine publisher drafted a response for the cardinal denouncing Hollywood's crass commercialism. However, unlike in those previous episodes, Spellman decided to deliver the statement himself.

At a mass at St. Patrick's Cathedral on 16 December 1956, Spellman publicly condemned the film from the pulpit of the hallowed cathedral. He told the estimated two thousand people gathered that he was "shocked" to see the release of "another motion picture [that] has been responsibly judged to be evil in concept and which is certain to exert an immoral and corrupting influence upon those who see it." He further found it "astonishing and deplorable" that Hollywood's leading authorities had passed *Baby Doll* for general viewing. "It is," the cardinal thundered, "the moral and patriotic duty of every loyal citizen to defend America not only from dangers which threaten our beloved country from beyond our boundaries, but also the dangers which confront us at home." Indeed, Spellman had visited those selfless soldiers who protected the nation from afar; what enraged him was the cancer that seemed to be festering from within. The cardinal had personally spoken like this only two other times: to attack Communism and to discuss the imprisonment of Josef Cardinal Mindszenty in Communist-controlled Hungary. Revealing his frustration, he concluded: "It has been suggested that this action on my part will induce many people to view this picture and thus make it a material success. If this be the case, it will be an indictment of those who defy God's laws and contribute to corruption in America."[3]

Spellman's sermon was unusually harsh and unusually public. His indictment of both a movie and anyone—Catholic or non-Catholic—who dared to see *Baby Doll* was unprecedented. The Catholic Church had opposed movies before, *The Miracle* being the most significant of those cases. But the fury with which New York's cardinal attacked *Baby Doll*—a mediocre picture at best—indicated that something more serious was afoot within the Catholic Church. During the period between *The Miracle* and *Baby Doll*, the church's authority on matters such as movies had grown increasingly tenuous. The Supreme Court's decision in *Burstyn v. Wilson* weakened the church's power to exercise Catholic influence through state censors. And the kind of movie culture that took shape in New York City illustrated a predilection among moviegoers—many of whom were Catholic—for more mature and, therefore, potentially controversial subject matter. The church watched worriedly as Hollywood responded to the new tastes emerging among a better-educated and perhaps more daring audience. Thus, underlying the crisis of Catholic cultural authority was a sense that culture by its very nature belonged to the people who made it important. Many New

Yorkers believed that movies belonged to the moviegoers, not priests. As New Yorkers grew increasingly less tolerant of Catholic denunciations, protests like Spellman's simply struck many people as sanctimonious at best and authoritarian at worst. Indeed, the Catholic Church had to decide whether it wanted to be regarded as a moral curator or an American fascist.[4]

Historian Una Cadegan explains that during the 1950s the Catholic hierarchy realized it could no longer rely on its influence behind the scenes in Hollywood or among state censorship boards in its fight against crass consumer culture. Its traditional avenues closed, the church took its fight to the public, hoping that popular action—spearheaded by the laity—would convince Americans in general to stand with the church on matters of culture. "Defenders of the Legion [of Decency] and the National Organization for Decent Literature," Cadegan writes, "maintained that their program reflected the values of all 'decent' or 'right-thinking' people. They claimed to be speaking for the majority of their fellow citizens, a cultural majority powerless in the face of amoral, monied conglomerates. Further, they were affirming their own right to define mid-century culture against, as they saw it, both Eastern sophisticates and West Coast moguls." But Spellman's explosion failed to win converts. "The public to whom the rationale was ostensibly addressed was alarmed rather than energized by the communal prescription of individual action, by theological imperatives toward social action," Cadegan notes. While Catholics defended their actions in language that played upon democratic notions of public life, the arguments they used and the actions they took undermined the spirit of their defense.[5]

Into the breach between Catholic action and democratic culture strode the editors and writers at *Commonweal*. The journal *Commonweal* had consistently been a source for moderate and liberal Catholic views on the most pressing issues of the day, including film censorship and the role Catholics played in constructing popular taste. Sensitive to the crisis of authority that racked the church, writers at *Commonweal* prepared Catholics for the postcensor world. By using their journal much like Crowther used the Arts and Leisure section of the *New York Times*, these writers addressed a public that had grown tired of censors and restrictions. *Commonweal* offered pluralism and criticism. And in doing so, the journal created a new kind of Catholic critic, one who illustrated that it was possible to judge culture without moralizing it, to lead people without threatening them with eternal damnation. In fact, *Commonweal's* work was so successful it made tactics such as Spellman's thunderous declaration against *Baby Doll* obsolete.[6]

In the early postwar period, *Commonweal* had earned a reputation for being liberal and Catholic, two traits that had often seemed at war with each other. Starting in the 1930s, *Commonweal's* editors had opposed the prevailing Catholic position on Spain's fascist dictator, Francisco Franco, sharply criticized the tactics of red-baiting Senator Joseph McCarthy, and taken a view contrary to that of church hierarchy on how best to regulate and regard motion pictures in America. It was a record, the editors admitted, that had earned them the label of "liberal" by both supporters and foes. But if they were tagged for valuing the American Constitution and opposing "any interference with due process of law," then, the editors said, they would accept it. At base, they offered a simple explanation for their position: "We think Catholics have not given enough thought to what it means to live in a pluralistic society and we consider it imperative that they repair this omission." But they also made clear that while such a position offered them editorial guidance, they never imagined that their views stood for or reflected official Catholic doctrine. *Commonweal* represented "not a movement but an attitude," they explained, and although it was a Catholic attitude, the journal "frequently represent[ed] a minority point of view — or at least a point of view quite different from that found in many diocesan papers and magazines." In other words, this wasn't the Legion of Decency.[7]

Commonweal was unabashedly liberal and cosmopolitan. And it could act unlike any other Catholic periodical of the day because it operated in a city that was unlike any other in the country. *Commonweal* relied on the intellectual community in New York for its readership, its staff, and its inspiration. While Spellman and the Legion believed that through their work they helped save their faithful from the immoral influence of sordid movies, the editors at *Commonweal* hoped to rescue Catholics from the intellectual straitjacket that such a mission had created. In picking this fight, *Commonweal* did not simply parrot the liberal press or the ACLU or other opponents of Catholic pressure, though. Rather, the journal stood firm on a principle that was part of the Catholic intellectual tradition, though often overlooked — that

Catholics were one of many groups that contributed to a larger discussion on the limits of a free society. The editors did not contest that the church should serve as a moral check on immorality, but they did contend that Catholics could not afford to dismiss modern culture as categorically illegitimate. Part of modern culture was the debate over how to control movies.

William Clancy, the editor who had staunchly defended Bosley Crowther, positioned himself as one of the three chief spokesmen, together with John Cogley and Walter Kerr, for the journal on film censorship. The three were concerned about the perception non-Catholics had of Catholic thought. With good reason, all three worried that situations like the ones sparked by *The Miracle* and *Baby Doll* had made it appear that Catholics were not good democrats. Kerr's fellow theater critics often doubted whether he could be a credible critic and remain a Catholic.

In a piece published in April 1950, Kerr contrasted criticism of art as "a thing made, not a thing done, and hence not subject to moral evaluation" with the approach assumed by the Legion and most priests who investigated the "immorality" of books, plays, and movies. The article revealed his trepidation about the Legion's guidance: "When I made a lecture tour among Catholic organizations recently," Kerr told readers, "not a single question was asked me regarding the artistic merits of anything." The readership of *Commonweal* was unique in that it had as many non-Catholic subscribers as Catholic readers. Thus, Kerr's observations must have only reinforced preconceived notions of Catholics as moral watchdogs. "The only questions were moral questions, morally phrased," Kerr sighed. "I think it is fair enough to say that, among rank-and-file Catholics, the moral evaluation of art is the only evaluation now being made." Kerr acknowledged the bind that the parish priest was in: "His duty is to concern himself with prudence, and if he succeeds in prudently guiding all who come to him in his lifetime, it will not really matter very much if he has ignored or helped to destroy the norms for evaluating art, and the art itself as a consequence. The prudence *is* more important."[8]

Kerr consistently explored the consequences of the general Catholic approach to art: that because Catholics seemed so reluctant to accept aesthetic judgment, their attitude encouraged the production of outright bad art and discouraged those who had been inspired to produce something extraordinary. He argued that in the end the loser was the integrity of art. In an attempt to protect society from a perceived harm—even though such harm might not exist—the moralist "must ignore or abandon aesthetic norms. He must discard the notion of integrity for fear of the damage integrity may do. Having done away with the appropriate artistic norms, he must fill the gap with moral norms, the only norms with which he is familiar. In place of a truth which beauty requires, he substitutes an ideal of untruth, as though an untruth were less capable of doing damage." Kerr's strong position was not merely a defense of art against ill-tempered moralists, it was, as Clancy and Cogley also emphasized, an attempt to elevate the general opinions Catholics had of art beyond simply placing it within a moral quandary. Kerr hoped that by improving the intellectual integrity of Catholic opinion in regard to the arts, he would also educate Catholics so that their reactions did not seem so provincial and irrational. In the long run, Catholics might be able to take credit for encouraging rather than discouraging the production of better art.[9]

Commonweal offered a synthesis of liberal and Catholic approaches to society and culture that did justice to both sides. In historical terms, that achievement served as an intellectual bridge, spanning different eras of Catholic thought and moving the church toward Vatican II. John Cogley received confirmation of *Commonweal's* significance when in 1963 he participated in the proceedings of that historic undertaking in Rome. He learned from one of the Vatican's prelates that the journal "had been read carefully" over the years, and that he should be proud of the fact that "the magazine [had] sensed the mood of the universal Church long before it found expression at the Vatican Council." Rodger Van Allen, the author who related this story, called what Cogley and others at *Commonweal* did a "nonmovement movement" that "achieved certain dimensions of a sect quality in its relationship to the Roman Catholic Church." Integral to the journal's unique reputation was that it illustrated the potential of Catholic laity to influence the church. Vatican II was the official opening of the church, a figurative as well as literal turning of the hierarchy toward—rather than away from—the faithful. In this sense, *Commonweal* competed with and beat out organizations such as the Legion of Decency for influence with Catholics.[10]

During its most active and vital period, from the mid-1930s through the 1960s, the journal's chief editor was Edward S. Skillin. Born in New York City and educated at Fordham and Columbia universities, Skillin promoted a unified editorial policy by bringing together junior editors and contributors that shared his background—almost all were working-class kids who went on to study in New York City universities. And they all championed the protection of constitutional liberties in order to steer American Catholics toward a better understanding of their country. "When the magazine saw American Catholics ignorantly attempting to coerce fellow Americans into a morality stemming from a particular religious group," Martin Bredeck explains, "*Commonweal* realized that American Catholics had still not grasped what America meant as a nation." Skillin intended to correct that notion. "The editor gloried in his acceptance of the principle of American pluralism," Bredeck writes, "and hoped that such outspoken admission would, perhaps, shock his fellow Catholics into realizing that to be an American Catholic meant to live at peace, and at home, with both religious faith and with a man-made principle of government which recognized the separation of the two." Prior to 1950, such issues as fascism, Communism, and liberalism had occupied the pages of *Commonweal*, until *The Miracle* forced Catholics to face the issue of church-state relations through the practice of censorship.[11]

Six months after *The Miracle* case was settled, *Commonweal* ran an issue devoted to motion pictures in contemporary America. The editors introduced the issue under the title "The Critics and the Guardians," suggesting that perhaps it was time to consider movies from a perspective different from the one promoted by the Legion and apparently accepted by most Catholics. It was clear that Walter Kerr's critical view guided the issue. In his flagship article, "Catholics and Hollywood," he contended that the standards by which Catholics seemed to judge motion pictures had little to do with aesthetics or intelligence and much to do with how simplistic, pro-Catholic messages were projected. As a consequence, Kerr explained, "the identification of good will with good work is commonplace in the Catholic press. Unfortunately, the sort of art which Catholics are urged to admire is commonplace, too— and the power which Catholic spokesmen have come to wield over the motion picture has helped make the motion picture even more commonplace than it need have been."[12]

What the Legion in particular had done to Catholic opinion, Kerr

believed, was truly disheartening because it had engendered a "petri-
faction of taste," which "discredits the entire Catholic intellectual tradition." But rather than offer an alternative aesthetic judgment, Catholics
instead turned to a different weapon—the threat of economic boycott.
"The only persuasiveness we have been able to whip up is the persuasiveness of the dollar," Kerr shrugged. Thus, rather than join in the
debate over the complexity of art, Catholic opinion had simplified the
situation to an extent that would do long-term harm to the opinions of
Catholics. "Our fear that any recognition of the claims of the 'esthetic'
may undermine the Catholic accomplishment to date, our reluctance
to encourage any study of the nature of art as art, our insistence that
the Catholic contribution stop dead at the cautionary level, have also
brought about [a] second penalty . . . the discouragement of the creative film-maker pursuing the ultimate possibilities of his craft." Like
Bosley Crowther, Kerr, too, believed that moviemakers had to be able
to "follow the bent of human nature honestly through its aberrant as
well as its generous impulses, through its virtues and vices alike, until
all fall into place in a complex, but truthful pattern."[13]

Father Gerald Vann, a Dominican priest, took issue with Kerr's argument in an essay *Commonweal* published a few months later. He
questioned Kerr's premise that aesthetics and morals existed in two separate spheres and asked the rather provocative question of how much
aesthetic ugliness was allowable before such "trash" affected the moral
integrity of society. "It is bad theology to regard aesthetic values as lying
wholly outside the realm of morals," Vann asserted, "and when we fight
for better standards in art and literature we are doing something which
is not merely humanistically valuable, but which in the last resort is
part of the total process of redeeming and renewing the world."[14]

Although Kerr did not directly respond to Vann's contentions, the
critic clearly had in mind the kinds of issues the priest had raised in a
book published a year later based on the Gabriel Richard Lecture he
gave at Trinity College. Kerr had consistently acknowledged that with
any kind of freedom came responsibility, so he did not advocate a value-
neutral world in which anything goes. But in order to get to a stage in
which such a debate about artistic values could happen, he stated in no
uncertain terms that "what must be discredited and defeated is not the
isolated instance of unjustified censorship, but the principle of censorship." Why? Kerr did not defend art for art's sake. Rather, he connected

the need for aesthetic judgment with Catholic participation in a democratic culture. To be good democrats, Catholics needed to understand that acceptance of aesthetic criteria was the only basis on which to have a broad public discussion. Using morals, as Vann and many other Catholic priests and officials demanded, undermined the pluralistic nature of cultural criticism. Thus, Kerr's position on censorship and art and motion pictures echoed the general concern of *Commonweal*'s editors and contributors that Catholics were not simply attempting to impose their moralistic views on non-Catholics; they were rejecting even the possibility of having a civil debate with anyone who did not share their theological vision.[15]

To illustrate the specific bind Catholics were in, Kerr explained that one night he overheard two respected playwrights discussing whether he, as a drama critic for a large New York daily newspaper, could like the play they were about to present. What caused them to wonder was not, as it should have been, whether the play was any good, but whether Kerr as a Catholic would approve of it. But since one playwright reminded the other that Kerr wrote for *Commonweal* and therefore was a "liberal Catholic," some ambiguity entered into their conclusions. Reflecting on this instance, Kerr explained, "The Catholic who practices criticism outside the Catholic press is, in fact, suspect in both of the worlds he inhabits. The secular mind distrusts him because it fears that he will sooner or later abandon his pretense at criticism and reveal himself for the censor he is. And should he not begin to show the traits of a censor . . . he will as promptly be distrusted by Catholics."[16]

So where was the middle ground? If we extend Kerr's dilemma to represent Catholic opinion in general, how could Catholics participate in cultural debates democratically? And how could Catholics contribute without either raising the suspicions of non-Catholics or losing their identities, which had been shaped by their faith? For Kerr, the first thing that needed to happen was recognition that "the diffusion of the censorial mind over the whole community [was], to be blunt about it, a sign of sickness." So was "the hysterical refusal of the critical and censorial camps to attempt any sort of mediation." Ultimately, Kerr offered, "the defender of art and the defender of prudence are actually interested in the same objectives. . . . Each really wants good art, though neither has as yet been careful to make explicit his idea of good art. Each really wants a good society, though neither has as yet attempted to explain to the other his concept of art's function in creating the good society."[17]

Kerr, in some ways, got part of his wish—the set of assumptions that allowed the Legion to function effectively had begun to fall apart. Laws supporting state censorship weakened (though they did not disappear) under challenges from distributors and exhibitors. Throughout the 1950s, the Supreme Court hinted at a future devoid of state censorship boards, and thus a world far less structured and more ambiguous. The Catholic Church had to prepare for a time when it could no longer depend on state censors and a Hollywood code to exercise its will.[18]

In this new world, it was clear that filmmakers willing to court controversy could test the limits of what was acceptable, not necessarily what was good. And so Americans got to see films such as the racy *The Moon Is Blue, The Man with the Golden Arm*, which portrayed drug addiction, and of course Elia Kazan's *Baby Doll*; and audiences, particularly in cities like New York, could watch foreign films such as *La Ronde* and *M*, both of which required legal intervention to earn the right to be distributed. The appearance of these films and others like them was significant, but not necessarily for reasons that might seem apparent. Following the legal precedent set in the *Miracle* case, it became increasingly possible for moviegoers to see once-forbidden subjects on the big screen. But that didn't necessarily translate into a more sophisticated culture. It did raise an interesting question, though: "Is Decency Enough?"

Emmet Lavery, a Hollywood screenwriter and the founder of the Catholic Theatre Conference, asked that of Catholics in a piece he wrote for *Commonweal*. During the production of a film he wrote on the persecution of Hungarian cardinal Josef Mindszenty, Lavery related a conversation he had had with a priest who knew Mindszenty. The man asked, "What is this concern of yours [in America] to get the big A from the Legion of Decency? Better you should be condemned by the Legion! After all, who goes to see a picture that the Legion thinks is wonderful?"[19]

Lavery laughed off the comment but wondered, in light of the tension created by the Legion's influence, whether Catholics could ever simply "support the good films and ignore the ones they don't like," leaving film criticism to film critics. Yet that kind of approach, the Legion warned, would only encourage more smut. Would it? Lavery asked. He had just learned that Warner Bros. had purchased the screen rights to John Steinbeck's *East of Eden* and that Elia Kazan had been hired to direct the movie. "Already," he noted, "the tom-toms are beating and we may expect, in due time, a sizzling controversy the like of which has not been seen since David Selznick set out to do 'Duel in the Sun.' In the end, of course, Warners will make some adjustment. . . . It won't really change the basic tone and atmosphere, for those who know the original story, but it may save the studio a painful listing in the C category. The controversy will be good for a lot of copy in the newspapers and it will also be good for many extra dollars at the box-office." He intimated that this situation would continue to replay unless the church removed itself from the business of restricting movies. Without the church, though, who would contain movies?[20]

Martin Quigley editorialized that changing Hollywood's Production Code would be "tantamount to calling for a revision to the Ten Commandments." The editors of the *Catholic World* argued that recent court decisions on movie codes had ominous portents for the future. Not only would the "states . . . abdicate their responsibility as guardians of public morality," but Catholics would "have to be more vigilant than ever in guarding against immoral films. The sad prospect is that Catholics will have to be critical and censorious," the editors declared, "for the moral future of the movies is not bright." Underlying such statements was the assumption that the editors of the clerical *American Ecclesiastical Review* noted: those "who chose to attend salacious motion pictures are motivated, not by the artistic or aesthetic urge, but by the desire of sexual thrill." Was tolerance of carnal appetites the price to be endured for a democratic culture? William Clancy thought so.[21]

William Clancy believed the time had come to get beyond the idea held dear by the Legion and other Catholic officials that "the Supreme Court of the United States by practically ruling out all censorship has practically ruled out the concept of immorality." This position was to him untenable because it implied a view of the world that was not realistic. The constitutional issues decided in these cases were valid. But the larger issue that Catholics seemed to get wrong was the way to protect society from a culture of which they were a part. He found the absolute defense of the Production Code symptomatic of this larger problem. "The question of whether or not the present Hollywood Code should be revised is obviously not world-making, but the attempt to commit

Catholic opinion, *en bloc*, against even the possibility of revising it has interesting historical parallels. It is symptomatic of a tendency among us which is 'reactionary' in an almost classical sense."[22]

Clancy seemed to suggest that Catholics engaged in fights over the movies that were grossly disproportionate to the potential consequences involved. "The dire predictions of moral ruin for the nation should all official censorship of motion pictures be ended, leads one, inevitably, to a certain conclusion: that a rather shocking misunderstanding of the metaphysics of a democratic society (which include, by definition, the notion of limitation and hazard) still exists within a large body of American Catholic opinion, and that this misunderstanding is joined to an estimate of human nature that is more Calvinist than Catholic in its pessimism. To believe, for example, that if the Supreme Court rules out prior censorship it has, in effect, ruled the concept of immorality out of our national life is to reveal an attitude which would make democracy itself impossible." He declared that the Court, far from harming the public, was "protecting this medium from the exercise of arbitrary power by limiting, further and further, the area in which such power can operate." And while he recognized that "due process" and "freedom" "involve certain risks," it seemed to him "time to recognize that without risks there can be no freedom. Democracy can never be made completely 'safe.'"[23] Clancy had struck at the heart of an issue that was, in almost every sense, more significant than the bogeyman fear of declining morals. To Clancy, Catholics had much bigger problems than the possible appearance of "salacious" motion pictures; they needed to affirm for their fellow citizens that they understood how to participate in a pluralistic, democratic society. If they did, perhaps non-Catholics would begin to respect Catholic opinion, instead of discounting it as uneducated and nearly medieval. In the best case, improvement of the popular perception of Catholic intentions would lead to wider acceptance of Catholic cultural criticism.[24]

Martin Work, executive secretary of the National Council of Catholic Men, called Clancy's argument "superficial" and his liberal position "dogmatic." In Work's eyes, Clancy was willing to allow any kind of picture to be made and unleashed on a vulnerable public in the name of some abstract idea of free speech. To Work, such a world simply returned the debate to familiar ground: a liberal society abdicated its obligation to protect people from the damaging effects of immoral pictures. Furthermore, he believed an unregulated movie industry threatened "the moral fabric of democracy"—a democracy "whose freedom we are trying to 'protect,'" he wrote with evident indignation, "by eliminating the right of the state to safeguard public welfare through prior licensing of motion pictures."[25]

The editors of *Commonweal* had problems with both positions. "This magazine would suggest that in dealing with this problem [of a free screen] both camps—liberals and Catholics—tend to fall into certain simplistic errors." Interestingly, the editors concluded that on balance, "the error of the liberals seems to us more dangerous for democracy, however, than does the error of the Catholics." The journal castigated liberals for their naive construction of a democratic culture. "The freedom of the artist is a noble thing," the journal allowed, "but so is the freedom of any group to influence, as best it may, the course of public events. In a free society the answer to pressure we don't like is not to denounce its use or its right to exist (as liberals usually do in the case of religious pressure) but to organize counter-pressure. This is how democracy works." The editor, presumably Skillin, advocated a Christian realism that saw the church as a check on the darker aspects of society and the human nature that produced it. But he also took a shot at the church for the way it moralized culture. Thus, "if liberals are frequently simplistic about freedom," he remarked, "Catholics are frequently simplistic about art."[26]

Which side would Catholic moviegoers choose? The Legion had depended on parishioners as a last resort when its influence over the industry and theaters failed. According to historian Frank Walsh, "the growing independence of a better educated laity" undermined that power. The industry was increasingly defiant in the face of Legion intimidation, the laity was increasingly ambivalent about Legion condemnation of certain films, and owners had begun to care less about the Legion's support. One owner explained: "I have no objections to the Legion [advising] the people of yours or any other faith as to what you consider morally objectionable, but I resent the implied threat of a boycott as being totally irreligious, immoral or un-American." Moreover, Walsh suggests, "the real danger was that millions of Catholics who saw [condemned] films might begin to doubt the reasonableness of the church's other decisions." For example, the Legion mustered as much of its power as it could to go after Howard Hughes and his film

The French Line in 1954. This action, too, failed. Walsh notes that the owner of the Park Theater in Orchard Park, New York, met another Legion threat of a boycott by publishing a promise to pay the "reform school tuition" of any member of the audience "corrupted" by the Jane Russell vehicle. Hughes's movie made almost double what it cost to make, and, according to a report filed by the Legion's director, such success had to be attributed to a good many Catholics attending the movie.[27]

American Catholicism was changing, and the Legion had either to adapt or suffer being disregarded. "A new generation of better-educated Catholics valued pluralism and rejected the parochialism of the past," Walsh explains. "A growing number of Catholics, who felt they were better able to judge the moral implications of film than their parents, wondered if the Legion had outlived its usefulness." Martin Quigley, in particular, became alarmed by the laxity of priests toward the Legion pledge. Much like the code, the Legion pledge worked only if those supposedly beholden to it believed in it and followed it. In 1956, Quigley wrote to Cardinal Spellman of a shocking development. He had heard Father Joseph Moffitt of Georgetown University "tell a congregation at a mass that the pledge was voluntary and that those who did not wish to take it could stand with the others but not say the words." But "what was especially startling [to Quigley] was his [Moffitt's] declaration that although Catholics should avoid going to condemned films to satisfy their curiosity, it was not a sin to see such films." Walsh points to a National Catholic Welfare Conference study done in 1956 that "suggested that Catholics were not abiding by the Legion's rulings." The report was not published for fear of alerting the industry and reaffirming the public's suspicions that many Catholics were quietly disregarding the code and even the condemnation that followed from such an act.[28]

In the summer of 1956, a few months before the Christmastime release of *Baby Doll*, an essay appeared by one of the guiding lights of liberal Catholic thought. In "Literature and Censorship," John Courtney Murray echoed the anticensorship, pro-democratic line that had made *Commonweal's* contentiousness so significant. However, in this case, Murray published his statement with "ecclesiastical approval." Prior to John Cogley's experience with the Vatican II council, Murray's essay was the clearest indication that *Commonweal's* editorial stance had made a difference in Catholic officialdom.[29]

Of the many fundamental questions Murray asked, one was particularly significant: "What requirements of public order can be made valid against the claims of freedom?" His answer spoke to the core of the Legion's legitimacy, for its work was based on the notion that not only did it need to speak for all Catholics but it also needed to pressure any groups that might affect Catholics. "Law seeks to establish and maintain only that minimum of actualized morality that is necessary for the healthy functioning of the social order," Murray asserted. "It does not look to what is morally desirable, or attempt to remove every moral taint from the atmosphere of society." The Legion and church officials had very little legal ground on which to make a stand against the erosion of prior censorship of motion pictures. They had, according to Murray, operated under a basic misunderstanding of the law.[30]

"A human society," he reminded his clerical and lay readers, "is inhumanly ruled when it is ruled only, or mostly, by fear. Good laws are obeyed by the generality because they are good laws, they merit and receive the consent of the community, as valid legal expressions of the community's own convictions as to what is just or unjust, good or evil." Trying to decide what is best for the community, Murray counseled, was a task as difficult as trying to determine what laws that community should follow. He acknowledged that various churches would inevitably clash over moral views and the definition of rights. And he suggested that since all religious groups in the United States were minority groups, no one church could possibly think that its way should define all rules for society. At base, he contended, each minority group had a right to create and enforce rules among its own members but did not have the right, as part of a pluralist community, to impose such systems on society in general. Thus, when considering the issue of censorship, he stated frankly: "We need not quibble over the word; the frequent fact is that many of them [pressure groups] achieve the results of censorship, even when they refuse the name."[31]

But such limitations did not mean that minority groups such as the Catholics could not voice their opinion or attempt, in a democratic forum, to influence outcomes of debates. "No one can show," he acknowledged, "that such an action lies beyond the limits of a primeval American right to protest and object . . . [even when] the action may indeed be strenuous." But he advised that prudence should be a factor as well. Why? Because of the fear many moderate Catholics had that the rest of the country was beginning to think that all Catholics were closet (or not-so-closeted) fascists. Such tactics as boycotts had the potential, he argued, to obscure "from the public view the true visage of the Church as God's kingdom of truth and freedom, justice and love." To Murray, what pressure groups did through coercive power was censorship. And censorship, unfettered by "intelligence" and "prudence," produced results that were "ridiculous," "stupid," and open to "ridicule as well as resentment." Thus, he advised that "censorship is no job for the amateur . . . [and] there is no room for the personal, the arbitrary, the passionate. The censor is not called upon for a display of moral indignation." In civil as well as religious realms, Murray believed that caution, professionalism, and judicious thought would serve the people well. He even imagined, considering the Code of Canon Law, that all Catholics could judge "whether a particular work is obscene"; he emphasized that he believed an "ordinary Catholic" could figure this out "for himself."[32]

Where did that leave the Legion? One can only imagine the mood Martin Quigley must have been in after reading (or hearing about) Murray's strong dismissal of the logic that had supported Quigley's brand of censorship. And then he looked out of his Times Square office window and saw Baby Doll. His Production Code was steadily disintegrating; state laws were gradually evaporating; and the last bastion of moral guidance, the Catholic Church, was undergoing profound changes. But all was not yet lost.

The week before *Baby Doll* opened, the *Brooklyn Tablet* ran two pieces on the dangers lurking within motion pictures. On Saturday, 8 December 1956, *Tablet* readers would have understood the significance of both articles, for the next day was the Sunday each year when Catholics all over the country were asked to stand and take the Legion of Decency pledge. The *Tablet*'s editors suggested that Hollywood could no longer be counted on to keep movies with condemnable material off American screens. "It is therefore most heartening to hear," they exclaimed, "a renewed call to action which would revitalize the Legion of Decency and encourage our people to become more consciously aware of this disgraceful record. The clarion call we hope will awaken those Catholics who in their support of 'B' films particularly have helped to create this deplorable condition." The Catholic hierarchy had attempted to reinforce the notion that each individual Catholic had an obligation to "form a right conscience before attending any movie and that natural law commands us to avoid evil." In other words, the editors continued, "All informed Catholics know that there are *absolutes*, even if they are lacking in some of the decisions of the highest court of our land."[33]

It was clear from the editorial that the church was acutely concerned about the weakening of the web of control. It was no longer able to rely on the courts, the PCA, or Catholic intellectuals. "The corrupting influence of many 'B' films and the public's apparent apathy in regard to right moral standards on the screen have been a source of great concern to the executives and reviewers of the Legion of Decency," the editors explained. Thus, in this particular light, *Baby Doll* was the type of film that required Catholics to rise to the challenge that both the PCA and the state would not meet. The editors called the passage of the film by the PCA the "mystery of the century" and asked, "How can an ailing world look to this Country for moral leadership when such immorality is spawned in our film capital?" The editorial concluded with an appeal that was special to Catholics: because the next day was the feast day of Mary, the editors hoped that all Catholics would take the opportunity to commit themselves sincerely to the Legion's work.[34] William Mooring, a Catholic cultural conservative, took a different tack regarding *Baby Doll*. Anticipating that the movie would be defended as an artistic enterprise, Mooring scoffed, "Nowadays almost any film in which sordid human experience is realistically projected gets hailed as 'artistic' and 'adult.' Beauty and art, it seems, are no longer on speaking terms." But then his tone shifted to one of resignation. *Baby Doll*, he seemed to almost sigh, was "a most depressing and sordid film." And what, he asked rhetorically, do the men who made it hope to achieve by it? "Profit would be a legitimate objective assuming the product were worthy. They do not speak of profit, however. They speak of truth and art, claim the film is 'true to life.'" It was clear that Mooring had a skeptical view of art, one that he thought his readers shared.[35]

The Knights of Columbus reprinted a telegram sent to its journal, *Columbia*, as a statement of church policy on *Baby Doll*: "Because of your interest in the moral health of our nation, especially our American youth, permit me to inform you that the National Legion of Decency today, November 27, condemned the Elia Kazan–Tennessee Williams motion picture production 'Baby Doll,' which is being released through Warner Brothers, for the following reasons: "The subject matter of this film is morally repellent both in theme and treatment. It dwells almost without variation or relief upon carnal suggestiveness in action, dialogue and costuming. Its unmitigated emphasis on lust and the various scenes of cruelty are degrading and corruptive. As such it is grievously offensive to Christian and traditional standards of morality and decency."' The journal editorialized, "Nothing more need to be said about 'Baby Doll.' No Brother Knight nor any member of his family, of course, will patronize the picture or theaters where it is shown. All are urged to make known to their friends the Legion of Decency's condemnation of the film and strong reasons stated." As similar statements were read in Catholic churches around the country, a formal boycott began of theaters that dared to show *Baby Doll*.[36]

Initially, the results of Catholic action were mixed. The film opened with strong box office returns, grossing $51,232 in its first week at the Victoria Theater, on Broadway and 46th Street, where on 18 December the film premiered. Its opening night had gone off without any controversy, though the theater staffed an extra ten people in anticipation of the large crowds of curious moviegoers. The audience didn't seem particularly shocked by the film, either. *Look* magazine, a knockoff of *Life*, ran a piece on audience reactions to the issues swirling around the film. These snippets provided an almost perfect cross-section of timeless reactions to movies. And they illustrated in ways that no editorial or court case could why universal censorship was impossible.

Mrs. Marian Balestrieri (an older woman from Jersey City) said the movie was "very good . . . and not immoral." As if prompted by *Commonweal*, she added, "I don't think the Cardinal is fair to judge a film he has not seen. I'm a Catholic but I believe people must make up their own minds." Thelma Fox, a black City College student, said she didn't find the film offensive except for one part in which Baby Doll is ordered away from a cotton gin because she might become the object of attention of the black workers. Mike Fezza, a middle-aged laborer from Brooklyn, exclaimed: "Nothing happens and I thought this would be really something to see after all the stuff I read in the papers. I enjoyed it, though. That Carroll Baker is pretty nice." But Frank Daley, a Boston bureaucrat, declared the film "immoral. There is no doubt of that. And I don't think it is up-to-date. These are days gone by, maybe, but it certainly is not the way things are down there today." Mrs. Ida

Shindelman called the film "trashy . . . but not immoral. The people, the lives they lead are so dirty. Why does anyone want to make a picture like that? How can they live in such filth?" Russian-born Harry Tarasinsky declared it a "world-wide truth." Actor Arthur Perlin thought it "disappointing." And Memphis-born Edgar M. Wilmoth cautioned that it was "completely false." *Look* noted that in New York the movie was a box office sellout partly due to its notoriety; yet that same notoriety had sparked a flood of letters to the offices of Warner Bros. (the distributors) protesting both the film and the advertising. The Reverend Timothy J. Flynn, director of Radio and Television Communications for the Archdiocese of New York, reported to Cardinal Spellman that a harsh review of the film by Howard Whitman of NBC's *Home Show* generated more than two thousand letters, three quarters of which endorsed Whitman's view.[37]

Bosley Crowther thought it was "less on the order of an American movie and more on the order of a 'foreign film' — meaning, of course, the kind of picture we often see from Italy and France. Such selective observation," he explained, "is no doubt induced and justified by the film's realistic content and the brilliance with which it is directed and performed." The *New York Post* chose to focus on Cardinal Spellman's condemnation. The paper ran an editorial on 18 December 1956, defending the film and criticizing the cardinal. The editors acknowledged the right of any group to protest a movie, but, they added, "by the same token, it is the privilege of the rest of the community to challenge the general application of such standards without having aspersions cast on its patriotism." The *Post* took particular issue with the connection Spellman made between promoting the movie and being somehow unpatriotic. "It is hard to see how the ruthless enslavement of Hungary can be even remotely equated with the appearance of a movie here, even if it were generally agreed that the film was 'certain to exert an immoral and corrupting influence.' . . . Indeed," the editors provocatively challenged, "it might be more justly said that the terror to which the Legion of Decency has intermittently reduced Hollywood bears some authentic if minimal resemblance to the suppression against which the Hungarians have rebelled."[38]

There was no shortage of Catholics who sided with Spellman. From late 1956 through the summer of 1957, it became "obvious," the National Catholic Welfare Conference reported, "that [Warner Bros.']

'Baby Doll' [had] succumbed to the obstacle course prepared for it by the Roman Catholic Legion of Decency." There was little doubt that the boycotts and campaign of threats had paid off—the film played in only about a quarter of the total number of theaters that an A-list movie usually did. Warner Bros. received warnings from the Catholic War Veterans (the same organization that had led boycotts against *The Miracle*) to cancel distribution of the movie or face a nationwide boycott. Of course, the studio refused and watched with troubled amazement the reaction the film stirred.[39]

Vigorous protests erupted in three northern New Jersey cities, organized by officials of the Holy Name Federation and the mayor of Jersey City, Bernard Berry. Meeting with theater owners, the group negotiated for the film's run to be cut from three weeks to one and for advertising to be "toned down." Three bishops in Connecticut issued an "unprecedented" joint statement advising Catholics that they had an "obligation in conscience to avoid the motion picture." Speaking for the triad of Connecticut bishops, Archbishop Edward F. Hoban explained the boycott as an affirmation of the Ten Commandments: "The morality for which I speak is the morality of the natural law, of the Ten Commandments. It is the morality that binds all men. It is the moral law to which public life as well as private consciences must conform." Bishop William Scully of Albany, New York, the chairman of the Bishops' Conference on Motion Pictures, told his parishioners to avoid the Strand Theater, the city's premier movie palace, for six months because it had shown *Baby Doll*. Carrying out a similar campaign, churches in Yonkers reportedly distributed twenty-one thousand cards for parishioners to sign protesting the showing of *Baby Doll* at RKO's Proctor's Theater. The manager of the theater said he had received fifteen hundred such cards informing him that the signer "resented" the exhibition of the film and would "avoid your theater for six months." A priest in Yonkers explained that the protests were not a boycott but a "quarantine." "It's not a drive, and it's not an attempt to militate against the right of non-Catholics to see this picture," Father Fitzgerald asserted. "It is simply a fulfillment of the Catholic patron's Legion of Decency pledge, which requires that [Catholics] do not patronize a theater which shows a condemned film."[40]

There was disagreement on why the film ultimately failed at the box office. Catholic officials and the journals that reflected their opinion drew a clear conclusion. The editors of *America* declared: "Public opinion can be effective." It was their contention that "the conclusion is the obvious one that the campaign of the Legion of Decency has paid off. This in turn is a tribute to the obedience of American Catholics to the directives of their bishops and to their widespread determination to heed the (condemned) rating slapped on *Baby Doll*." *Ave Maria* editorially echoed this sentiment: "At least the movie studios will have something to think about next time they make plans to perpetrate another off-color picture on the American public in order to cash in on the movie's emphasis on sex. And perhaps someday decency will play as important a role in their thinking as dollars." But many Catholic and non-Catholic critics panned the movie, whether or not they agreed with the Catholic-inspired boycott. In the end, as many commentators would later conclude, the poor quality of the picture sank it as much as Catholic action.[41]

Responding to the coverage of the confrontation in *America*, Thomas Fleming made the astute observation that it was not moral suasion but threats of economic boycotts against theater owners that carried the fight against *Baby Doll*. Finding that approach "unethical and disgraceful," Fleming hit upon a significant revelation—the church had lost its moral authority in matters involving motion pictures. Not only had Kazan made *Baby Doll* more or less the way he wanted to, but Warner Bros., a major industry player, had distributed the film, and thousands of movie theaters had exhibited the film. Moreover, whether the church wanted to recognize it or not, thousands of the faithful, especially in places like New York, had watched the film. As Emmett Lavery had predicted, controversial films would continue to be made, seen, and debated—there was, as *Commonweal* had editorialized consistently, no way to order a pluralistic society around a minority point of view.[42]

From the start of the controversy over *Baby Doll*, *Commonweal* had attempted to advance discussion beyond the dichotomy that posed morality and free speech as the only options available. *Baby Doll* was not, the editors opined, another *Miracle*. They believed Spellman had every right as a bishop of the church "to warn Catholics against the movie"; this was not censorship. Thus, "the argument against the existence or rightness of this authority to teach on faith and morals can only be theological—not political." To argue otherwise, the editors offered, "would make the American way, not a framework or system within which people of various beliefs can operate together, but an ideology with a positive theological content." However, when the nature of the attacks against those who made the film and those who saw it tended to be ad hominem or grossly exaggerated, then a line had been crossed. "In this case, for example, many people not only could but did take Cardinal Spellman's remarks as a challenge to the patriotism of all who disagreed with him. Perhaps the controversy over 'Baby Doll' was inevitable, but if arguments over the motives and patriotism of those who supported the movie had never arisen in the first place, the discussion might have been carried out on the right issues."[43]

Indeed, when Spellman decided to play on patriotism he ended up confusing the issues at hand. By implicating *Baby Doll* in the much more serious concerns of the cold war, his response elevated an inconsequential movie to a place of heroic speech. He made it possible and almost necessary to defend a poor movie. *Commonweal* suggested that Kazan's sin was not one of immorality but of aesthetics. "If, in the case of 'Baby Doll' its producers consider it a serious and artistic treatment of an adult theme, they have no business advertising it in the way they have. If Hollywood wants to make adult pictures and to be taken seriously as an artistic medium, movie advertising should not suggest that the industry is simply a highly organized scheme to merchandise French postcards that talk." Yet because the Catholic hierarchy had chosen once again to condemn a film they considered salacious rather than inartistic, they set themselves up for a continuous war against all films that dealt with similar subjects, even if they were handled more competently. "Movies in the future can be expected to turn more and more to adult themes which cannot be handled on television," the editors astutely predicted. "Public confidence in the aesthetic competence as well as in the moral training of evaluating groups will therefore become more essential than ever. A certain tension will probably always exist between artist and moralist, but it hardly seems necessary for us to live in a state of constant crisis, passing from one 'Baby Doll' controversy to another."[44]

In the past, Catholic action against pictures like *Baby Doll* had emerged, supposedly, out of a fear of the effects immoral movies had on society. After this latest controversy, though, the character of that fear seemed to shift. An exchange between Martin Quigley and Cardinal Spellman indicated a new reason for concern. In January 1957, Quigley wrote to Spellman asking him to use his influence with the pope to ensure that the Italian authorities in charge of reviewing and approving films would provide the "appropriate attention for the film." Through his contact Count Enrico Pietro Galeazzi, a friend and confidant of Pope Pius XII who dined with the pope almost every evening, Spellman hoped to motivate the Vatican to take action against the film in Italy. The cardinal of Paris had already allowed the film to be classified as acceptable, though for adults only, and clergy from other faiths in New York City had come out strongly against Spellman's blanket condemnation of the film and those who wanted to see it. Most notably, James A. Pike of St. John the Divine (the Episcopal Church's equivalent of St. Patrick's Cathedral), although "he found the film 'unsuitable for any but adult minds' . . . , argued that the church should not condemn 'portrayals of real life' but try to solve the problems they raise.'" *Life* reported that when its reporter asked a rabbi and two Protestant ministers what they thought of the film, all remarked that although the movie might be in poor taste, it did not warrant the kind of response Spellman had issued. John A. Burke, ecclesiastical director of the Catholic Film Institute in England and a priest, told the faithful that he could see no reason why adults could not see the film. Considered in the light of such reactions from other clergy (even within the Catholic Church), Quigley's letter to Spellman and Spellman's appeal to the pope revealed a fear of losing control. Both Quigley and Spellman understood that their views on movie censorship were becoming increasingly anachronistic, even irrelevant.[45]

Ever rational, *Commonweal*'s John Cogley complained that the controversy played out like a "classic dance. . . . The 'rational debate' one might have hoped for was doomed almost from the beginning. . . . Catholics speaking against 'Baby Doll' occasionally sounded as if they were finally in grips with a really big evil in an age of totalitarian horrors; some liberals rushed off to the barricades as if they were saving the Republic from Torquemada." What was all the fuss about? Cogley wanted to know.[46]

But what about Spellman's attempt to involve non-Catholics in the issue as well? Cogley addressed those who claimed that the cardinal had no *right* to condemn the film and those who went to see it. One could disagree with Spellman's opinion of the danger such movies presented to America and still be loyal, Cogley offered. But one could also understand Spellman's statement if Americans assumed that those who were loyal did not want to hurt America—under his logic, loyal Americans would not want to patronize a movie that could hurt their country. But the question that seemed to linger for Cogley was why Spellman felt compelled to make such a strong statement in the first place. Was it, he seemed to ask, because the Legion had grown useless in such matters?[47]

Indeed, his next essay on the controversy suggested it had. Cogley said he could not support the "use of naked economic pressure. The Church, seeming not to trust in her own strength, reaches out for the secular sword—in this case the economic weapon. Then she has to step down to the level of worldly struggle and look suspiciously like any other power center." Indeed, did this case reveal to the church that it had lost its power? "The Church has to rely on moving the hearts and minds of men. It must persuade. It can not use force and coercion without hopelessly clouding and distorting its own image. The world has changed radically since spiritual authority was wont to turn to the 'secular arm' for support. In our society economic strength is the rough equivalent of the Inquisitional power." By using economic leverage, the church had left itself open to criticism not merely from those outside but from its own people who expected it to rise above such tactics.[48]

The damage, though, could not be measured merely in terms of criticism. By accepting boycotts and threats, Catholics had shown themselves once again to be poor democrats. This was a serious failure, Cogley believed, because "a democratic society needs the Church too, and the Church loses in meaningful influence to the degree that it hides its own bridal identity behind swagger and cockiness." After all, he concluded, "living in a pluralistic society involves self-restraints beyond the law. All the major religious bodies in America are minority groups; each is potentially dependent on the prudent use of power by the others. As with Christianity, it is the spirit of the law rather than the letter which quickens the democratic life."[49]

Much to the surprise of many American Catholics, the Holy See chose prudence over power. A few months after *Baby Doll* quietly faded from movie screens, the Catholic Church changed its tune on movies. In November 1957, a meeting of American bishops in Washington D.C. approved of a revised rating system that did away with the B category in favor of more A categories. The Office catholique international du cinéma (OCIC) sponsored the meeting in its role as the international Catholic organization that monitored and commented on the role of mass communication, especially movies, in modern life. Greg Black writes, "The delegates to the OCIC, like many of the leading intellectuals within the Catholic Church in the United States, believed the Legion of Decency was hopelessly out of step with the modern cinema." There were two key results from this meeting: Quigley was pushed further out of the inner circle, and the church planned to revise its approach to movies, making it more positive. Pope Pius XII's September 1957 encyclical *Miranda Prorus* reinforced this new direction, as did a meeting in November 1957 of the Episcopal Committee on Motion Pictures. That body, Black notes, provided written appreciation of the work of progressive forces within the church's intellectual class to guide the Legion's work in a new direction. It was clear by late 1957 that the Legion no longer dictated church doctrine on movies. The editors of *Commonweal* praised this apparent transformation: "The changes in the Legion render obsolete much of past criticism and enlarge the areas of possible agreement."[50]

In the summer of 1962, reaction to another saucy blonde on a billboard revealed the changed Catholic position on movies. A giant billboard advertising *Lolita* went up on Broadway, and once again it was likely that Martin Quigley saw the oversized picture of yet another young actress posed seductively in an attempt to attract moviegoers. Yet, unlike *Baby Doll*, whose content was actually mild in comparison, *Lolita* was not condemned, theaters showing it were not picketed, and Quigley did not fire off memos to Cardinal Spellman predicting the fall of civilization. This time, Quigley was working for those making the film by helping to secure approval from both the PCA and the Catholic Church. Yet, by the early 1960s, Quigley's role as an intermediary between the industry and the church had come under increased scrutiny from church officials. Many wanted him to defend not simply the picture but his rather lucrative financial relationship to Hollywood, which had sustained him throughout the history of the Legion.[51]

Unlike state censors, the Legion was relatively unaffected by legal decisions—it followed a higher law. Yet, as the controversy surrounding *Baby Doll* revealed, the Legion had hit a wall: its actions had become disproportionate to the significance of the situation, and its overblown rhetoric lessened the effectiveness of those actions. It was not lost on many Catholics that Cardinal Spellman seemed to suggest that the exhibition of a movie should cause as much concern as the brutal oppression of Hungarian freedom fighters. Starting in December 1959, Catholics would reaffirm their commitment (whatever of it was left) to the Legion's mission by reciting a new pledge. In her study on this transitional phase in the Legion's history, Mary McLaughlin explains: "If we look back at the first Pledge, the difference is most evident in the positive statements exhorting the pledgers to *do* something, the major change being 'to promote good motion picture entertainment.'" The Legion tried to become a more accommodating, even encouraging, force within movie culture. Moreover, the Legion's reviewers were given a new category, or "Separate Classification," under which they could list those movies not modest enough for the A-III but not depraved enough for the dreaded "Condemned." Federico Fellini's film *La dolce vita* became an example of the kind of film that, even though it appeared controversial enough to earn the Legion's wrath, had artistic merit that the Legion's reviewers could not dismiss. In an interview with McLaughlin, the Reverend Thomas F. Little, the priest in charge of the Legion's affairs, admitted that the church had to respond to the more educated Catholic laity—a generation that by the 1960s had gone or were going to college and were therefore "better able to interpret the content of films than their parents had been."[52]

In the fall of 1962, the Legion came to an inglorious though unofficial end. At a dinner hosted by officials for Loews Inc., Legion officials were told that Loews's theaters were "no longer interested in Code Seals for films which it books" and that "a Legion Condemned rating or no rating at all from the Legion means nothing." The picture in question was *Boccaccio 70*, a forgettable Italian film starring the sexy Anita Ekberg. In the past, Legion officials would have been asked to dinner in order to negotiate a resolution to the problem of censoring the film—this time they were told flatly that their opinions no longer mattered. By 1963, the organization had erected yet another category, A-IV, to classify those movies that were "Morally Unobjectionable for Adults with Reservations." What, one might wonder, was left to condemn?[53]

The convoluted and increasingly qualifier-heavy policies of the Legion foreshadowed its demise as a formidable force. In order for the church to represent its more urbane and educated population, it had to alter the way it approached that population. In the past, of course, the Legion had conceived of its role as a moral protector more than simply a moral guide. But that had changed. As Una Cadegan explains, in response to charges that the Legion was antimodern and anticapitalistic—and therefore anti-American—the church "shifted its focus away from organized 'pressure group' activity and toward the formation and encouragement of individual taste and judgment." An expression of that understanding came in 1964, when the church began publishing the *Catholic Newsletter.* Besides reducing the role played by the once-omnipotent *Tablet,* this was a way to provide parishioners across the country with fairly thorough reviews of new films. "The Legion," Mary McLaughlin notes, "was beginning to promote the idea that good films had a value in themselves."[54]

The final change came when the Legion lost its name, adopting the nondescript title National Catholic Office for Motion Pictures (NCOMP). In a press release on 8 December 1965, the NCOMP explained that although "its work [was] once limited to the moral classification of films, [it] now also embraces the positive endorsement of outstanding films and concentrates more and more upon the promotion of film education." But wasn't that what film critics did? Indeed, the statement echoed the general sentiment of modern movie culture, democratic undertones and all: "In our free society," the NCOMP statement read, "appreciation and support of good films on the part of all members of the community are essential to the future of the motion picture industry." Catholics, it seemed, had been allowed to join without penalty of sin those other parts of the moviegoing community that attempted to enjoy rather than fear their entertainment. Father Little conceded to McLaughlin that the Legion's old way had made it appear a "stubborn, antiquarian, unrealistic defender of Catholic movie-goers against moral corruption." By 1965, such battles no longer needed to be fought.[55]

A sign of the changed times was the appearance of Moira Walsh, a movie critic for *America.* In a two-part article in 1964, Walsh made clear that she was not the successor to Legion stalwart Mary Looram. Rather than "invite" the public to accept Catholic positions on movies, Walsh questioned the entire philosophical edifice upon which the church had built its "right conscience about films." "There is," she wrote, "literally almost no such thing as a movie that is 'safe' or 'harmless' for the passive, undiscerning spectator. As far as I am concerned, this is not a controversial or 'far out' opinion but a simple statement of fact." Walsh's views would have sounded quite familiar to the contributors and readers of *Commonweal*. Referring directly to the changes made in the years after the *Baby Doll* debacle, she reminded her clerical and lay audience that "seven years ago, the Legion took its giant leap forward and since then has been judging films in the rational humanistic, Christian terms that befit an art form with a right and even a duty to confront the actualities of human experience." However, echoing the rationale first put forth by Walter Kerr, William Clancy, and John Cogley, she contended that Catholics would be dealing with the legacy of the Legion for years to come. "The main problem," she argued, "is that so few of the Legion's constituents (and so few of its critics, for that matter) know what a moral film is or how to go about forming a right conscience about films." The Legion had failed to educate moviegoers, who had been a captive audience, and instead had used threats to control movie culture. Walsh concluded that movies had to be taken seriously because "being 'deeply shocked' by a movie is often a salutary human experience, not a morally harmful one." The best place to have learned that lesson was New York City.[56]

4

Amos Vogel and Confrontational Cinema

ONE OF THE unique aspects of postwar New York was the existence of parallel movie worlds. The first world had Hollywood premieres, influential daily critics, and censors. The second world operated underground, outside the traditional bounds of criticism and censorship. Of course, there was interaction between these two worlds: foreign films often thrived in both, and a few critics and censors were aware of, if not actively engaged with, the underground. Yet because the cinematic underground did not operate under the same constraints as the mainstream, it proved to be especially influential in determining how American culture might handle controversial films. While Crowther and the *Commonweal* critics fought to dislodge the censoring attitude, the underground attempted to free moviegoers of mainstream assumptions about cinema. During the first decade of the postwar period, few places did that better than New York's Cinema 16 and its creator, Amos Vogel.

The audience, Amos Vogel wrote to independent filmmaker Kenneth Anger, sat in "dead silence . . . much more pronounced than usual, indicating the close attention they paid to the film." And once the film ended, "there was at first a sort of stunned silence, followed by a scattered applause of the more intrepid among the audience and by a prolonged and pronounced 'buzzing' . . . indicating that everybody had been in some way stimulated or provoked or disgusted or fascinated by the film. This type of reaction occurs," Vogel added, "very infrequently." One man left the screening in obvious discomfort; he

even berated Vogel for showing a film designed, it seemed, purposively
to provoke him. The head of the National Board of Review was there
with his wife; both "thoroughly disliked" the film, which the woman
referred to as "fairy propaganda."[1]

The film was Kenneth Anger's *Fireworks*, a homoerotic fantasy film
shown in April 1952 as part of a special event held by Cinema 16, a
film society in Manhattan with the largest membership in the United
States. Vogel explained to Anger that because the evening was devoted
to "damned" (or controversial) films, it attracted "practically everybody
in the art and avant-garde field you can think of." New York's Cinema
16 was also the first to provide a public exhibition of Anger's film. Marcia Vogel, Amos's wife and partner in the society, remembered it as one
of the films that "moved people so much that they had to get up and
leave." That was not an uncommon occurrence at Cinema 16. "I'm a
strong believer," Vogel explained, "in showing essentially anything that
has human and aesthetic validity and relevance." The program was
billed to the film society's members as "Les Films Maudits: An Evening
of Damned Films" and besides Anger's film included Georges Franju's
ultrarealistic documentary on French slaughterhouses, *The Blood of
Beasts*.[2]

Vogel introduced *Fireworks* to his audience with laudatory comments from Tennessee Williams, who called Anger's film "the most exciting use of cinema I have seen," and Lewis Jacobs, who wrote for the
one serious American film journal at that time, *Hollywood Quarterly*.
Jacobs claimed that "despite the difficulties of 'forbidden' subject matter, the film's intensity of imagery produces an effect of imaginativeness
and daring honesty which on the screen is startling." Vogel noted that
judges at film festivals in Brussels, Cannes, and Paris had concurred
with such praise by honoring Anger throughout 1951.[3]

As with most showings at Cinema 16, the filmmaker was not present
at the screening, but the audience had a detailed set of program notes
for edification. Vogel had asked film critic and artist Parker Tyler to explain to those in attendance what they were about to see and why they
were seeing it. Tyler was a smart choice. He was among the few critics
of the time who wrote sensitively about the cinematic avant-garde and
what he called the "poetics" of film. "Anger's film," he suggested, "is a
more or less a direct attempt to deal with typical homosexual fantasies,
and because his method is virtually automatic . . . the result is a film

closely resembling the standard variety of a wish-dream." Sometimes Anger's attempt was too direct, Tyler thought, such as in a scene in the "Gent's Room," which was a bit too literal for a work characterized by visual puns and allusions. Because of such material, Tyler was concerned that the audience might dismiss the picture as simply a gay film rather than appreciate it "as though it were *any* kind of erotic fantasy." This concern was not misplaced; Tyler explained that "psychiatrists had been interested in the film for use "as 'clinical therapy' in the cure of homosexual neuroses." He hoped the audience at Cinema 16 could see beyond a simplistic view of homoerotic images and acknowledge Anger's "courage to give them any artistic status at all."[4]

Films such as *Fireworks* had no chance of a mainstream theatrical release. The art house circuit also rejected such material because of its limited market appeal. The only option for this kind of alternative film to be seen was through a project like Cinema 16. Vogel started the film society in order to showcase what he called "invisible" filmmakers. Shortly after Vogel and his wife, Marcia, started Cinema 16 in the fall of 1947, Amos contacted Anger, who replied that he "would be most happy" to have Cinema 16 present his films, as Vogel's new organization was "exactly what is needed for the independent film movement in America. . . . We experimental film makers are particularly indebted to such a project as yours as it constitutes practically the only means for our works to reach the public."[5]

The Vogels began Cinema 16 because they shared a passion for avant-garde films, not to show dirty pictures. They had come to their idea for a film society as patrons of New York City's most influential avant-garde filmmaker, Maya Deren. The Vogels had seen one of Deren's shows in 1946 at the Provincetown Playhouse, a theater in Manhattan's bohemian district, Greenwich Village. Amos had been impressed with Deren's programs because she had proven that there existed an audience ready to experience such films, and (just as important to Vogel) her shows were professionally done, ran smoothly, and seemed well planned. Based on that precedent, the Vogels tried showing films they knew were not being seen with any regularity in the city. Their venture scored instantly: "The two hundred seat auditorium [of the Provincetown Playhouse] was filled for 16 evenings, two shows an evening," Vogel remembers. "It was a huge, smashing, immediate success" because "the idea . . . fulfill[ed] a real social need."[6]

However, they needed money to run and advertise the shows, and they had to contend with state censors. A representative from the state board of censorship queried Vogel about his project after seeing an advertisement in the *New York Times*. Vogel admitted that he was so naive that he had never heard of the board or the procedures by which all exhibitors and distributors had to abide. To satisfy the censors, Vogel had to provide films and scripts. That meant paying someone to type up scripts, including those for such films as a French children's cartoon that included such racy language as "baba" and "booboo." It also meant enduring the tedious process of renting films from distributors for the length of time it would take to submit the films to the board, get its approval, advertise the program that would show the films, and then schedule the exhibitions. Some of the films, Vogel admits, had nudity and "some sexy business," which of course did not get past the censors. But the state even rejected a documentary that included a cat giving birth. Deciding that this was no way to operate their fledgling film business, Vogel and his wife "had some discussions with a civil-liberties lawyer and decided that we were going to start a private membership club. When you do that, you're not subject to censorship." He also noted that while the film society designation allowed him to avoid prior censorship, it did not prevent the authorities from shutting down the screenings after he had shown an "obscene" or "offensive" film. "Had I desired to show hard-core *porno* films at Cinema 16," he explained, "I certainly would have had access to them, but we would have been closed down by the police, even if we were a club. In any case, I had no desire to do that, not because I'm against porno—it just wasn't what I was interested in showing."[7]

Vogel thus avoided the web of control that had snared many other films that were far less controversial than a picture like *Fireworks*. Existing outside the bounds of mainstream movie culture allowed Cinema 16 to operate in a kind of cinematic vacuum. Vogel might have solved his financial problems by showing films that pandered to prurient tastes, but to his credit, he chose to attempt something even more radical than creating scandal—he wanted to create a new cinematic aesthetic. "I had hoped that by showing these films at Cinema 16," he reasoned, "and by making audiences more and more familiar with them, I would develop more tolerance. I'm sure I succeeded, but only within certain limits. Always there was the complaint, especially with abstract films,

'I got a headache from looking at it.' They said it then; they say it now. It's obviously an ideological headache." Over the course of his career at Cinema 16, Vogel constructed an approach to his film programs that balanced provocation and education. He would bring moviegoers face-to-face with all kinds of movies, from the truly great to the truly terrible. This was confrontational cinema—an idea that made moviegoing an intellectual exercise rather than a passive experience. As such, confrontational cinema suggested a way to move beyond the staid limits of mainstream movie culture without obliterating the limits that made it a shared culture.[8]

Film historian and documentary filmmaker Scott MacDonald writes of this era: "Instead of accepting moviegoing as an entertaining escape from real life, Vogel and his colleagues saw themselves as a special breed of educator, using an exploration of cinema history and current practice not only to develop a more complete sense of the myriad experiences cinema makes possible, but also to invigorate the potential citizenship in a democracy and to cultivate a sense of global responsibility." When Vogel began his film society in 1947, even the most cosmopolitan city in the United States barely accepted the notion that motion pictures could be significant as an art. Cinema 16 helped to change that. It entered New York City's movie culture at a propitious moment, when trends in moviemaking and moviegoing were beginning to explore new dimensions. And it built a new tradition out of those trends. Vogel pushed audiences and filmmakers to take their roles in movie culture more seriously. As he explained to MacDonald, "When I started, there were *no* such showings in New York, but when I did start, almost immediately I found a lot of people who were anxious to see such material and who came to screenings. It's always a direct interaction between some kind of social agent and the surrounding social situation at the time." Vogel's programming became a social agent, moving movie culture in a direction that allowed more diversity of opinion and, ultimately, participation by moviegoers.[9]

"When my mother gave me a membership for Christmas, I was fifteen," poet Robert Kelly remembers. "My friend, Arthur Pinkerton, and I both had memberships. Going to shows involved a long trip for us—we both lived in a remote section of Brooklyn—to the Paris Theater. But it was a wonderful occasion to get into Manhattan on Sunday mornings, when nobody else was about, and go to this elegant little movie theater. We were already getting to know all the movie theaters in the city that played art films. Events started about eleven in the morning and lasted until about one, when the regular features began, and Amos Vogel would at times . . . say a few words about the program." Kelly's experience was part of an uncommon, significant, and edifying era captured by the relatively brief history of Cinema 16.[10]

At the height of its popularity, Cinema 16 had an estimated seven thousand members, each of whom paid a $10 subscription for a year's worth of screenings. Vogel also distributed films from a collection that grew to thousands of films. One estimate is that the film society filled over 2.2 million seats and rented to another 2 million people over the course of its sixteen-year history. "Its success over the years," Cinema 16 historian Stephen J. Dobi believes, "indicated to ever-timid commercial exhibitors that it was now 'safe' to show certain kinds of films they wouldn't have touched before." Vogel made an art out of programming series of short films, and to the wider world, his distribution practices enabled New York City's movie culture to expand exponentially. "Some of our most absorbing classes . . . are 'Experimental Film I and II,'" explained Boston University film professor Robert Steele. "Were it not for Cinema 16, we would have to drop these courses from our curriculum. We owe Cinema 16 a debt of gratitude for having given us access to these remarkable films from here and abroad." A generation of independent filmmakers whose work was first shown at Cinema 16 owed that same debt.[11]

Perhaps the most recognized facet of Cinema 16's history is the list of filmmakers whose work premiered in the society's programs. Scott MacDonald contends that Vogel "implicitly established a canon of independent cinema that subsequent generations of programmers have debated and revised." Many of the filmmakers showcased by Cinema 16 were not familiar to most moviegoers at the time, but they became vital to the postwar avant-garde movement. The list includes Kenneth Anger, Stan Brakhage, James Broughton, Carmen D'Avino, Curtis Harrington, Julian Huxley, Norman McLaren, Sidney Peterson, Hans Richter, Joseph L. Stone, Willard Van Dyke, and Herbert Vesely. Cinema 16's influence was felt in two ways: first, as *the* outlet for new independent filmmakers; and second, as one of the only sources of inspiration, distribution, and education for other film societies in the United States. Cecile Starr, a writer at that time for the popular *Saturday Review* and a great champion of film societies, confirmed that second point when she edited a volume in the 1950s on film societies. A regular attendee at Cinema 16's Sunday morning screenings at the Paris and Beekman theaters, Starr said that "at first [Vogel's] group was small but it was extremely influential from the very start." She noted that when she read essays contributed by founders of other film societies, "almost all of them acknowledged that they got their inspiration from Cinema 16."[12]

At the height of their business, Amos and Marcia Vogel combined made $15,000 a year. Their first program took place at the Fifth Avenue Playhouse. That venue seemed relatively small once Vogel moved his operation to its more permanent home: the sixteen-hundred-seat Central Needle Trades Auditorium (later known as the Fashion Industries Auditorium). Cinema 16 also used various art houses around Manhattan, including the Paris Theater and the Beekman. Members of Cinema 16 signed up for a yearlong film series held on Wednesday evenings at the Central Needle and Sunday mornings at an area art house.

Its membership was among the most distinctive things about Cinema 16. It drew from a wide variety of New Yorkers—everybody from New York's avant-garde to secretaries and, later in its history, Hollywood luminaries such as Marlon Brando and Elia Kazan. The members paid for the society; Vogel noted that he never used outside money, mostly because no federal or state agencies existed to help finance an organization like his. When asked by Scott MacDonald whether the lack of external funding might have helped Cinema 16 because it forced Vogel to build a loyal audience base, he acknowledged that he programmed with the audience in mind, not so much to please members as to avoid overwhelming or boring them.[13]

It was Vogel's programming as much as the fact he exhibited independent and avant-garde films that made Cinema 16 unique and significant. When asked about the process of selecting films, Vogel explained that he cataloged every film he saw—no matter how short or obscure—in a folder. By the end of Cinema 16's run in 1962, he had amassed between twenty thousand and thirty thousand folders. He would pull films from catalogs, contacts, and submissions. "An entire year's programs—sixteen different events," Vogel explained, "would be put together in advance. It might consist of two hundred or fifty films, depending on length." Vogel did have help sorting through hundreds of films. Besides his wife, Jack Goelman, a war veteran and one of the city's growing population of movie buffs, saw most of the films. "I don't know how many films we'd look at in a day," Goelman says. "I just remember films being all around the room—science films, experimental films, travel films, foreign films without subtitles." He recalls enjoying the challenge of programming a film series with six or seven films out of the dozens of films that he and Vogel had chosen as possibilities. "What I most admired about Amos was his range of feeling about film; I've never met anyone with such a broad approach." That approach, though, was one that aspired toward a particular goal. As Goelman explains, "Of course, Cinema 16 was not a democratic organization. The audience didn't decide things. But it was always a question of who *are* we? What is our relationship to the audience? What do we owe them? What do they owe us? How often do we listen to them?"[14]

Having a membership-based film society allowed Vogel to approach moviegoing in a way that was intellectually different from the commercial theaters. "I was able to present programs which I knew in advance would antagonize most of the audience," he explained. "But that was okay; there were other programs they would like. People soon learned that when they went to Cinema 16, they had to expect to be displeased sometimes." Vogel admitted that some members would quit and ask for their money back, and he would get angry phone calls or letters, but, he added, that was a small minority.[15]

One example that illustrated Vogel's ethic was the exhibition of Fritz Hippler's movie *The Eternal Jew* (1940)—an anti-Jewish screed that made clear the Nazi ideology of hatred. Federal customs officials actually hesitated to let the propaganda piece into the country but did so after German film scholar Siegfried Kracauer assured the agents that Vogel was going to show the film as part of an educational program that included extensive notes written by Kracauer himself. As the author of a highly regarded work on German films, *From Caligari to Hitler*, Kracauer possessed the credentials necessary to broach a topic as controversial as anti-Semitism. Showing the film with Kracauer's notes made the experience of watching it an intellectual enterprise on a level that would have been foreign to most moviegoers in November 1958. In his discussion, Kracauer contended that the film could be seen as an indication of the waning ideological domination of the Nazis rather than as a flat reflection of the regime's terror. "The film amounts to a wholesale condemnation of the Jews and all that is Jewish," Kracauer acknowledged, "yet achieves this goal in a very forced and artificial way." It was, he told the audience, a "conscience-saving propaganda message issued at a moment when the Nazis prepared the death camps in Poland. . . . I have the distinct feeling," Kracauer ominously concluded, "that this film served to rekindle hatred against the Jews in a period when many Germans were wavering and entertaining heretic thoughts."[16]

For the audience, the screening of the film had the kinds of effects Vogel both expected and wanted, though those two reactions were not the same. Many Jews in the audience questioned Vogel's decision to screen such a picture. Ed Emshwiller found the evening "extraordinary." The film "was such hideous propaganda that you had to wonder whether by showing these films you were encouraging socially undesirable behavior." But Emshwiller remembered that "it was a terrific program because you didn't leave feeling, 'Oh sure, I'm against censorship': you really were conflicted about where one draws the line. That kind of programming had educational value: pat attitudes were challenged, and without anybody preaching—just by showing films and asking the question."[17]

That kind of evening had been rare in the movie culture of New York before the advent of Cinema 16. Even though New York City was the undisputed center of serious film culture in the United States, home to multiple film societies, art house theaters, university film programs, and—most significant—the film library of the Museum of Modern Art (MoMA), there was little confrontational cinema. Before the rise of Cinema 16, MoMA's film library was the single best source for unusual moviegoing. Jonas Mekas, a Lithuanian immigrant who became a major force in New York's postwar avant-garde film scene, told an interviewer that when he arrived in New York in the 1940s he attended three "universities" to learn about movie culture: Cinema 16, Times Square (for commercial features), and MoMA's daily film programs. The Vogels, too, were influenced by the museum's shows. Marcia Vogel explained that when she and Amos were dating, they often went to see films at MoMA; she would rush to the museum when she finished work to get tickets for the 5:30 P.M. show because Amos had to work until 5:30. They got the idea for Cinema 16, she said, by considering how films like the ones they saw at MoMA might also be seen at other places and at other times. They even handed out fliers for Cinema 16 in front of MoMA. Marcia Vogel also credits Richard Griffith, the film curator at MoMA from 1951 to 1965, for giving Cinema 16 a big boost by introducing the Vogels to the famous documentarian Robert Flaherty, who agreed to sign a letter Cinema 16 sent out to attract sponsors.[18]

By the 1950s, however, MoMA had earned a reputation for playing it conservative, for having a somewhat restrained position in New York's movie culture. It had not always been that way. The museum had been the first place in the United States to promote the conservation and presentation of old films. In the mid-1930s, the film library had formed around a fiercely intelligent and energetic British film critic named Iris Barry. She and her husband, John Abbott, fought to secure a place for motion pictures among the treasures of modern art. That notion was radical in the 1930s—the art community in which they operated was not easily convinced that movies were art. Part of the arrangement made to preserve old movies at the museum was the public role the film library would play. In the postwar era, the museum showed films that simply were not available elsewhere. Television and revival houses were still in their infancy when MoMA was running two daily programs of films from its expanding library of domestic and international classics. Yet MoMA was criticized by many as living in the past and contributing to an incomplete understanding of film art.[19]

During the years immediately after the war, MoMA launched film programs including "The Art of the Motion Picture, 1895–1941," "The Documentary Film, 1922–1943," "The Film till Now," "The Art of the Film," "The Work of Robert Flaherty," and other series that combined classics and socially significant documentaries. It was not, to repeat a common criticism of the time, a daring approach. Iris Barry and her successor, Richard Griffith, had chosen a mission of preservation as much as exhibition. Vogel's kind of provocation was of no interest to them, though that did not mean that the film library lacked significance. Griffith explained that because circulating programs touched universities, high schools, and film societies, "the Museum has played some considerable part in the creation of a culture of the film in this country—a world of discourse where comparison, analysis, and study help formulate taste of young and adults alike, a development of which Hollywood . . . is not aware." Moreover, as Griffith noted in 1956, when the film library began its programs in 1939, there "was one fully-accredited academic course in motion pictures. Today, there are almost 75 accredited courses in more than 50 colleges and universities throughout the country." The museum, he clearly implied, had played a major role in educating the public about how and why to take films seriously.[20]

Charles Turner, a film enthusiast who had been involved with MoMA and the Theodore Huff Memorial Film Society after the Second World War, remembered that "people coming in didn't know how to react to silent films. . . . The reaction of some was to laugh at anything that wasn't absolutely current in style or performance. . . . Early on at the Museum this caused real conflict between members of the audience, to the point of verbal outbursts and things thrown. There was enough of a disturbance from audiences that Iris Barry had a slide projector permanently set up in the extreme right port of the Museum's projection booth with a slide that read something to the effect 'If the disturbance in the auditorium does not cease, the showing of this film will be discontinued.'" Complaints about the audience, inability to get tickets, and the odd scheduling of showtimes also marred the reputation of MoMA among those most serious about movie culture in New York. Many who wanted to see the programs were unable to attend at inconvenient times such as late afternoon, and those who could make it to the 5:30 screening would find shows constantly sold out. The problems that Turner and others identified at MoMA were one source of inspiration for the Vogels to begin Cinema 16, which had two shows on Sunday mornings and evening shows on Wednesdays.[21]

Another source was clearly what Barry and especially Griffith had been programming. Amos Vogel had praised the film library in an article he wrote on running a film society because the film programs available through the museum were among the best in the country, including one that Frank Stauffacher of the San Francisco Museum of Art recommended called "Art and the Experimental Film." However, not until 1952 did MoMA run a program devoted to experimental films for the public. Cecile Starr was among the attendees for the show entitled "Why Experimental Films?" which covered twenty films from 1921 to 1952 and was organized and guided by Edward Steichen, a famous photo artist who directed the museum's department of photography. The presentation lasted a marathonlike three hours. "To be sure," Starr lamented, "it was over by midnight, and the Cinderella presumably returned to the attic or basement or wherever it is that the abstract film artist hangs out. Yet while it lasted it was an exciting occasion for everyone present." Unlike most film programs at the museum, this one lasted only a single evening. It would not be until 1954 that Richard Griffith decided to program a series devoted exclusively to contemporary avant-garde film: "The American Scene, 1945–1953."[22]

In his official report about the film library published in the fall of 1956, Richard Griffith defended the museum's programming decisions, particularly in relation to the lack of attention given avant-garde films. He made it clear that he was responding to inquiries (and most likely criticism) he had received regarding the acquisition and exhibition policies of the film library. He pointed out that MoMA had run programs twice daily in the museum's auditorium since 1948. The decision about what to show related to what the museum had decided to preserve. "Priority [was given]," he said, "to films which, by general agreement, are of the highest importance and merit, while collecting when possible films which by their success—or failure—have had profound impact on the history of motion pictures, and films which, by reason of their social or cultural influence, have attained significance." This was the policy that earned MoMA and Griffith a reputation for being a bit stodgy in comparison to film societies such as Cinema 16.[23]

Griffith and his predecessor, Iris Barry, had created a film canon—one that was not, though, universally agreed upon within a movie culture that was undergoing rapid and dramatic changes. Griffith explained that as the museum's collection grew, the film library focused shows on a particular filmmaker—Griffith, Chaplin, Eisenstein—or a national cinema or a genre, such as documentary film, to suggest that film had a history, past masters, and great works that should be familiar to the public in a way that was similar to the other arts housed in the museum. That explanation, though, only alluded to why he had eschewed the contemporary avant-garde. In a statement seemingly designed to anger the avant-garde community, he reasoned: "It would seem in the logic of things that the Film Library should signalize this development." After all, it was clear that Griffith considered MoMA a kind of cinematic gatekeeper. Thus, the absence of postwar avant-garde films could be understood, Griffith suggested, by understanding the context in which he worked. "It is a paradox of this new *avant-garde* movement, lively and assertive as it has been," Griffith contended, "that its actual productions have been, with striking exceptions, in large part literal duplications of the ideas, imagery and cinematic achievements of the Paris avant-garde of thirty years ago." To him "it seemed best to wait for the passing of this period of prentice work and 'agonies and indecisions' and to wait for the emergence of a genuinely personal expression." MoMA was, after all, still a museum, even if it claimed to be "modern."[24]

Film critic Andrew Sarris found MoMA a bit too stuffy. Sarris came of cinematic age during the 1950s in New York City. He was among a handful of critics who changed the way Americans thought about movies. In the late 1950s and early 1960s, Sarris became the most vocal and eloquent champion of a critical style referred to as *auteur* criticism. That approach originated in France with the work of critics writing for the journal *Cahiers du cinema* and working within the collections and programs at the Cinémathèque française, an institution that MoMA's film library was constantly compared to, though often unfavorably. Sarris recalls: "I do not know exactly when I began to be restive with the MOMA 'line,' but gradually through the '50s I began to discover that film history was far more copious and complex than I had imagined." MoMA had created and maintained a position on film history: before 1929, film was art; after the emergence of the talkies, it became a sociological experiment. For Sarris and others like him in New York's movie culture, the notion of art was much more expansive, including contemporary Hollywood directors and, for Vogel and Mekas, avant-garde and independent filmmakers. With other outlets available in New York, including the revival houses in Manhattan, television, and film societies such as the Theodore Huff Memorial Film Society, MoMA's dominant position in film culture began to wane. And then film theories arrived from France: "Almost simultaneously," Sarris explains, "the development of rationales for Pop art in America and England sounded the death knell for antikitsch attitudes. . . . The directorial retrospective became a staple of revival programming, and gradually even MOMA began to make this policy more the rule than the exception." The museum had gone from changing elite and popular attitudes toward motion pictures to being a target itself for a new wave of ideas about film. And, somewhat ironically, the generation that had been raised on MoMA's programs eventually challenged it.[25]

Vogel's efforts at Cinema 16 were an example of that. Vogel, like Barry and Griffith, had positioned himself as custodian of New York's movie culture. His was not the only film society in the city (and certainly not in the country), but it was the most successful and the most influential. One photograph taken of an audience for one of Cinema 16's Wednesday evening programs illustrates this point. Vogel used the sixteen-hundred-seat auditorium at the Central Needle Trades building in lower Manhattan. The night this photo was taken, Alfred Hitchcock made an appearance to discuss his filmmaking techniques. The house was packed. All seats were taken, and running along the entire side of the enormous hall was a mural depicting the fruits of democracy done by artists as part of the New Deal–era Works Progress Administration. The congruence of images—the masses toiling for democracy and the masses supporting the democratic art—suggested that there was a connection between the democratic nature of the country and the democratic atmosphere that the cinema created. Institutions such as MoMA and Cinema 16 were built on a spirit that challenged an older order of authority—in this case, the notion that movies were not art or should not be taken seriously. Both institutions proved that assumption wrong and in the process produced generations of moviegoers who enjoyed challenging prevailing opinion.[26]

Audience involvement has always been a fundamental aspect of movie culture. Iris Barry had boldly argued in the mid-1930s that movies were significant because the people who watched them made them so. Amos Vogel proved that there was a relatively large audience for films not made with popular consumption in mind. The folks who patronized MoMA's film programs received an education, an academic treatment of motion pictures. The people who attended Cinema 16's screenings had a different experience, and their reactions illustrated why Vogel's project was a departure from anything that had come before it or, for the 1950s, around it. Vogel's crowd learned to engage film actively, to embrace it, reject it, but most of all to wrestle with it. The audiences for Cinema 16 did not passively submit to the atmosphere of the cinema—that behavior was expected in more conservative institutions such as MoMA and, frankly, commercial and art house theaters. Vogel was, I suspect, all too pleased to have a rowdy audience.

In the fall of 1953, Vogel published a synopsis of member responses to a survey. The audience for Cinema 16 was typical for the era and the city. It was composed of college graduates, most of whom (59 percent) were under the age of thirty. Vogel noted that a survey conducted a year before had revealed a larger percentage under that age—the film society had attracted an older crowd and lost some of its younger members. Audience preference in programming was not surprising considering the crossover attendance from patrons of MoMA's screenings. The most popular kinds of films were documentaries; the least popular were abstract and psychological films. Vogel added that the "worst liked film of the year" was *Psychotherapeutic Interviewing*. I imagine he wasn't too surprised.[27]

In an attempt to explain his radical approach to programming, Vogel wanted his members to understand that the difference between a film society and the commercial cinema meant that Cinema 16 would aim "to further the appreciation of films and of new experiments in the film medium," no matter how painful that process might be. In somewhat strained logic, Vogel seemed to suggest that any film that was unpopular was also controversial. Thus, he stood firm on his commitment to "welcome" controversy and made it clear that "neither applause nor the absence of applause [could] determine . . . program selections." Vogel could defend his approach by citing the rise in membership. Cinema 16 was so popular that he had to arrange for two evening screenings on two nights, both Tuesday and Wednesday, to accommodate the influx of members, in addition to two screenings held at one of the city's art theaters on Sunday mornings.[28]

One might assume that Vogel was preaching to the converted, yet one of the most interesting aspects of Cinema 16 was the fact that it really did operate as confrontational cinema. One patron asked if something could be done "about people constantly walking out during a showing. It is most annoying to those who are enjoying the films, or speakers. They never go quietly." One of Jack Goelman's jobs as Vogel's assistant was to evaluate audience reactions. He remembers a mass exodus during the showing of Willard Maas's tragically slow film *Image in the Snow* (1952). Goelman estimated that out of a crowd of twelve hundred, around four hundred to five hundred people walked out, loudly voicing their opinions as they left. Carmen D'Avino, an experimental animation filmmaker whom Vogel championed in the

1950s, exclaimed that the "audience was wonderful. . . . They'd boo; they'd walk out; they'd scream for joy. It was a volatile and beautiful audience to present anything to. I was thrilled to have work shown at Cinema 16."[29]

According to P. Adams Sitney, a devoted Cinema 16 fan, the Wednesday night screenings were the rowdiest because people had time to have dinner and a few drinks before showing up. The 11:00 Sunday morning shows were more subdued and seemed to attract a more refined crowd. Sitney explains that as a Catholic, he usually reserved Sunday mornings for church. But in the late 1950s, Cinema 16 was "like going to church. . . . All these people were dressed up in jackets and ties, coming to see the latest Japanese film or a collection of short films from the Polish Film School." Writing in the magazine *Holiday,* Al Hine described a young man waiting outside the Beekman Theater one Sunday holding up a sign that read: "Will anyone sell or swap me their membership to Cinema 16?" About the audience in the theater, Hine wrote that while they were "probably . . . a little younger than the crowd at [the] nearest art theater," they were "not noticeably more eggish of the head nor horned of the rim than the folks who pass through the portals of the Roxy or the Music Hall." If the audience members were clearly not unique, the film society they belonged to was: Hine noted that "whereas almost all major film companies shun even the thought of controversy, Cinema 16 lives and waxes fat on it."[30]

For some members, Vogel's programming was a very positive experience, exposing them to movies they would not otherwise have been able to see. Others resisted the steady diet of "important" and "serious" films. One patron complained that the films were "too 'off-beat' or [were] for very avant-garde collegiates," and that Vogel had failed to "cater enough to those of us who are not starry-eyed and immature and a trifle decadent but just intelligent interested human beings who want to be informed or amused or touched." Another half-jokingly asked if the program notes could be "a little less lyrical. I can decide for myself if the film is 'filled with delicate visual poetry' or is a 'sensitive evocation' of something or other." Many in New York had a creeping suspicion that Cinema 16 was a bit too pretentious for its own intellectual, artistic, and ideological aspirations. "Superficially you have attempted to create an esoteric social idea," one person wrote, "but actually you have succeeded in doing nothing but to overcharge a few bewildered neurotics by making them feel like intellectuals."[31]

Reception by film critics echoed such mixed sentiments. From the beginning, Vogel's greatest supporter among New York critics was Archer Winsten of the *New York Post*. By the time he retired in 1986, Winsten had written reviews for the *Post* for fifty years. He was in many ways a beatnik version of Bosley Crowther: he wrote for a large daily newspaper but woke late, kept his schedule on the back of a used envelope, avoided advance screenings, and liked movies that Crowther panned, most notably Carl Dreyer's *Day of Wrath*. He also liked Cinema 16. Crowther did not actively oppose the film society—in fact, he was on the Robert Flaherty Award Committee, a group sponsored by Cinema 16 that honored selected documentary films each year. Winsten, however, consistently plugged Cinema 16 from its beginning. Writing about the scientific film *Monkey into Man* exhibited at Cinema 16's first show, he declared, "If Cinema 16 can find more like it its success will be sensational." After attending the second show, Winsten suggested, "The strength of Cinema 16 programs thus far has been that they have thrown a wide net of taste. . . . And if abstractions, in some unimaginative cases, do no more than whet the appetite for bone, meat and gristle of the fact film, they have functioned as efficiently as many a fiction powder puff in the major movie palaces." After attending *The Blood of Beasts*, Winsten reflected on the role other critics might play in supporting an effort as worthy as Cinema 16. "Audiences still do want to see good things," he argued. "This is a cornerstone of belief. Creators are still making new, fresh films. Those have been seen. But between the two there are roadblocks, deceptive directions, all kinds of discouragements. If a critic doesn't stand up and fight occasionally, who will?" The question for other critics, however, was what exactly were they fighting for when they praised Cinema 16?[32]

When James Agee lent his help to Vogel's cause, he did so, as he suggested in the weekly *Nation*, in the "hope [that] the idea [would] spread." Agee was not a regular at Cinema 16 and his connection to it was indirect at best, but Vogel did show one film that Agee had helped make: *In the Streets*, about Spanish Harlem. And as much as Vogel was appreciative of Winsten's support, to have Agee in his corner was a different kind of endorsement. When it came to movie criticism in the 1940s and 1950s, Agee was in a league by himself. There was a perceptible sense in New York that Agee was too good a writer for movies. Whereas Bosley Crowther's power came in large part from his position at the *Times*, Agee had cultural cachet in New York's art community because of his considerable literary talent. Yet Agee's endorsement of Cinema 16 was tempered by his fear that such a project could easily slide toward pretentiousness.[33]

His brief review of the first six months or so of Cinema 16's operations emphasized its pluralistic potential. Here was an opportunity to see films that were almost impossible to find, let alone see on a regular basis. Thus, filmmakers who produced works without immediate marketability had a chance to get reactions from audiences who were consistently fed products with proven commercial viability. That was, on the surface, a good thing, Agee believed. However, he cautioned, "One of the biggest mistakes that can be made and which appears to be made remarkably often, is to assume that uncommercial or relatively uncommercial motives guarantee a good film or a good minority audience for it. Instead, such motives guarantee special temptations and liabilities, as grave at least as those imposed by rankest commercialism." Agee worried that Cinema 16 would be "dull." In an effort to dignify commercially untenable pictures, Vogel and his colleagues came perilously close to taking the joy out of watching movies. Agee pointed out that "there are inevitable drawbacks about this kind of showing which so exclusively assembles the specially interested: the danger of a kind of churchy smell to the whole business which seems to me essentially much more hostile to vigorous work and vigorous enjoyment and criticism than the good honest stench of the average movie theater—the odor, if not of sanctity, of cold, arrogant, uncritical self-righteousness in the audience, in the pictures, and in those who make them." Was Cinema 16 doomed because of the nature of film societies or because of the nature of its founder? Agee suggested that the problem lay in the awkward convergence of a popular medium and unpopular content. That assessment appears delicate compared to criticism leveled by one of Agee's successors fourteen years later.[34]

Dwight Macdonald thought he was too good for movie criticism. Mass culture and the "kitsch" attitudes that it produced disgusted him. He spent the better part of his career as a critic dismantling the pretentiousness of what he called "masscult." He wanted either art or entertainment, not the bastardized offspring of the two. In his monthly film column in *Esquire,* Macdonald declared that it was "time to cast a cold eye on what is known as 'the art film.' Its ideals are high and it is dedicated to truth—no escapism, no box office. I am in favor of high ideals, but why are they so seldom entertaining in art films? I am also in favor of Truth and Realism, but why are they here always depressing? Above all, why are most art films pooh?" Macdonald was fed up with the attitude that if a film had little to no commercial value, it was worthy of an intellectual's time and praise. Cinema 16, he believed, had become blind to this fact. It had not, Macdonald argued, contributed in any significant way to the cultural progress of film. Rather, "the more distressing aspects of life are so frequently on view at Cinema 16 that I have often wondered just who its four thousand devotees are. Masochists? Psychiatric social workers on a busman's holiday? Whoever they are, they have taken a lot of punishment."[35]

Amos Vogel could not believe what he had read. He wrote a letter to Macdonald listing the famous avant-garde filmmakers who had had their premieres at Cinema 16. He called Macdonald a social conservative and wondered why he seemed to defend commercial cinema, which certainly did not need the assistance. "You accuse us of not being entertaining enough," Vogel shot back. "We have never claimed to exist for the sake of entertaining our members; we leave this to the neighborhood houses." After all, Cinema 16 had developed a niche between commercial theaters and MoMA; it had created for itself a role in a movie culture that had grown crowded with alternatives to Hollywood products.[36]

Macdonald enjoyed Vogel's reply, and his rejoinder was an example of intellectual mismatch. He dismissed much of what Vogel argued as sadly lacking in a basic understanding of the intellectual terms of debate. "No foe, I, of Angst," Macdonald wrote back, arguing that angst and entertainment were not mutually exclusive cultural positions. "Art must be entertaining, that is pleasurable, or it isn't art." Macdonald ended his reply to Vogel with a quip from a new critical darling, Pauline Kael. She had remarked recently, "After an evening of art films, I often want to see a movie." To which Macdonald added, "Me too."[37]

Ernest Callenbach, the editor of *Film Quarterly,* followed the Macdonald-Vogel tiff with some interest. His journal depended on the kind of movie culture created in New York City and by organizations like Cinema 16. Even so, "experimental offerings may on the whole be among the worst," Callenbach admitted. He pointed out, though, that "they are far from the dominant note in Cinema 16 programming, which has included work by Antonioni, Bresson, Cassavetes, Clarke, Franju . . . and a variety of 'classic' film-makers." Callenbach could not understand why Macdonald would go after Vogel and Cinema 16 when there existed "extreme deficiencies [in] our present film distribution," and when "we have one regular serious magazine," no national film institute, underfunded museums, and meddlesome censors. To prove his point, Callenbach turned to "serious" movie culture's favorite villain: "In such a situation Cinema 16 is a positive beacon of enlightenment—compared, say, to such a force for constriction and dullness as Bosley Crowther."[38]

Macdonald found Callenbach's defense weak and indicative of a larger problem. While he thought Vogel "a very nice fellow," Macdonald also believed that because he couldn't "tell junk from gems," an organization such as Cinema 16 was "worse than none because it alienates the more intelligent movie-goers from the art film." One could be "charitable" about the general idea of Cinema 16, Macdonald argued, but "it's when the specific is in question that the problems arise." "It seems to me," he wrote, "that the slightest pretensions to being 'serious' is [sic] given A for effort and one is considered immoral and not a good fellow if one points out that a movie can be both serious and a mess. What we need is more birth control in every branch of art; the young should be discouraged on principle, since most of them are as ungifted as their elders have proved to be; in fact, I really think critics should judge the art film by the same standards they judge the Hollywood film; at least that's what I try to do."[39]

One filmmaker Macdonald had in mind when he leveled his criticism at Cinema 16 was Jonas Mekas. "I must confess," Macdonald wrote of Mekas, "I rate dedication lower than acumen and enthusiasm lower than talent." One of the films the critic viewed on his visit to Cinema 16 in April 1962 was Mekas's *Guns of the Trees* (1960). The movie had been preceded by "an impassioned leaflet by its creator . . . [that] raised considerable expectations." What Macdonald saw, though, was a film with "two contrasting love stories which were all too easily followed (once one got used to *avant-garde* cutting) since they represented Good and Bad, Creative and Destructive, Life and Death, or, existentially speaking, Authentic and Inauthentic." He told Ernest

Callenbach that he found most of the films he saw at Cinema 16 "maddeningly bad."[40]

In a single review, Macdonald had identified the paradox of Cinema 16—its greatest strength was also its greatest weakness. Vogel did not merely show films, he forced moviegoers to confront them. That approach was one of the truly radical features of Vogel's confrontational cinema—it sparked real debate and forced moviegoers to take a side. When Vogel's programs were strong they worked on multiple levels— exposing, challenging, and educating Cinema 16 members in a way completely unique in the city. When they were weak, as Macdonald noted, they came across as pedantic and pretentious, more a threat to the art of cinema than an illustration of it. One way to avoid this pitfall was simply not to take an ideological position at all. Of course, Vogel could never do this; his project lived (and would die) based on his devotion to strict programming. If the public rejected a series of films, they were rejecting him.

In the early 1960s, challengers emerged who proved much more damaging than mere criticism. Scott MacDonald says of Cinema 16: "Even if audience members didn't enjoy particular films, they knew that they were privileged to see films almost no one else got to see." Although this was true for almost fifteen years, by 1960, new venues had opened and new provocateurs offered an alternative to Vogel's approach. Vogel had shown that a community existed in New York that hungered for films out of the mainstream. He also became a model of how to run a fairly successful business without being either inside a museum or tied to the box office. Vogel was a pioneer who led others to a different kind of world. The next generation of film enthusiasts tapped into a world made evident by Vogel's work. Yet this group did not merely improve upon or cut into Vogel's market. A deeper difference existed between them that was fundamentally ideological.[41]

The new generation was represented by two film entrepreneurs who became fixtures in New York City movie culture. The first was Daniel Talbot, whose New Yorker Theater and, later, New Yorker Films exhibited and distributed an eclectic mixture of films for an eclectic population of moviegoers. The second was Jonas Mekas, the filmmaker who was so inspired by the programs of Cinema 16 that he hoped to turn the entire city, and then the country, into one large film society. Both Talbot and Mekas avoided the rigor of Vogel's programming in favor of fluidity. By doing so, they wanted to accomplish what they must have perceived was Vogel's goal—exposing people to a myriad of film experiences. But in their appeal to freedom they abandoned the more serious—and, it seems to me, more significant—point of Cinema 16: building a forum in which a moviegoing public was forced to confront and create a cinematic aesthetic.

Talbot took over the Yorktown Theater in early 1960, changing the name and the programming philosophy. The New Yorker Theater officially opened in March 1960, and its first program paired *Henry V* and the French silent children's film *The Red Balloon*. His thousand-seat theater on Broadway and West 88th Street near Columbia University and City College filled up. The neighborhood had a large Hispanic population that probably would have preferred a theater that showed Spanish-language films, but Talbot reasoned that college students and bohemian migrants from Greenwich Village had begun to live in the area in numbers large enough to make his repertory cinema a hit. He was right.[42]

On a single Friday evening in its first full week of operation, the theater drew over two thousand moviegoers paying $1.25 a ticket—a very healthy return for films long gone from first-run screens. The two-week total for the first twin bill was over $10,000, a tidy sum when compared to what was on Broadway. Talbot continued to use the two-movie format as the model, coupling like films and films that had no similarity whatsoever. This was an approach to programming that resembled nothing else—the New Yorker did not operate like a traditional art theater or Cinema 16. And Talbot certainly did not abide by the same rules that governed the big commercial theaters. His style of selecting and pairing films, though, did have an internal logic—Talbot described it to *Variety* as "fragmented programming."[43]

That approach, of course, stood as the alternative to Vogel's confrontational cinema. It was clear that Talbot represented the younger generation who had been educated in Cinema 16 and art houses and now wanted to add a new twist to the movie culture created by those institutions. Where Vogel had crafted an agenda that pointedly expressed his radical politics, Talbot and his coconspirators were more interested in simply expressing themselves. They hoped to shake up moviegoers rather than to build a new kind of moviegoer. The New Yorker was what Cinema 16 would have looked like if the audience had kicked out Vogel and taken over programming. While not giving his audience everything it wanted, Talbot did give New York's moviegoing public its due. The place had a kind of populist feel that reflected the maturation of those who came to see the movies. It was as if New Yorkers, having received their primary education through MoMA's programs and taken advanced courses in movie viewing at Cinema 16, had now graduated into the world of the New Yorker, where they were expected to use their filmic wisdom to appreciate the diversity of the movie culture all around them. Both MoMA and Cinema 16 had been quite intentional in their efforts to educate the viewer, assuming that audiences needed to be led toward significant films. The New Yorker was a house of discoveries without an intentionality that assumed the existence of a canon of films that all moviegoers had to accept. In his first year of operation, Talbot illustrated this new relationship to film and his audience.

Throughout 1960, the New Yorker attracted around seven hundred patrons on Friday nights and close to a thousand on Saturdays and Sundays, with patrons paying as much as $1.25 for a ticket on weekend nights. The theater grossed around $350,000 for the year, which meant that Talbot had succeeded well enough financially to remain open and that he had found an audience. Fragmented programming worked. He followed up the first eclectic twin bill with another of equal disconnect, pairing the Orson Welles classic *The Magnificent Ambersons* with a film from two Greenwich Village bohemians entitled *Pull My Daisy*. The pair of films sold over seventy-three hundred tickets during its two-week run and had people cheering from their seats. In May, Talbot ran Chaplin's *Modern Times*, grossing more than $17,000 over three weeks. James Monaco writes of this era: "There was an electric atmosphere about the place, which was full of audiences who were virtually all young people who had a real hunger for film that couldn't be satisfied with Times Square junk." Talbot claimed that all the shows in the early years were applauded, which might suggest something about both the audiences' tastes and the respect Talbot had for those tastes.[44]

Like Vogel, Talbot had help programming, working closely with Bill Everson in New York and future *New Yorker* critic Pauline Kael out in Berkeley, California, to locate and nab old films that would have quietly disappeared if this group of devotees had not rescued them. During the first three years of operating the New Yorker, Talbot also used the expertise of his friend Peter Bogdanovich, a young film aficionado. A future auteur himself, Bogdanovich screened and wrote program notes for Hollywood classics by John Huston, Orson Welles, and Sam Fuller. The diverse interests of this group and the great diversity of tastes among the New Yorker's audience found expression on the screen. Over the course of his career, Talbot showed everything from W. C. Fields and Charlie Chaplin to Jonas Mekas, Kenneth Anger, and Jean-Luc Goddard. And to his credit, Talbot responded fairly sincerely to his patrons' suggestions, giving them musicals and Dietrich, Disney and Lindsay Anderson. There were foreign films and Hollywood films, the most popular movies of the year and the most underground. And Talbot was also not averse to repeating those films he believed had significance, such as *Blue Angel*, *The Magnificent Ambersons*, *Grapes of Wrath*, *8½*, and *Alphaville*.

There was little identifiable ideology to be found in the theater—which, of course, created a new kind of filmic sensibility. There was no rigid devotion to the French New Wave or to Hollywood's classical era or to Charlie Chaplin, for that matter. One wall of the lobby had framed photos of directors and large photocopied reviews from New York critics. Outside the theater, Talbot posted program notes written for each series by his relatively young cohort: Bogdanovich, Kael (once she moved to New York), Everson, and *Post* critic Eugene Archer. Roger Greenspun, who also wrote program notes for Talbot, gushed that "an extraordinary amount of creative energy went into the theater, and one way or another the theater paid that energy back." It was not, Greenspun noted, "much of a glamour spot." Its seats were uncomfortable and the theater was just simply old. Nevertheless, "on off hours, [it was] the least dead looking movie house in New York."[45]

Exhibitors who ran theaters like those on Broadway operated on the assumption that audiences came for the popcorn as much as the pictures—and many would thank God that the American public liked popcorn. The lobby of the New Yorker provided its audience with a different treat—a chance to record in large accounting ledgers their thoughts about the movies, the theater, the management, and their wishes. The first page of the first book set the tone for this unique interaction. Near the bottom of the page, Talbot had inscribed, "In the beginning . . ." (a prelude to many movies). His patrons responded with characteristic wit: "This is a great Book but not quite the Bible," to which another added, "Go to Hell!" with an arrow pointing up to the quip about the Bible. Talbot treated moviegoers with a special kind of respect that acknowledged their cultivated tastes in films and their need to talk about them. Over the course of the theater's existence, the ledger books became synonymous with the New Yorker experience: hundreds were filled up with musings, doodlings, demands, and, most basically, names and addresses of patrons. While not quite a salon for talk about movies, the books did provide Talbot a glimpse of part of the city's movie culture.[46]

Not surprisingly, there were a fair number of pages filled with complaints. For example, one patron wrote, "Have you ever considered switching to silent films? Your projector seems to be ideal for them." On the opposite page, this same person scratched out the "see" in the page title "Films I would like to see" and wrote "hear." On another page, a patron wrote: "How dare you make me captive audience to a miserable bore like the 'Ivan' film—a hideous Russian pot-boiler." Below that comment was written: "Really not too bad—and rather charming if you take it in the right spirit. Of course the print was extremely poor and its very choppiness made sitting through it a tedious experience."[47]

Most of the gripes, though, were about the selection of movies. One could find requests and testimonials written in Spanish, Russian, French, Italian, and Japanese. Patrons from Manhattan and Brooklyn seemed to dominate the audience list. People wanted everything from Eisenstein films to Laurel and Hardy, from *Lolita* to *Lady and the Tramp*. It was not unusual to see requests for foreign and domestic films in the same list, as well as old and contemporary films, serious and comedy. There were pages of ridiculous pencil drawings of Hayley Mills from *The Parent Trap* and Elizabeth Taylor in *National Velvet*. And then there were the names of New York's literati and intelligentsia sprinkled throughout. Robert Schuman, the recently appointed president of a recently built Lincoln Center, asked in 1960 for Russian opera films and film productions of Chekhov. Future avant-garde film guru P. Adams Sitney (who was at Yale at the time) made a telling request: besides wanting Luis Buñuel films, he asked that "if any one from New Haven environs sees this, please get in touch with me, if interested in a films society." It was a desperate plea from a film fanatic. Al Goldstein, the future editor of the city's largest smut magazine, *Screw*, scrawled: "Don't Repeat 'Cinema #16' or the 'Thalia,'" an art house in the same neighborhood. Talbot obliged. Rex Reed signed the book and offered a preview of the kind of stinging reviews that would make him a popular New York film critic. "Whoever decided on a double bill of 'The Golden Coach' and 'St. Joan' should see a good analyst," he snapped. "Never have 4 hours passed so tediously! The former was incredibly boring, artless and presumptuous," Reed wrote with characteristic tact. "'St. Joan' proved to be a horrid sort of bad joke which the audience yawned through with complete dismay." Apparently not every show had the audience cheering from the seats. Reed's fellow critic John Simon came to the New Yorker and so did Susan Sontag, who requested *Queen Christina, Zéro de conduite,* and *Germany Year Zero* (a brief dissertation could be written on what this selection of films meant to Sontag). Even folk singer Joan Baez paid a visit, thanking the management for a "lovely evening" in June 1967.[48]

What made this record of popular opinion most impressive were the running debates over a myriad of issues, sometimes tending toward the personally offensive. There was an ongoing discussion of Charlie Chaplin's politics, with patrons alternatively defending the great film comedian and condemning him as a Communist. One scribbled during a Chaplin series, "Who needs the Red rat—Chaplin?" Another took the time to answer: "I for one am not interested in his political life. I like his work as a performer. To me a movie house is to enrich art not to have a political discussion." Trying to sound serious, one person used the better part of a full page to express "dismay" that "Americans would request that Charlie Chaplin films be shown at 'The New Yorker.'" This person, who signed the book "Eight [*sic*] Generation American," wanted others to remember that "America has been good to you Eastern European Jews, Catholics, Orientals. Do reciprocate." One thing that the writer could be assured of was that people would read and respond. "You crazy hysteric Americans!" one person wrote. Another asked: "How can any of Chaplin's films make one Communist?" There was a more direct response that many patrons used throughout the book—they scribbled out the original offending comment and called the person a name ("schmuck," "idiot," and the like). Along these offending lines, an audience member demanded that "no Negroes should be allowed in the or this [*sic*] Theatre." The usual response was given by another in the audience: "Whoever wrote that is a smuck or shmuck or schmuck," obviously wanting to make the point clear.[49]

The books also became an open forum, even a referendum when certain movies were playing, on the "politics" of *Cahiers du cinema*. Among the most lively debates in New York's movie culture in the early 1960s centered on the emergence of the auteur theory, an approach to film criticism that drew on close watchings of many films by a single director in order to discern patterns of style. The French journal was the birthplace of this particular idea, and its chief American importer was a young *Village Voice* and *Film Culture* critic, Andrew Sarris. At the New Yorker, the auteur theory found expression in the programming policies of Talbot and Bogdanovich, both of whom were friends of Sarris and at least familiar with, if not devoted to, the *Cahiers* line. So, too, it was clear, were the patrons. One asked rhetorically, "What are you, an official theatre of the *Cahiers du cinema?* What's the use of having this book if you ignore all the requests? Why don't you invite those idiots of the *Cahiers du cinema* over to see that junk (most of it) that you're showing?" The response? "Angel Face is *not* Junk!" If one sifts through the hundreds of pages of requests and recommendations, statements and replies, something becomes very clear. All this name-calling and list-making illustrated, if nothing else, that New York City had a movie culture full of lay theorists. Patrons were able to argue passionately for *The Best Years of Our Lives* and a series of William Powell films. They could thunder about Otto Preminger and ponder over the connection between Ingmar Bergman and *la nouvelle vague* (the French New Wave). The New Yorker was an outlet, a refuge, and an alternative for all those moviegoers who, by the 1960s, were beginning to embrace a new sensibility about movies and American culture in general. It was an energy that had broken the older mold of moviegoing—going to the movies was neither a passive form of recreation nor an opportunity for cultivation. Talbot's theater allowed a certain amount of anarchy to thrive by breaking away from the commercial and even intellectual concerns that had contained movies. Thus, it was not surprising that at the same time the New Yorker took off, so did a group dedicated to channeling some of this anarchic energy into a new type of movie culture.[50]

On 28 September 1960, Amos Vogel's domain was directly challenged by a group collectively known as New American Cinema and led by the endlessly energetic Jonas Mekas. Part of Mekas's plan was the creation of the Film-makers' Cooperative, an organization that would exhibit and distribute the avant-garde and independent films of the New American Cinema. Unlike Vogel, Mekas was "less concerned with audience size than with the integrity of individual film artists' cinematic visions." Vogel was both a businessman and a self-appointed authority on independent film. He took a larger cut from the exclusive contracts he signed with filmmakers, and he chose which filmmakers to distribute, resisting the impulse that pervaded the co-op to promote those who wanted exposure. Siegfried Kracauer explained what made Vogel's operation unique: "Whenever I attended the screenings of Cinema 16, I felt elated about the intensity with which a huge audience watched the spectacles you offered them—films in a daring mood, films with a serious purpose. You yourself are an educator, and your own passion for the cinema is contagious." To Vogel, audience taste for films mattered as much as the filmmakers.[51]

Vogel told Scott MacDonald: "I would say that the historical catastrophe of the American avant-garde movement is precisely the fact that Jonas and I were *not* together, that Jonas excluded me at a time when I was doing a very big and very successful project in New York." Mekas countered: "No matter how open Amos would have been, he could not have accommodated all the filmmakers in the group. We needed an outlet controlled by ourselves, where no film would be rejected and all would be available. And so the Film-makers' Cooperative came into existence." Mekas explains the decline of Cinema 16 this way: "It was the Madison Avenue world and the fine arts crowd. It was not . . . the lower middle classes. But *whatever* it was, it exhausted itself after a decade and attendance naturally began falling off."[52]

The break between Cinema 16 and the New American Cinema might best be summed up by P. Adams Sitney. He characterized the rivalry between Vogel and Mekas as the difference between what was showing at Cinema 16 and what was showing at the Charles, at that moment the theater that Mekas used to exhibit work of the New American Cinema. Sitney was pretty much on the outside of the fight because of his age (he was sixteen in 1961) and because he was a devotee of both places rather than a filmmaker. The break came when Vogel refused to show *Anticipation of the Night*, even though the film's director, Stan Brakhage, was a hero among the angry independent film community.

"*That* position fueled the moral polemic of Jonas and all the people who were wild about Brakhage." Vogel's decision and Mekas's opposition to it indicated the great differences in their intellectual and even ideological approaches to programming. In relating those differences, Sitney recalled a show Mekas did for Marie Menken, the wife of explosive filmmaker Willard Maas. "She [Menken] was up all night putting them together. Some had soundtracks, some didn't. Gerard Malanga was making titles; Willard was running around screaming and cursing everybody out. This is a mode of operation that Jonas could handle: midnight at the Charles—no announced program. Cinema 16 simply didn't operate that way." And by 1963, it didn't operate at all.[53]

The demise of Cinema 16 was part financial—other options such as the New Yorker simply competed successfully with Vogel—and part intellectual. Vogel's confrontational cinema had defined limits that offered a modicum of protection from censors and for audiences. While he challenged his patrons to engage films of varying subject matter and quality, Vogel did so to encourage a certain type of conversation about taste. At Cinema 16, moviegoing was challenging—moviegoers saw unique offerings but not necessarily ones they liked. Vogel sought to construct a movie culture that incorporated not merely avant-garde films but avant-garde attitudes. To accomplish such a feat, though, meant taking the avant-garde and Vogel seriously. That proved to be too much to ask in a culture that was into cool and camp.

5

The "Flaming" Freedom of Jonas Mekas

ON THE EVENING of 3 March 1964, at the New Bowery Theatre in the East Village, New York City police detective Arthur Welsh observed what he considered an "indecent, lewd and obscene film" and, acting in his capacity as an officer of the court, arrested four people on the charge of obscenity. The film was Jack Smith's *Flaming Creatures*, and those arrested included two ticket takers, Garry Sims and Florence Karpf; the projectionist, filmmaker Ken Jacobs; and Jonas Mekas. In Welsh's initial report of the incident he listed Mekas first, as the defendant who "did supply and distribute [the] lewd and obscene film . . . for exhibition at the New Bowery Theatre." Mekas rejoiced in his arrest. It was a moment of persecution that he hoped to turn into a movement for liberation without end.[1]

Jack Smith's film was small and campy and would have gone unnoticed by the vast majority of moviegoers in New York and elsewhere if not for Mekas's efforts. Smith shot it on grainy stock and it looks amateurish. Its story line is a combination of kitsch playfulness and avant-garde bizarre. A group of actors—some in drag, some half naked (the women topless, the men bottomless)—romp and dance and even simulate rape in a world that seems one long hallucination. Smith originally made the film for his friends in Greenwich Village as a homage of sorts to the gay cinematic underground, a world that was almost completely unknown to most New Yorkers in 1964. And yet Mekas chose to take a heroic stand on this film, to challenge not merely the traditions of narrative cinema and the enforcement of anachronistic censorship laws but also the existence of a public culture. Mekas inverted the questions that had guided debates over art throughout the modern period. Rather than investigate the relationship between the artistic fringe and the mainstream, Mekas decided that there need not be a relationship; the idea of the avant-garde subverting order was unnecessary if the vanguard became the new order. New York's movie culture had undoubtedly been progressing through a revolution during the postwar years, and that revolution had produced rising expectations. Moviegoers in New York City certainly enjoyed more freedom to see more types of films than at any point in history. Mekas wanted to find out whether such freedom could ultimately match his expectations. In this way, *Flaming Creatures* was indeed the perfect test.

Mekas was as much a creation of his moment as he was a creator of it. He had a Beat sensibility—iconoclastic and fiercely independent—and mass movement ambitions. Every controversy he generated was a both a personal test of authenticity and a potential political statement with broad implications for American culture. Mekas was one of those figures in whom one can see a transition from the internal struggles over identity in the 1950s to the external production of image in the 1960s. Mekas was not content to offer a way for individuals to change how they experienced films; he hoped to create cinematic experiences that would make all moviegoers part of his revolution. And that was an unfortunate ambition because the grandiosity of it made such sweeping change nearly impossible. As a result, Mekas's projects were often reduced to courting controversy as an end in itself.[2]

Thus, Mekas made it possible to imagine that conflict rather than criticism was the organizing principle of culture. That stance could appear avant-garde and even heroic—Mekas battling the forces of repression in the name of freedom—but unlike Amos Vogel in his attempt to educate moviegoers, Mekas had little interest in merely promoting a different way to look at films. Rather, Mekas embraced cinema in a way that more closely resembled Cardinal Spellman and Martin Quigley's view. Like them, Mekas believed movies could transform society and even destroy it. However, he looked forward to the consequences of such destruction, fighting against all standards of taste and art with the same kind of fury with which Catholic moralists had defended codes intended to protect Western civilization from the menace of movies. However, at least censors employed some kind of critical criteria when evaluating

movies, even if that calculus was seriously flawed. Mekas rejected all
cultural authority in the name of a freedom that seemed boundless. His
stance implied that any film could be legitimate and that controversy,
such as the one caused by *Flaming Creatures*, was an end in itself. In
his management of the flap over *Flaming Creatures*, Mekas exposed the
unfortunate implications of defending art as a heroic endeavor.

The controversy caused by *Flaming Creatures* ushered in a new
period in the heroic age of moviegoing during which the quality of
the material being defended mattered less and less. Rather, what mattered was the act of championing the right kind of material—it had
to be subversive and transgressive. In this way, Mekas personified the
heroic artist in Susan Sontag's essay "The Pornographic Imagination."
He embraced film as an abstract principle—film as life, film as spirit. It
was not enough to argue that films were serious; they had to be, in Mekas's mind, almost untouchable or unimpeachable. But this passion,
perhaps inadvertently, sparked a strange kind of cultural competition
in which it became necessary to defend increasingly more outrageous
films, though not necessarily better films. Taste could not factor into
Mekas's approach because taste required discrimination. And discrimination required a measure of discipline that ran against the kind of
flaming freedom that Mekas embraced.

Jonas Mekas has consistently claimed that he was not looking for a
fight when he promoted, exhibited, and distributed *Flaming Creatures*,
but a fight is what he got, and the controversy surrounding this case has
become a landmark in the history of the culture wars. Even though
Flaming Creatures was initially a most unlikely film to achieve notoriety, it was perfect for Mekas's purposes. He knew that he could make
out of it what he needed, and in the process, the fight over the film
would help make Mekas into a hero.

In retrospect, it seems clear that New York City's movie culture had
been waiting for Jonas Mekas to appear. "Far from being without film
culture," film historian David James contends, "the city to which Jonas
Mekas came was the country's—and perhaps the century's—center of
independent cinema." Mekas and his brother Adolfas, Lithuanian by
birth, had arrived in New York in October 1949, having spent the previous four years as refugees in displaced persons camps in war-torn Eu-

rope. When the brothers first arrived in the States they lived together in the Williamsburg section of Brooklyn, working factory jobs. Early on they gravitated to MoMA film programs, where Jonas became friends with avant-garde filmmaker Hans Richter, who taught courses at the City University of New York. Some of Jonas's earliest film projects documented the experiences of Lithuanian refugees around the city. And, of course, he was an earnest devotee of Cinema 16.[3]

During this early period, Mekas possessed boundless energy when it came to film. He was working in a factory, living off meager wages, but seemed to visit almost every theater in Manhattan. By the mid-1950s, he decided to channel his passion into writing about the cinema. Amazingly, his first effort was the founding of the journal *Film Culture* in 1955. With a small regular staff, almost no budget beyond the production of a first issue, and a desire to create a serious American film journal, Mekas set out to treat movies as a legitimate art form. Though the early issues of the journal bear almost no resemblance to what would come later, *Film Culture* immediately established itself, and its editor in chief, as an intellectual force in the motion picture world. In its first few years, *Film Culture* included pieces by stalwarts of the establishment such as Gilbert Seldes and Bosley Crowther. The film historian and foreign film subtitler Herman Weinberg was on the editorial staff, as was a young Andrew Sarris. In short, the journal comprised a microcosm of New York City's movie culture—its past, present, and future.

Sarris met Mekas in late 1954 through Roger Tilton, an instructor at Columbia College. "[Mekas] was very open about everything," Sarris remembers. "There was no money for editing, which I understood. But he gave me the opportunity to write." And even though he thought the title of the journal a bit "pretentious," it was at least a serious attempt to look at film. "The aesthetic emerged out of the seriousness, out of experimental film, out of foreign art films," Sarris explains. Mekas and his coeditor, Edouard de Laurot, introduced Sarris to the French critics they were reading, which reflected the desire—especially Mekas's—to create a magazine that projected a sense of newness: it was glossy and "we had complete freedom; we could write anything we wanted." Sarris admits that he was lazy as an editor and writer; de Laurot was the "heavy hitter" theoretically, and Eugene Archer was the "big pieces" writer. "There really was very little linking the different segments at the magazine. There were the political people, the antiquarian people [Weinberg], experimental people, there was the gay subculture, much less political than it is now."[4]

In these first few years, Mekas harbored an almost vitriolic dislike for avant-garde films. He called most efforts "adolescent" and scoffed that most of these films were filled with "zombie-like characters" and a "superexcess of unintelligible details . . . that are . . . full of significance to the makers but . . . convey no definite meaning to the viewer." In retrospect almost mocking his later views, he even expressed great annoyance over the use of a "stream-of-consciousness" style that was devoid of "moral stand." "Being incoherent in their very intention," he argued, "these films necessarily remain shallow and incomprehensible. It is not important to decide here whether or not these neurotic and homosexual poems can be called art. What I want to stress is that this art of abnormality is unmotivated, unresolved and lacks a moral dimension." Such attacks, Mekas later explained, were a direct reflection of the influence of Edouard de Laurot, whose Marxist criticism had little tolerance for what he considered the apolitical musings of many avant-garde filmmakers. However, once his colleague had left the journal, Mekas was free to pursue a different intellectual avenue—to be reborn through a new influence. By the late 1950s, Mekas had become the most outspoken champion of a movement to "free cinema." But to free cinema from what?[5]

That question became the intellectual focal point for Mekas's other writing job—as the regular movie critic for a small upstart weekly called the *Village Voice*. The *Voice* began in the mid-1950s as a very small paper, only ten to twelve pages an issue in its first year, but immediately lived up to its name as "the voice" of New York's historic bohemian enclave. The first issue that included Mekas's column "Film Journal" also ran a review by Beat poet Allen Ginsberg of Beat novelist Jack Kerouac's *The Dharma Bums*. The *Voice* had also carried an acerbic and short-lived column from its one true celebrity (and financial patron), Norman Mailer. It was a paper that from a very early point in its history reflected the passions, interests, and tenor of its neighborhood—evident in the style as well as the content. Mekas's writing fit that character perfectly, for he loudly championed the cinema he adored and in so doing sought to convert his readers to movements in New York's movie culture.

In his first review, he took a shot at New York's biggest critic, Bosley Crowther, and generated his first hate mail. Mekas praised the Indian film *Pather Panchali*, arguing that because "it is so fresh . . . it caused some of our daily reviewers to lift their brows: 'It has no structure!' 'It has no plot!' (as if the art of the film could be equated with that of the novel)." Mekas scoffed at Crowther's comment that the movie seemed "unprofessional." Mekas jeered, "After seeing so many 'professional' films one longs for the freshness of the 'non-professional,' one who has not yet become 'a traitor to his wild and lonely youth.'" Jerry Talmer, one of the early editors of the *Voice* (and later an editor at the *New York Post*) remembered that Mekas's column constantly provoked readers. One wrote in to lambast the "small brain" writing movie "commentary" for the paper.[6]

In the late 1950s, Mekas underwent a conversion (and he does compare what happened to him to the experience of St. Augustine): he became a passionate promoter of a cinematic sensibility emerging in New York's underground. Like St. Augustine, Mekas had an epiphany. It came at the Cinema 16 screening in November 1959 of two new films: *Shadows*, from a young auteur named John Cassavetes, and *Pull My Daisy*, a humorous effort put together by painter Alfred Leslie and Beat poet Robert Frank. The films are important cinematically for what they came to represent in movie culture. Content was no longer an end in itself, as it had been in previous battles over movies. The new debate was over what a moviegoer was willing to accept from a cinematic experience. After watching these films, Mekas went revolutionary, calling for the "*complete* derangement of the official cinematic senses." He wanted to subvert the traditional ways of making, selling, and seeing movies.[7]

A year before that momentous night at Cinema 16, Mekas had been among a relatively small group of about three hundred people at a midnight show of *Shadows* at the Paris Theater. The screening, though, fell far short of success; much of the audience left before the film ended because the sound and projection were so poor. But Mekas stayed. Director John Cassavetes recalled that Mekas ran up to him and the cast, praising the film. Unmoved, Cassavetes determined that his movie was a flop because it was all "cinematic virtuosity" and lacked almost any narrative or character development to draw in audiences. So he decided to reedit the film and shoot additional scenes, made more necessary by the fact, Cassavetes biographer Ray Carney notes, that the director had destroyed almost all extra footage. He shot more than eighteen hours of new film, weaving the new scenes into the finished work, screened on 11 November 1959 at two evening shows for Cinema 16. Amos Vogel was so impressed when he previewed the film that he rented *Shadows* for $250, four or five times the traditional rate, and created a buzz that attracted some of New York's artistic intelligentsia, including Parker Tyler, Arthur Knight, Paddy Chayefsky, Kenneth Tynan, and Meyer Shapiro. This time, the director, the audience, and the distributor were all pleased.[8]

Jonas Mekas was not. To him the more polished film was a sellout. He had been blown away by the first, rough version of the film. "*Shadows* breaks with the official staged cinema," he declared, "with made-up faces, with written scripts, with plot continuities. Even its inexperience in editing, sound, and camera work becomes a part of its style, the roughness that only life (and Alfred Leslie's paintings) have. It doesn't prove anything, it doesn't even want to say anything, but really it tells more than ten or one hundred and ten other recent American films." To Mekas, the reedited version betrayed the essence of the emerging American underground. "They succeeded in persuading Cassavetes to re-shoot and re-edit the film, to make it more suitable for the commercial theatres," Mekas lamented. "The result was a bastardized, hybrid movie which had neither the spontaneity of the first version, nor the innocence, nor the freshness." And therein lay the sin—Mekas believed that the purity of such vision would free American cinema from its compromise with commercialism. Years later, Cassavetes told Ray Carney that he had edited the film and worked off a script in part to make the film more commercially marketable. It wasn't Mekas's nefarious "them" who had changed the film—it was the filmmaker himself.[9]

J. Hoberman, the current *Village Voice* film critic, has noted that the controversy Mekas created over the two versions of *Shadows* was "the first great debate of Mekas's career at the *Voice*." It also gave Mekas "license to wipe clean the slate and reinvent the movies, virtually from scratch." Mekas wrote, "*Shadows* proves that a feature film can be made with only $15,000. And a film that doesn't betray life or cinema. What does it prove? It proves that we can make our films *now* and by *ourselves*. Hollywood and the miniature Hollywoods of our 'independents' will never make *our* films." *Shadows* was a revelation to Mekas—

the future of independent cinema had opened up to him. "A $15,000 film is financially unbeatable," he proclaimed. "Television cannot kill it. The apathy of the audience cannot kill it. Theatrical distributors cannot kill it. It is free."[10]

Here was the next stage of cinematic freedom: the realization that filmmaking is not a business or even an art; it is simply, profoundly, and personally an act. In Mekas's cinematic world, films existed as an extension of an individual's soul—this was filmmaking and moviegoing as personal theology. In *Film Culture*, Mekas pronounced a "New Generation of Film Makers" who would "mistrust and loathe the official cinema and its thematic and formal stiffness," who would be "primarily preoccupied with the emotional and intellectual conditions of their generation as opposed to the neorealists' preoccupation with materiality; [and] seek to free themselves from the over-professionalism and over-technicality that usually handicaps the inspiration and spontaneity of the official cinema, guiding themselves more by intuition and improvisation than by discipline."[11]

In a piece for England's most influential film journal, *Sight and Sound*, Mekas echoed his *Film Culture* editorial in a regular column entitled "New York Letter," announcing that a small core of filmmakers were pioneering "spontaneous cinema." He mentioned Cassavetes, Leslie, Frank, and Stan Brakhage and rejoiced in the idea that "the new generation of film-makers is governed by the feelings and winds of this transitional period." The "aims and purposes of the previous generation have betrayed them," Mekas decided; thus, the best alternative was "to throw away all inhibitions and lose oneself completely in the spontaneous improvisations that lead into the inner regions of our being: where, after all, everything rests." His vision of cinema, he hoped, would usher in a period of freedom that valued transparency rather than movie magic and was ultimately ethical rather than commercial. It was almost a spiritual movement for Mekas, since for him cinema could reveal—perhaps even must reveal—the soul of the artist and the nature of his or her society. "I would call a fool anybody who would demand of this generation works of art that contain clear and positive philosophies and esthetics. There will be nothing of that! This generation is too young, too alive for that. . . . This decade will be marked by an intensified search and by the further loosening of sensibilities for the purpose of reaching still deeper into less contaminated depths

of man's soul, trying desperately to escape the clichés of art and life."
Such freedom allowed no room for traditional standards, especially
those enforced by censors. This was freedom of expression taken to
anarchic ends.[12]

The testy battle over the iterations of *Shadows* mirrored a deeper
struggle in New York City's movie culture between more traditional
forces for change and the rather energetic, anarchic, and loosely organized forces for complete "derangement" represented by Mekas. In
1960, Mekas sought to channel such energy toward "breaking the frozen cinematic ground." He hoped that through his informal leadership,
something new and vital would emerge from New York's underground.
In September 1960, Mekas formed the Film-Makers' Cooperative in
order to distribute films without interference from Amos Vogel, New
York censors, or any regime of taste. A dispute over Vogel's refusal to rent,
exhibit, and distribute *Anticipation of the Night* from Stan Brakhage
finally separated Vogel from Mekas and divided Cinema 16 from a new
era of independent film. Brakhage explained that the "independent
filmmakers felt Amos wasn't showing enough of *their* work and other
work that they felt related to, and they often felt like they were being
used in a freak show environment." At base, Mekas rejected the authority Vogel exercised over film selection, considering Cinema 16 a slightly different version of commercial movie houses that stifled creative
energy by always seeming to have an agenda. Mekas argued that the
cinematic underground had simply outgrown venues such as MoMA
and Cinema 16, both physically and artistically. Many New York avant-
garde filmmakers agreed; they aspired to be part of a global community, to push beyond the bounds of their city's bohemian quarter.[13]

In the Summer 1961 issue of *Film Culture*, Mekas officially introduced the American version of Europe's avant-garde: the New American Cinema Group (NAC). In his initial statement, Mekas recounted
the September meeting at which twenty-three filmmakers and others
interested in the cinematic underground met to discuss how best to nur-
ture the next stage in movie culture. "We don't want false, polished, slick
films," he declared. "We prefer them rough, unpolished, but alive; we
don't want rosy films—we want them the color of blood." Most of all,
this group wanted control over making, exhibiting, and distributing films
without any impediments. The New American Cinema rejected censorship, licensing, and traditional distribution and exhibition schemes;

there would be no outside influence on the creative process, and the connection between funding and the "ethical and aesthetic" value of films would be erased. Mekas said he wanted to "blow up" the old system that controlled and contained movies—his co-op was to fill the void.[14]

If Vogel had developed confrontational cinema, Mekas called for destructive cinema. A signature of Mekas's modus operandi was his periodic violent pronouncements. Besides calling for "breaking" frozen cinematic ground and "derangement" of cinematic senses, he also called for "shooting" screenwriters and studio presidents. He imagined producing a movie called *The Massacre* during which the director would "place all movie critics on the set [and] machine gun the critics" and then "announce completion of the shooting." He also advised blowing up a studio once all motion picture equipment in Hollywood had been gathered in it. The film could be entitled *Destruction of Hollywood*. Of course, Mekas meant none of this literally, but he was serious in a figurative sense. And that helps explain how the "pied piper" of New York's underground attracted a growing cohort of young revolutionaries who staunchly rejected mainstream movie culture as innately corrupt and corrupting. That same energy struck just as many, though, as bravado, rather than heroism, which was why Mekas also alienated allies like Amos Vogel and prompted some of his staunchest supporters, such as critics Andrew Sarris and Parker Tyler and filmmakers Stan Brakhage and Jack Smith, to love the man but hate his movement.[15]

In his "Film Journal" column for the 8 April 1963 *Voice*, Mekas wrote of seeing *Flaming Creatures* at a private showing. He was sure that it would never make it to the commercial cinema because "our social-moral-etc. guides are sick." In the early 1960s, a few venues allowed the underground to show its work. Among those theaters were a collection of somewhat rundown places in the East Village and Daniel Talbot's New Yorker Theater. Critics and film historians J. Hoberman and Jonathan Rosenbaum write that the movies shown in these places were "distinguished from both commercial movies and the earlier avant-garde by a combination of willful primitivism, taboo-breaking sexuality, and obsessive ambivalence toward American popular culture (mainly Hollywood)." The Charles in the East Village was among the first to be transformed in 1961 into one of the city's eclectic theaters, showing everything from B movies to underground cinema. The Lower East Side was peppered with these theaters, and the atmosphere at the Charles reflected the patrons, who were helping to create a new cinema environment. Vogel said it was a "properly bedraggled beat audience spitting in the face of the bourgeoisie." Among the young filmmakers shown publicly for the first time there were Andy Warhol devotee Paul Morrissey, Brian De Palma when he was a Columbia University student, and B-movie satirist Robert Downey. Here could be found an eclectic mix of "Madison Avenue types . . . among beards, black leotards, and sloppy sweaters." The Charles ended its run as an underground theater in late 1962 and reopened in January 1963 to show the nudie-cuties of racy auteur Radley Metzger—a trend that would characterize New York's transition from the era of Mekas to the era of porn entrepreneurs.[16]

Smith's *Flaming Creatures* fit nicely into the seriously informal, chaotically programmed group of "midnight movies" shown at places like the Charles. Hoberman and Rosenbaum explain that Smith used "grossly outdated black-and-white film stock, which gave the images a striking ethereality, [to present] a discontinuous series of tableaux accompanied by a sound montage of Maria Montez dialogue, 'hacienda' music, and rock 'n' roll. His 'creatures' . . . included mock Arabian odalisques, sultry Spanish dancers, and vampirelike Marilyn Monroe clones, among many others not so easily classified." The movie ran about forty-five minutes and was completed for a proudly reported $300. Smith once claimed that he made the movie specifically for a screening at the Charles. The Charles had closed by the time his farce was ready for its premiere, so Smith held the first public screening at an equally offbeat theater, the Bleeker Street Cinema, on 29 April 1963.[17]

But later, Smith's film prompted Marshall Lewis, the manager of the Bleeker Street Cinema, to send Mekas a letter expressing his concern over the bad publicity his theater received from shows of the NAC. Mekas and his revolutionary cinema had to find another home. "I regret . . . that the experiment has not been successful," Marshall wrote; "however, my concern for the reputation of the theatre comes before any personal feelings I might hold about *every* film-maker (good or bad) having access to a showing place." Thus began Mekas's heroic fight. Whereas Amos Vogel had helped to promote art theaters, Mekas was closing them down in the name of his art.[18]

Writing in the *Voice,* Mekas compared Smith's style to cinema giant Joseph Von Sternberg's in "imagination . . . imagery . . . poetry."
But Mekas thought Smith had much more. "This movie will be called
pornographic, degenerate, homosexual, trite, disgusting, etc. It is all
that, and it is so much more than that. I tell you," Mekas proclaimed,
"the American movie audiences today are being deprived of the best
of the new cinema, and it's not doing any good to the souls of the
people." Smith's film was one of a string of new films that announced
the arrival of a more sexually provocative underground. Nudity, homosexuality, and the frank flouting of contemporary social mores seemed
as much a part of these films as the unorthodox shooting and editing
and the extraordinarily low budgets. Mekas anointed this movement
"Baudelairean Cinema," a reference to the nineteenth-century French
critic Charles Baudelaire (whom Mekas clearly identified with), who
had prophesied that the rise of popular arts would eventually transcend
and subvert more traditional cultural categories. "It is my duty," Mekas
thumped, "to bring this cinema to your attention. I will bark about it
until our theatres start showing this cinema." He compared what these
new filmmakers were doing to the achievements of Marquis de Sade
and Arthur Rimbaud. And like the works of these writers, pictures from
the underground "tread on the edge of perversity" and are "dirty mouth"
movies—they all contain homosexuality. "So there is now a cinema for
the few, too terrible and too 'decadent' for an 'average' man in any organized culture. But then, if everybody would dig Baudelaire, or Sade,
or William Burroughs, my God, where would humanity be?"[19]

Perhaps a better question to have asked was where would the artistic fringe be—the vanguard and modernism, for that matter—if "everyone" accepted what Mekas embraced? The point of being on the
edge was to stay there, to remain an annoyance rather than become the
thing to attack. The nature of movies, though, disturbs that relationship because moviegoing is supposed to be—almost must be—a public and even commercial experience. Mekas wanted controversy to do
more than tease mainstream culture and the laws keeping it in check.
He wanted controversy to replace mainstream culture.[20]

In the pages of *Film Culture,* news and criticism of the cinematic
underground was fed into a loop—some praise led to more praise,
which led to the defense of the underground against attacks from the
enemies outside the pages of the journal. In the latter half of 1963,

the mainstream provided fodder. Veteran New York City reporter Pete Hamill wrote "Explosion in the Movie Underground" for the *Saturday Evening Post*, at that time among the most popular magazines in the country. He called the NAC "amateurish and ill-conceived" but significant enough to attract some attention from the Ford Foundation and a small and loyal group of cineastes. The *New Yorker* ran a short piece on a Film-Makers' Co-op show that had been canceled at the Bleeker Street Cinema. In it, Mekas brazenly embraced the notion that the NAC was "disorganized, unsophisticated, and anarchistic" and hinted that Jack Smith probably stole the film stock on which he made *Flaming Creatures* because his budget was so small. When asked if there was anything that the NAC feared, Mekas and others with him intimated that they were not afraid of the censors or the city's license department but were "terrified" by the prospect of becoming part of the "Establishment."[21]

Well-known critic Arthur Knight also filed a report on the underground, this time from Los Angeles, where he was treated to a screening of *Flaming Creatures*. In what became a famous condemnation of Smith's film, Knight exploded: "*Flaming Creatures* . . . is far from boring—it is merely repulsive. A faggoty stag reel, it comes as close to hard-core pornography as anything ever presented in a theatre. In depicting the revels of its assorted perverts, the film studiously avoids imagination or suggestion. Everything is shown in sick and sickening detail, defiling at once both sex and cinema." This from the critic who just a few years later would write a groundbreaking series for *Playboy* on sex and the cinema. "What emerged from Hollywood's first encounter with the New American Cinema," Knight suggested, "was the suspicion that its advocates are less film makers than anti-film makers, rebels without either cause or purpose. Technically, they may be accused of sheer incompetence, while thematically they seem to be leading the way to a blind alley of self-indulgence and self-satisfaction from which there is no escape."[22]

Such critiques probably inspired Mekas to embrace Smith's film even more. Writing in *Film Culture*, Mekas mused, "In *Flaming Creatures* Smith has graced the anarchic liberation of new American cinema with graphic and rhythmic power worthy of the best formal cinema. He has attained for the first time in motion pictures a high level of art which is absolutely lacking in decorum; and a treatment of sex which makes us aware of the restraint of all previous film-makers. . . . He has lit up a part of life, although it is a part which most men scorn."[23]

Ken Kelman echoed Mekas's praise in the same issue, gushing that Smith's film "beats with total life. It is not a mere collection of whimsical actions or striking images [as were other avant-garde pictures]. It is a realized vision. The others have the same style, but not the imagination, the articulateness, the poetic concentration." The others also did not have "what tamer creatures would call the 'perverse' pleasures, the 'violent' joys, the 'dark' raptures." Although few in the audience clapped at the film's conclusion, Kelman assured his readers that what they saw was something higher than common Hollywood titillation. On the page opposite this review was Jack Smith's singular comment: a page blank but for a huge "CENSORED" printed diagonally across it and the title "From 'Flaming Creatures' By Jack Smith."[24]

That was Smith's reply to the New York City Department of Licenses. In August 1963, Mekas angrily huffed that he had to find yet another venue to show films from the NAC, because the censors—the police and license officers—had begun to pester him again about exhibiting unlicensed films. "They have disregarded the fact that most of the films screened are unfinished works-in-progress and cannot be submitted for censorship or licensing. We are not in the business of making money: We are running an experimental film workshop, and we don't care what the bureaucrats say we are doing." Especially irritating to Mekas was that such harassment clearly illustrated that city officials considered these films anything but art. For surely, the license commissioner did not treat new installations at the Museum of Modern Art this way. "We are only reminding you that neither as men nor as artists can we grow by compromises. But that's what you are asking of us," Mekas pleaded. "You are telling us to go into the rat holes, stay away from the public. You are asking your artists to sell themselves out, to give up, to go to Hell." This was a delicate moment for the NAC. Mekas understood that in order for his cinematic avant-garde to appear legitimate, films such as Smith's needed air to breathe.[25]

In October 1963, Mekas published a discussion he had had with filmmakers Storm De Hirsch and Louis Brigante in which he intimated that New York City was ripe for a cinematic revolution. He conceded that Smith's film probably appealed to a very small number of people and should not be forced down anyone's throat. Yet he also clearly believed that there would come a moment when the New American Cinema had to make a move against cinematic tradition and create a new future for movie culture. "This gained freedom puts on us a huge demand to go all the way out (or in). And very few of us are doing that at this moment," Mekas acknowledged. "We are still too locked up in ourselves, too hung up on something or other." One wonders if it was taste, standards, and boundaries keeping Mekas back. If so, he proved up to the challenge of undermining such notions.[26]

On 12 December 1963, Jonas Mekas used his weekly column in the *Village Voice* to announce that his journal, *Film Culture*, had attempted to award Jack Smith the Independent Film Award. However, the presentation had to take place on the roof of a car rather than inside the Tivoli Theater because the theater's management had been threatened with police action if it allowed Mekas's group in. A thousand people, according to Mekas, gathered outside the Tivoli, and a few hundred forced their way into the theater. The police were called and the audience was threatened with arrest. Was this the storming of the cinematic Bastille?[27]

Soon after, Mekas took a copy of *Flaming Creatures* to the Knokke-le-Zoute film festival in Belgium, hoping to make the NAC an international force. Belgium's minister of justice advised the festival's selection jury, on which Mekas sat, that national law forbade public exhibition of overtly obscene material. Stymied once again by the "state," Mekas resigned, making threats of his own. Waving cables of support from American filmmakers, he told festival officials that he had the power to pull from competition American entries from Stan Vanderbeck, Gregory Markopoulos, Robert Breer, and Stan Brakhage. Film festival officials worked out a compromise that allowed Mekas to arrange a private screening, not a public exhibition, of *Flaming Creatures*. Consequently, Smith's film received a "special prize of the censored film." Mekas began samizdat screenings in his hotel room for European filmmakers such as Jean-Luc Godard, Agnes Varda, and Roman Polanski; *Variety* journalist Gene Moskowitz was on hand to record the event. Over forty people packed into the room, though some, especially Agnes Varda, were none too pleased to be barred from walking out on the screening by a rowdy crowd that had gathered to praise it.[28]

Mekas next attempted to take over the projection facilities at the casino that housed the festival. He and his gang hid *Flaming Creatures*

in the can of Stan Brakhage's *Dog Star Man* "on New Year's night,"
hoping to slip Smith's film in between one of the many reels that made
up the eight-hour screening of Andy Warhol's aptly titled *Sleep*. Mekas
and his band of American anarchistic cinephiles "stormed the Crystal
Room and took over the projector," but the manager cut the lights.
Recounting his adventure for his *Voice* readers, Mekas claimed that he
"ran to the switchboard room, [tried] to push off the house detective,
[while] holding the door, trying to force the fingers of the bully who
was holding the switch." Elliott Stein of England's *Sight and Sound*
reported that Mekas "called out for help 'from all those present who
believe in freedom of the screen.'" At that point, the main switch to the
casino was thrown, plunging the whole building into darkness. When
light returned, another showdown took place, this time between radical American filmmaker Barbara Rubin and the Belgian minister of
justice, M. Pierre Vermeylen. "Do you want to see the film?" Rubin
shouted to the audience. "Yes!" the voices returned. But Vermeylen
would have none of it. According to Stein, he delivered a "curt lecture"
on free expression, explaining that Belgium was the only country in
the world without an official film censor. He considered Smith's film,
though, to be "both pornographic and [as if this mattered] inartistic."
Rubin told the Belgian minister of justice to "fuck himself" and called
for the film to be projected onto his face.[29]

Mekas rejoiced when the details of these events had "blown across
the world." He had wrapped himself in the flag of freedom—his cause
was a screen that knew no bounds—intellectually, aesthetically, and
geographically. "It has become very clear," he wrote in the *Voice*, "that
it makes no sense to hide art under a film society membership or other
cloak. To look for ways of getting around the law, instead of facing it
and provoking it directly and openly, is dishonest. That's why bad laws
exist. If Knokke left any lasting impression on me, it is the realization of
the dishonesty of artistic 'freedom' that is relegated to clubs, societies,
membership groups. That includes the Loves and Kisses to Censors
Film Society." (That was the umbrella group he created under which
to show unlicensed films.) When Mekas compared the American films
he brought over with the others in the competition, he concluded for
perhaps the first time in his career that "the only truly creative work in
cinema is being done by Americans."[30]

On 14 January 1964, *Variety* ran a small headline that read, "Belgians Balk NY Creatures," reporting that "Flaming Creatures divided the delegates, the critics and the Belgians. Comments ranged from terming the film a crude stunt, a stag film, a misnamed 'artie.' . . . And what was it finally?" *Variety* asked. "Smith had made a sort of high camp transvestite affair showing a group cavorting in a kind of 1920s setting. And the cavorting was seducing one woman among them, who was also somewhat hermaphroditic. There was manipulation of sex organs shown." A reporter from the *London Financial Times* predicted "the battles currently being raged about 'Flaming Creatures' at Knokke will almost certainly have significant reverberations for the future of film censorship."[31]

It was in the context of his international success that Mekas seemed to have a second epiphany. He returned to New York determined to face off against the city's officials. On 3 March 1964, Mekas and three of his colleagues spent an evening in jail for exhibiting *Flaming Creatures*. The Manhattan district attorney's office had gone undercover with plainclothes officers to view the film when it opened at the New Bowery Theatre at St. Mark's Place. The next night, the police returned to make arrests. Mekas was not at the theater when the police arrived, but after a friend phoned him to alert him to the bust, he rushed to the theater and demanded to be taken into custody as well. The revolution in New York had begun. A trial date was set for 16 March.[32]

Mekas seized the moment. Rather than demur in the face of what he considered illegal and immoral harassment, he returned to exhibiting movies, smartly choosing to screen French poet Jean Genet's homoerotic prison film, *Un chant d'amour*. The police took the bait. On 7 March, Mekas was arrested a second time, at the Writers Stage Theater, for showing what was clearly a controversial and provocative film. It was a way, J. Hoberman explains, "to link the suppression of *Flaming Creatures* to the suppression of a film . . . by a famous European artist." Mekas attempted to impress upon the arresting officers that Genet was an "international artist." The cops laughed at him, of course; how could they have known Mekas was leading a revolt to free the human soul? This second arrest in less than two weeks was a good deal more violent and vindictive than the first, though. According to Mekas, the police kicked him, confiscated his possessions, and generally treated him shabbily. He was even threatened with death: "One of the detectives who arrested me told me . . . he did not know why they were taking me to the station: I should be shot right there in front of the screen." To them, he was a "pink" who exhibited "gay" films. "This is just a small taste of Justice at Work, and it makes me puke," he growled. "The time is here for a total change. But nobody really believes it will or can be done. The corruption is almost total, from top to bottom."[33]

Officials from the New York City license department returned to the New Bowery and cited it for showing more unlicensed films. The owner of the theater, Theodora Bergery, attempted to break the lease she had signed with Mekas's American Theatre for Poets, telling the *Voice* "she would prefer commercialism to a film like 'Flaming Creatures' which to her is 'not art.'" Her sacrilege seemed to confirm Mekas's mission—New York needed him to rescue it from the philistines. A case in point: when asked if she had seen the film, Bergery responded, "Anything that's bad enough for Detective O'Toole is bad enough for me." This was only the latest in a line of theaters that had broken with or attempted to break with the NAC. On 19 February, two weeks before the scene at the Tivoli, Mekas had been told by an attorney for the Gramercy Arts Theatre that his group could no longer use that theater, either.[34]

Mekas used his column in the *Voice* to list the theaters in 1964 where such action had taken place, including the Pocket Theatre, the Gramercy Arts Theatre, the New Bowery Theatre, and the Film-Makers' Cooperative, and declared that "the Co-op screenings have been and will continue to be, unlicensed because we do not believe in lice-nsing [*sic*] works of art. It is very possible that most of our films could safely pass the censors. But that's not the point. There are other works which wouldn't pass, and we are not willing to sacrifice a single one of them." It was police action against film that represented the real obscenities: "Works of art are above obscenity and pornography—or, more correctly, above what the police understand as obscenity and pornography." Art, he argued, had simply become more frank (pure), not more lewd or crass. "The existing laws," he added, "are driving art underground." "The detective from the District Attorney's office who arrested us last Tuesday with 'Flaming Creatures' told us that he was not interested in the film as a work of art; he also admitted that he was not competent to judge it; he said he was looking at it strictly as a matter of 'duty'; he was looking only for 'objectionable' images according to his interpretation of the law." Mekas went on to appeal to the constitutional right to expression and to declare that the obscenity laws were ridiculous in a society that should value art. He asked, "Who among you dares pose as judge of our art, to the degree of dragging our art into the criminal courts? In what times do we live, when works of art are identified with the workings of crime? What a beautiful insanity!"[35]

It did seem a bit crazy to suggest that *Flaming Creatures* broke the law but *Lolita* (which had come out two years before) did not. Or that police officers and criminal courts were the appropriate arbiters to determine which obscure film had violated laws established to protect the public. But it was equally ridiculous to buy Mekas's view of art and criticism. Thus, if censors failed to appreciate art and taste, Mekas failed to appreciate the value of standards and limits. And whereas censors had created a culture that feared controversy, Mekas had emboldened a culture to want nothing but controversy. In either case, movie culture suffered because these extreme positions came to define it.

That situation was summed up on 9 April 1964, in a statement made by the Film-Makers' Cooperative Anti-Censorship Fund in the *Village Voice*. "An important shift in the ways of life, in moral attitudes is about to take place in America. Really, the shift has been going on for some time: what's lacking is the official stamp. That's what this is all about. The clash between a going away generation and a coming generation. Much of what the Old Generation calls immoral and obscene; much of what it calls non or anti-art—to us is Beauty, because it is part of our life. Old ways of life to us seem full of false morality; much of the art of Yesterday begins to look like a lot of nothing." How cynical this sentiment had become. The past was dead to Mekas and his group. All they could find worth commenting on was the repression they believed had unfairly targeted their work. How egotistical as well.[36]

Yet many people believed that Mekas had spoken "truth to power," that the only way to break the ridiculous web of control over movies and American culture in general was, as Mekas had demanded, to "break the frozen ground" of tradition. Far from standing alone on this issue, Mekas had supporters from various quarters of the city. He received letters and even money. One man contributed $5 to Mekas's defense. Joseph Carbone, a resident from the other end of city, in the Bronx, told Mekas that he "read with anger" the account of Mekas's arrest. Like many New Yorkers, Carbone believed that as long as people were given the freedom to decide what kind of movies they wanted to see, he could not "see any crime being committed in this case." Another letter writer informed Mekas that he had actually attended the infamous screening of Genet's film and wished to "praise your courage and good taste in making this beautiful film available." He thanked Mekas for letting him "participate in your crime."[37]

Gordon Hitchens, editor of *Film Comment*, wrote to wish Mekas luck with the upcoming trials but also reminded him that "American film makers are by no means united in their beliefs about 'legal restrictions placed upon works of art.' . . . Many of them will betray serious reservations about this word 'freedom' if you question them closely." Hitchens also asked Mekas why he had based his defense on the idea of art (quite an elitist view, in fact). "Cannot non-works of art be free as well?" Hitchens closed with a reminder that if Mekas intended to invite the "intelligentsia" to private screenings, *Film Comment* should be on that list as well. Likewise, Mekas received a letter from Randolfe Wicker, the public relations director for the Homosexual League of New York. He thanked Mekas for allowing him and Paul Welch from *Life* magazine to attend a screening of the two embattled films but hesitated to lend his full support to these films because, to him, they perpetuated "distorted" views of homosexuality. He asked, "Why don't film-makers produce an authentic film about a love affair or something between two boys which takes place in the contemporary homosexual setting?" In the end, Wicker was willing to fight for artistic freedom, even if that meant the right to present such distortions.[38]

Before the trials got under way, Mekas made a direct appeal to the one man in the city whose involvement could have settled the cases, Manhattan district attorney Frank Hogan. "I have thought much about these cases and I hope that you'll agree with me, after studying the enclosed material that there was more misunderstanding in these cases than crime," Mekas reasoned, "and that something more constructive could and should be done about it instead of wasting time, money and energy in courts." The case involving Genet's film was eventually dismissed; action against Smith's film, though, would continue for two years.[39]

Prosecution of Smith's film manufactured a curious cultural moment. Mekas sensed the appeal his heroic stance had among New York's literati and he capitalized on it. He invited cultural luminaries to see special screenings of *Flaming Creatures* and *Un chant d'amour* on 21 and 24 March, in the hope that those who attended the shows would be willing to lend their reputations in the fight to free cinema. Among those who responded were critic Rudolph Arnheim, journalist Bob Scheer, Eve Preminger (Otto's niece), and artists Roy Lichtenstein, Christo and Jeanne-Claude, and Robert Rauchenberg. Placed on the list of people who saw both films and were "willing to defend on the grounds of a work of art" were artists Salvador Dali, Andy Warhol, and Storm De Hirsch; filmmaker Elia Kazan (and his son Chris); poets Alfred Leslie, Allen Ginsberg, Diane di Prima, and Frank O'Hara; critics Elizabeth Sutherland, Nate Hentoff, Susan Sontag, Lewis Jacobs, Ken Kelman, and Herman Weinberg; Henry Geldzahler (curator at the Metropolitan Museum of Art); and writer Buck Henry. Among those listed as potential witnesses were New York intellectuals Lionel Trilling, Daniel Bell, Steven Marcus, and William Phillips. Others also ready to testify included Lewis Allen (a commercial film producer connected to the NAC) and Robert Hughes (editor of *Film*). Mekas noted next to the name of his former boss at the *Voice*, Jerry Talmer, that he "saw both films and liked both and he doesn't think any of them is obscene and he said he will come as a witness if we need. I think he should be used." Next to Amos Vogel's name was the comment: "I don't know his reaction." That soon changed.[40]

Amos Vogel found this whole affair profoundly disheartening. Vogel had the audacity and the experience to question what was truly at stake in this case and he did so in the *Voice*, no less. While the tone of his piece was not vindictive, Vogel did not pull any punches. The time had come to tell Mekas what many in New York's movie culture had been saying about the NAC. Part of the problem, Vogel believed, was that Mekas had lost sight of any tangible goal. Many in the relatively small community had "watched with growing concern a progressive narrowing of [Mekas's] perspective, an inward-turning which threatens to limit his sensibilities and insights to an ever smaller circle of elect." Mekas had championed a small number of filmmakers, both as a film distributor and in his *Village Voice* column, to the exclusion of many other worthy people. Vogel worried that "the inverted provincialism on the part of one whose pioneering position requires, quite on the contrary, the utmost sophistication and openness is both a symptom and a result of his rejection of history, the past, cultural community, all of which elevate the intentional 'ignorance' and primitivism of his followers to the status of an ideology." In his promotion of the NAC, Vogel believed, Mekas had become "more dogmatic, more extremist, more publicity-conscious." Vogel found it commendable that Mekas fought for certain figures in the underground but thought his approach had "also been accompanied by an absence of style and seriousness, a lack of concern for film form, rhythm, and theory which leads many people to view the existing works and pretension with an indulgent, amused air, smiling at the antics of the movement or somewhat repelled by the 'camp' atmosphere of its screenings."[41]

Vogel had been deliberate—intentional—in his use of film, and he applied that approach to this controversy. To him, Mekas's fight was little more than a series of "calculated provocations," designed as much to promote the NAC as a cultural vanguard as to advance any real ideas. At base, Vogel suggested that the causes Mekas championed were the wrong ones, at the wrong time, and pursued in the wrong way. Despite what Mekas seemed to think, New Yorkers did not consider the right to see *Flaming Creatures* akin to fighting for civil rights or cleaning up city politics. Moreover, the way Mekas carried on—antagonizing police, license officials, and the district attorney's office—had the potential to damage other movements in the arts without significantly challenging the way moviegoing operated in New York. Vogel couldn't imagine why New Yorkers would line up behind a movie like *Flaming Creatures*. "In New York today," Vogel wrote, "[the context] is one of apathy on the part of audiences and opinion-makers and the need to 'clean' the city for the World's Fair and the forthcoming election on the part of the authorities." More than that, although Vogel acknowledged that "'Flaming Creatures' is a valid and 'felt' work," he concluded, "alas, intentions and achievements are not synonymous."[42]

Three letters were published in response, two in support of Vogel and one in support of Mekas. Vogel's characterization of Mekas had struck a chord with some readers; one suggested that it was about time "to get rid of that pompous prattler," the other referred to Mekas as a "Bosley Crowther without inhibitions." Letters published and unpublished that supported Mekas spoke to the righteousness of his cause. One reader, Mel Garfinkel, was a part of the set that supported both Cinema 16 and the NAC. He was offended by Vogel's insinuation that Mekas had manipulated the whole fiasco to promote the NAC. "The naïve and bumbling quality of the actions by Mr. Mekas and the New American Cinema and their poor timing," Garfinkel wrote in long-hand, "should be sufficient proof of their honesty. Add to this the possibility of Mr. Mekas facing a prison term in a very hostile atmosphere, and I think that one would find a lack of calculating logic."[43]

In his own response, Mekas reveled in his lack of a strategy; it was what gave his movement energy. He implored Vogel: "Don't wait until the right time comes; nobody knows the time. Do what your conscience tells you to do: That's the right time." Returning Vogel's advice, Mekas counseled: "There is no democracy of conscience. One should go against the whole world, if needed. Follow your heart's logic as you did in your youth: It's your reasoning, your 'maturity,' your 'public' sense that are betraying you. . . . When you started Cinema 16 in your younger, 'unreasonable' days, you went against the world. . . . You did not care whether New York was ready for avant-garde films or not: You knew you had to do it, and you did it."[44]

Vogel would have readily agreed—he broke new ground by exposing a generation of New Yorkers (and others) to independent films with the hope that seeing such fare might broaden the taste of moviegoers. Yet it seems pretty clear that Vogel did not think he was liberating individual souls with Cinema 16. His great contribution to the debate over movie culture was to create a unique environment in which to engage movies: a place that was supposed to be difficult to replicate. In a sense, Vogel challenged the boundaries within the minds of his audience because he had established boundaries within his film society. Mekas's intolerance for limits was undoubtedly liberating at first, but it bred a kind of extremism that could only destroy the intellectual rationale for supporting the New American Cinema. One can reasonably understand why Mekas resorted to extreme pronouncements; after all, he faced authorities more accustomed to patrolling concrete streets than the imaginary avenues of the artistic mind. Moreover, this was the era of extremism—defended from both the left and the right. Mekas had set up an intractable situation in which his anarchic movie culture made it possible to seem heroic for defending almost any kind of freedom, including, as he would later find, commercial freedom. For the moment, he felt righteous. But that is not the same thing as being right.

Among Mekas's most enthusiastic supporters were writers at the left-liberal journal the *Nation.* "To our mind," the editors opined, "the only sound position must be rejection of censorship per se. Even the banning of hard-core commercial pornography invites trouble, for the censor can and has advanced his attack from this area to others where he has no business to be. This can be an uncomfortable position to maintain, for it requires defending the freedom for that which may be distasteful to some people—perhaps even to the majority. But what else makes sense in a nation taking pride in its heritage of freedom? And what else permits the exploration and experimentation which sustain creativity?" Here was the irony of the heroic age: art and speech existing in a vacuum of taste, devoid of any need to engage any kind of public culture because in the brave new world of freedom each individual was a "public" unto himself or herself.[45]

Also writing in the *Nation* was Susan Sontag. She took a different approach, one that avoided the intractable issue of dealing with mainstream sensibilities. Rather, she offered a riff on her "new sensibility." The forum for a debate over art had changed, she suggested, from one in which morality and legalities persisted to one in which aesthetics prevailed. It was as idealized a world as that suggested by Mekas, where the individual's imagination was allowed to play among the human senses without any pretense to standards of traditional taste. Thus, in such a world, she submitted, "even if [the film] were pornographic, that is, if it did . . . have the power to excite sexually, I would argue that this is a power of art for which it is shameful to apologize. Art is, always, the sphere of freedom." Sontag argued that "the space in which *Flaming Creatures* moves is not the space of moral ideas, which is where American critics have traditionally located art. What I am urging is that there is not only moral space. . . . There is also aesthetic space, the space of pleasure. Here Smith's film moves and has its being." Fair enough. Sontag imagined an alternative sphere in which mere mortals who evaluated art in the light of social concerns would no longer be allowed to tread. And yet here again was the use of the heroic model without a shade of irony. Did Sontag actually believe that movies—the great public spectacle of the twentieth century—could ever exist (should ever exist) outside the culture made by and for their public?[46]

She did when it came to protecting artists like Jack Smith. "The price the *avant-garde* artist pays for the freedom to be outrageous is the small numbers of his audience, the least of his rewards should be freedom from meddling censorship by the philistine, the prudish and the blind." Society should not fear this film, Sontag suggested, since it would never play at larger theaters (such as Radio City), but if it did, "it would be lost on today's mass audience as a puppet theatre is on a huge stage." Indeed, *Flaming Creatures* was a perfect illustration of camp—a cultural experience that Sontag had boldly written about in a 1961 piece for *Partisan Review*. "*Flaming Creatures*," she thought, "represents a different aesthetic: it is crowded with visual material. There are no ideas, no symbols, no commentary on or critique of anything. . . . Smith's film is strictly a treat for the senses." It might have seemed intellectually vacuous, Sontag suggested, but the refusal to stand for anything had become the next great stage in modern art. And therein lay the irony of Mekas's position—he defended something that by its very nature was not all there. Camp was part illusion, part inside joke. Mekas's defense was wildly disproportionate to the stakes in this case. Ultimately, *Flaming Creatures* vanished from the debate, and all that was left was the essence of a struggle.[47]

Mekas made it clear that controversy defined the moment. In response to numerous busts, arrests, and impending trials involving the NAC, Mekas posted ads in different places, including the *Voice* and *Variety*, asking for support. "One after another," Mekas explained, "the independent and avant-garde film showcases have been closed, either by the District Attorney, the Police, the State Division of Motion Pictures, or the Department of Licenses." Equipment had been seized, and the movies taken included two films from Jack Smith, *Flaming Creatures* and *Normal Love*, Andy Warhol's *Newsreel* (which was a mock documentary of *Normal Love*), and *Un chant d'amour*. The declaration informed readers that four different trials were in the works and noted that poetry readings, off-Broadway plays, theater groups, coffeehouses, and dance halls had all been busted for similar offenses.[48]

Many artists at that time felt persecuted by New York officialdom for flouting social norms. Conflicts of this nature had defined Greenwich Village since the early part of the twentieth century. By the late 1950s, the Beats had become the latest group to antagonize residents and city officials. The *Village Voice* seemed to have come into existence to report on this situation alone. An article in June 1958 alerted readers to the rash of police summonses intended to stop poetry readings in cafés on McDougal Street. Initially, the dispute was over the nature of the activity in these haunts—the city's department of licenses had authority to regulate establishments that provided entertainment, including poetry readings. The city's harassment of such places became ridiculous. For example, the proprietor of Café Figaro, Charles Ziegler, stood before a New York County judge for allowing a string trio to play on Sundays, a day typically of rest and quiet for the area's Italian Catholic residents. He explained that he did not serve alcohol—not even Irish coffee—and did not seek out these "beatniks." Calling them "hostile, exhibitionistic children," Ziegler argued that he had intended only "to bring a little culture" to his neighborhood, not the Beats. The *Voice* reporter also noted with tongue firmly in cheek that after the police had spent time actually listening to some poetry readings, they determined "that the readings did not constitute entertainment in any generally accepted sense of the word."[49]

These initial conflicts between Village establishments and the law indicated a growing problem. The Village was rapidly dividing once again along cultural lines: the south Village was still heavily Italian and traditional; the north and east Village was beginning to express its artistic nature in increasingly colorful ways. What began as occasional police patrols of coffeehouses grew into a concerted assault on a vibrant cultural community. Most observers at the time believed that preparations for the 1964 World's Fair were behind the increasing police presence and action. "The City is cleaning New York for the World's Fair," one flier announced. "Instead of helping the arts, the City, State, District Attorney, police, fire, and licensing departments are using all available means to drive the arts underground."[50]

Yet, by the mid-1960s, art was hardly the issue for either side. In the summer of 1964, Cardinal Spellman once again spoke out against the moral degradation of his city. Commenting on two recent Supreme Court decisions that had expanded the legal definition of obscenity—both had been handed down on 22 June in cases involving the film *The Lovers* and the novel *Tropic of Cancer*—Spellman thundered that such decisions reflected "an acceptance of degeneracy and the beatnik mentality as the standard way of American life." The nation's most powerful Catholic believed this was a struggle for the "innocent hearts, minds, and souls" of the young, and called for a general boycott of "dealers who traffic in pornography." He blamed "a few misguided high-ranking judicial officials" for the predicament and condemned those who launched "savage attacks upon our sense of moral decency." Spellman once again proved to be a useful straw man. Rather than suggest that works defensible only as free speech were poor and had little claim to significance as art, he provided the perfect rationale for their absolute protection. Without the First Amendment, culture was subject to the ravings of moral extremists who saw every transgression as a precursor to civilization's end. Next to Spellman, Mekas did appear heroic—at least he mentioned artists.[51]

Contributing to New York's cultural conflagration, a political battle also heated up in the Village between longtime Democratic Party boss Carmine DeSapio and members of an upstart Reform Party that included a young Edward Koch. The wholesale rejection of the "old way" that characterized the sensibility of Mekas and his group had a counterpart in the forceful rejection of "politics as usual" by New York City's Reform Party leaders. In the summer of 1963, future mayor John Lindsay, a liberal, reform-minded Republican, also weighed in on the problems in the Village, asserting that "while reasonable regulation and its enforcement is one thing, the wholesale efforts being made by some to close down the coffee houses is another." Lindsay warned against those politicians like DeSapio "who prefer closed doors, closed windows, closed deals, and a tightly controlled community to one that is free and open." If Mekas wanted to free cinema from its commercial and censorial restrictions, politicians like Lindsay and Koch hoped to free New York political culture from its entrenched corruption and what they perceived as overzealous law enforcement. The city needed to breathe, they believed. And while the Reform Party was certainly not bent on some anarchistic program—politicians such as Ed Koch did not really support most of the Village's bohemians—it was prepared to err more on the side of an idealized "freedom" rather than continue what its members viewed as an ethically bankrupt political arrangement.[52]

Throughout the spring and summer of 1964, the Village hummed with political and legal activity. Stephanie Gervis Harrington (Michael Harrington's wife) reported on these matters for the *Voice*. In March she noted that "the current zeal of the City's Department of Licenses for the strict enforcement of licensing regulation against small avant-garde creative ventures has so far resulted in the temporary closing of three off-Broadway theatres, the suspension of poetry readings at Le Metro, and a general malaise among culturally minded New Yorkers as to what may be afoot." Harrington speculated that such police action was probably as much a product of politics as of concerns about the city's image. Officials in the department of licenses were jockeying for the position of commissioner after Mayor Robert Wagner appointed their boss to a city court judgeship. In any case, cleaning up the Village had the effect of temporarily uniting the underground. Harrington reminded her readers that, ironically, Mayor Wagner had once remarked with pride that New York had replaced Paris as the world's avant-garde center. His definition apparently did not include comedian Lenny Bruce, who was arrested in April 1964 at Café Au GoGo for an indecent performance *before* he went on stage. Unlike *Flaming Creatures*, Bruce's case broke new ground against legal restrictions of obscene speech.[53]

Yet all was not heroic for the underground. At base were issues that needed to be addressed because their implications extended far beyond a Village poet's right to perform in a café. The residents of Greenwich Village shared one of the most distinct spaces in the country. Their neighborhood had always had a kind of coherency because it existed, as it still does, off the rest of Manhattan's grid street plan and revolved around a small green space, Washington Square Park. Rents had been reasonable in the district since the 1920s and thus had attracted those who made little money—artists as well as immigrants. But by the 1960s, the area also attracted its share of drug addicts, drunks, and itinerant hustlers. The New York City that frightened the rest of America by the 1970s had its origins in the changes that the Village was undergoing in the late 1950s and early 1960s. A combination of corrupt government practices and inept political leadership allowed the development of some of the worst aspects of a "free" society.[54]

A society of rules clashed with a culture of freedom. The residents who wanted to sleep at 11:00 at night screamed at those who wanted to dance in the streets into the early morning. New York University (NYU) and commercial real estate developers wrestled with old ladies and poor artists over plans to renovate and develop dilapidated buildings and loft spaces. At a public meeting organized by Koch in the summer of 1964, city representatives and members of the avant-garde, including Allen Ginsberg, all raised their voices like never before. Many in attendance denounced the "bongo drums, flashing neon signs, sidewalk barkers, coffeehouse crowds, open-front stores, roaring motorcycles, derelicts, drunks and other irritants that deprive the neighborhood of solitude and sleep." The meeting lasted over three hours and poured out onto a street in front of the NYU auditorium in which the audience had gathered. One man shouted that instead of a place of commerce and culture, the Village had become a haven for "people looking for thrills, kicks, and la dolce vita!" Koch shot back, sardonically echoing Republican presidential candidate Barry Goldwater, "Extremism in the pursuit of sleep is no virtue." Poet Allen Ginsberg was jeered when he asked, "Do you think we shouldn't read poetry here?"[55]

In the months that followed, Mayor Wagner appointed a new, more moderate license commissioner, Joseph C. Di Carlo, who acknowledged that "a young artist can't start at the Metropolitan Opera or at the St. James Theater; so coffeehouses do serve a useful purpose in the city." Koch promised to hold more public meetings and to address issues important to as many residents as he could. He also worked to get the city to commit more police officers to Washington Square Park. Part of that plan, reported the *New York Times*, was to employ "more 'effective' measures . . . to curb activity of homosexuals in Village Square . . . as well as annoyances by drunks and hoodlums." These proposed solutions failed to placate anyone.[56]

Many artists had already made it clear that there was little room for compromise. In March 1964, fliers and posters went up around the Village calling for a march on the district attorney's office. Declaring "We Protest Raids on Films—Picket With Us," the New York City League for Sexual Freedom called for the right to "show any kind of film or publish any kind of book, however repulsive, even if it has no 'socially redeeming' artistic qualities whatever." While this organization had only a short-lived stay in New York—it ended up thriving in San Francisco—it did echo the general sentiments of many other groups. Mekas helped form a group called the Committee for Freedom of the Arts, which hoped to "represent the combined voices of all those interested in defending the rights of our minority group." Its members planned to stage demonstrations, lobby politicians, and produce a newsletter in the struggle to stop "official interference with freedom of the arts in NYC." The group also accepted donations.[57]

Mekas and his allies managed to pull off one march on 29 April during which they handed out copies of a newsletter that detailed all the cases pending against filmmakers, poets, coffeehouses, theaters, and the Artist Tenants Association. Calling for "Freedom Now!" close to two hundred people joined in the demonstration. They had intended to carry a large black coffin on which was printed "Will Freedom Be Buried?" but the marchers had to disband their "official" demonstration after police officers informed them that they needed permits to march a coffin uptown to Lincoln Center. Michael Smith reported on the event for the *Voice*, observing, "The mood of free expression was so rampant on Wednesday that half a dozen different leaflets were distributed at large, to the apparent confusion of many passers-by." Mekas was on hand with copies of his "Film Journal" column, and the League for Sexual Freedom circulated a petition for volunteers to "go to jail for freedom of the press." Others advocated traffic-less city streets, free mass transit, and legalized pot. "In addition, [creator of the avant-garde Living Theatre Julian] Beck and his wife, Judith Malina," Smith noted, "wore placards headed 'F—k' and 'C—t' and bearing Partridge's definitions of those classic four-letter words." Diane di Prima encouraged the crowd to "make joy" and "speak truth, do your work, and everything else will take care of itself." Allen Ginsberg read a list of grievances and a poem for the occasion. Julian Beck was cheered when he declared, "As long as they continue to put people in jail, none of us is free. We will not be free until we open all the doors of all the jails." Taylor Mead read an antipolice poem. But Beck and di Prima had to admit that the march had failed to communicate a clear message to the general public when they were told that a radio show had just reported that a group of artists had been marching to express their unhappiness about a housing project.[58]

Mekas was heard in court, though. In May 1964, Jonas Mekas and his colleagues stood trial for exhibiting *Flaming Creatures*. Mekas declared that he considered "the police actions unlawful, unconstitutional and contrary to man's spiritual growth." "It is my duty as an artist and as a man," he asserted, "to show the best work of my contemporaries to the people. It is my duty to bring to your attention the ridiculousness and illegality of the licensing and obscenity laws. The duty of the artist is to ignore bad laws and fight them every moment of his life." Echoing the type of sentiments expressed during the march for "artistic freedom," Mekas pronounced: "All works of art, all expressions of man's spirit must be permitted, must be available to the people." Mekas wrote about his courtroom experience in the *Voice*, telling his readers that the judge presiding in his case had clearly missed the point—he had loudly reprimanded him for his outbursts and scolded his poor co-defendant Jerry Sims for failing to wear a necktie.[59]

In the *New York Post*, reporter Paul Hoffman recounted the scene of a three-judge panel composed of former New York mayor Vincent R. Impelliteri, Thomas E. Rohan, and Michael A. Castaldi "impassively" watching a print of *Flaming Creatures*, trying to determine the level of obscenity of the film's action, while "munching on cigars." Stephanie Gervis Harrington reported in the *Voice* that "the prosecution objected to expert testimony on the grounds that the film should be judged pornographic or not on the basis of community standards rather than on the opinion of experts." That meant that the defense attorney, Emile Zola Berman (later counsel for the infamous Sirhan Sirhan), was not allowed to refute the basic contention that the film was obscene. He was allowed to call a few expert witnesses, including Susan Sontag, whom the court allowed to speak for a longer period than any of the other witnesses—a group that included Herman Weinberg, Lewis Allen, Allen Ginsberg, and the new director of the MoMA's film library, Willard Van Dyke. Sontag was asked to define pornography and asked to identify something she thought was pornographic. She pointed to "posters outside Times Square movie theaters that advertised war movies with sadistic atrocity pictures." The judges yawned. When Allen Ginsberg gave his testimony, he was visibly nervous on the stand—Harrington noted it was his first time testifying in court—but was able to give a definition of avant-garde, which, Harrington suggested, gave the proceedings a place in literary history. The court refused the defense's desire to compare *Flaming Creatures* to other movies with frank sexual sequences such as *The Silence* and *The Virgin Spring*, which were licensed by the state. Berman, inexplicably but perhaps tellingly, kept referring to the movie as "Crimson Creatures."[60]

The prosecution did little more than show the film, and the judges took little time to find Mekas and his colleagues guilty. At their August sentence hearing, the three defendants (the fourth had been dismissed earlier) received suspended sentences, which allowed them to continue to go free but meant that they were technically guilty and were therefore not entitled to their equipment or to the print of Smith's film.

"It was so utterly unbelievable and silly that I couldn't even take it as an insult. We took it as comedy," Mekas wrote in a scathing piece for the *Voice*, "On the Misery of Community Standards." "It is the community that should be measured against art," Mekas argued, because "the innocence and beauty of Jack Smith is so far above the so-called community standard that his work should be a privilege to view in our courts." Mekas's impassioned defense of Smith's film had the curious effect of returning the debate over movie culture to a place familiar to cardinals and codes. His use of Manichean terms to describe the struggle echoed the exaggerations of older authorities. When he dismissed the positions and opinions of not merely the judges and police but of the community itself, he declared that they had committed "monstrous acts against man. Consciously or unconsciously, they are the true instruments of evil." Even if Spellman rejected Mekas's position, he would have had to appreciate his use of language. Sounding even more like a good seminarian, Mekas added that "we should not pass judgment . . . on the judges themselves: It is enough that we know the consequences; for the laws of life are such that one cannot commit a crime against another man's soul without committing a crime against one's own soul. As for *Flaming Creatures* and *Scorpio Rising*, they are being screened by angels in heaven with the perfumed projectors of eternity." One wonders which double bill God favored: the Catholic or the anarchist?[61]

Jack Smith probably groaned when he read Mekas's account. He had not been present for most of the controversy and would have been happier, he confessed, if the whole fiasco had never happened. In subsequent retellings of this seminal event in New York's cinematic underground, Smith grew increasingly furious at what he perceived as Mekas's exploitation of his film. He famously accused Mekas of making his film "into a sex issue of the Cocktail World." "The film was practically used to destroy me," Smith said. He leveled his own charges against Mekas, claiming that the co-op's leader wanted to elevate underground film in the same way literary material, such as Henry Miller's books, had been made prominent. "Uncle Fishook [Smith's name for Mekas in later years] wanted to have something in court at the time, it being so fashionable. It was another way by which he could be made to look like a saint, to be in the position of defending something when he was really kicking it to death. So he would give screenings of *Creatures* and make speeches, defying the police to bust the film. Which they did." Smith revealed that he wasn't permitted to be in the courtroom, lest he make a scene and cause trouble for the defense. Smith consistently contended that he had made the film for himself and his friends and had never intended it to become a centerpiece of a First Amendment fight.[62]

That didn't mean he wasn't angered by the case. In a diary entry most likely written during the tumult of 1964, Smith scoffed at how shabbily his film was treated in light of the simplistic rendering of sex found in commercially viable films, with their "rigidly self-consciousness beings smiling pleasantly, displaying a product and fainting with rapture all at the same moment." The city's sex industry was steeped in corruption, paying off the police and the city authorities in order to exist—which was more obscene, he suggested, than his obscure, grainy film.[63]

Each January, Mekas turned his *Voice* column into a retrospective of the preceding year's best films. In January 1965, he remembered the year just past as one that existed well beyond its films: "In 1964, film-makers left the underground and came into the light, where they immediately clashed with the outmoded tastes and morals of the Establishment, the police, and the critics." He detailed the raids, summonses, and closings, not so much as a great feat accomplished but to remind his readers how close he and the underground had come to complete collapse. There had been seven months without any screenings because of police harassment. But the underground did survive and would in the long run achieve a victory of sorts over those standards that Mekas found so detrimental to the human soul. Critic J. Hoberman writes that "as a social fact, *Flaming Creatures* may have ultimately made the world safe for Long Dong Silver." While this was probably not precisely what Mekas wanted, he seemed unable to appreciate the irony.[64]

In a conversation with Paul Krassner, Mekas unwittingly acknowledged the cultural world that he was helping to create. Krassner, a friend of political radicals Abbie Hoffman and Jerry Rubin, recounted that he had come to the apartment of George Plimpton, a New York writer and editor of the highbrow *Paris Review*, to watch *Flaming Creatures* with "guests [who] ranged from Andy Devine to Terry Southern." That night, Krassner joked with Mekas that he didn't think the film would be considered pornographic since "the penises were limp." Only philistines missed the artistic nature of flaccid genitalia. Four years later, Krassner mentioned that conversation to Mekas. This time Mekas replied, "Even if the penises were erect, I *still* wouldn't consider the film pornographic."[65]

6

The End of New York
Movie Culture

HOW DO YOU know when a revolution has succeeded? How should
progress be measured? By the mid-1960s, two developments in New
York City's movie culture seemed to signal the dawning of a new era in
American cinema: the regime of censorship that had controlled movies
since their inception had almost completely unraveled and an underground sensibility became popular. In New York City, the protagonists
who fought for a free screen and to "free cinema" had much to cheer
about, not least because they had done a great deal to make this revolution successful. In 1965, the two organizations that had restricted the
freedom of movie culture in the name of a larger social responsibility were finally overtaken by the society they had vowed to protect. In
November, the New York State Motion Picture Division—the state's
censors—called it quits. New York's highest court, the court of appeals,
decided the state had violated the Fourteenth Amendment when it
censored movies before they were released to the public. A month
later, the Legion of Decency officially changed its name in an attempt
to remain relevant to its audience. Hollywood reacted to these changes
by adopting a new ratings system in 1966 that, in effect, enabled mainstream American films to look increasingly like foreign films and underground cinema. Film historian Jon Lewis notes that in 1967, the
number of films that earned the designation "for mature audiences
only" rose from six to forty-four. Yet changes in laws and codes merely
provided legalistic cover for something deeper—a new sensibility that
was sweeping across American culture. Movies were evolving into a

152

brazen art, and the public began to expect—not merely tolerate—a measure of controversy, even obscenity, among the popular arts. The hope was that once movies were freed from legal restraints, they might finally exude a kind of intellectual—and therefore artistic—prowess. Movies were indeed free—but to do what?[1]

The demise of censorship, *New York Times* editor Anthony Lewis confidently declared, "moved [the United States] from one of the most timid countries in dealing with sex in the arts to what many believe is now by far the most liberated in the Western world." He credited the Supreme Court for that development. "Nine no-longer-so-old men are responsible," he thought, for creating a culture in which "the voice of the sophisticated critic is dominant, and the Philistines are on the run." To him, the decline of censorship was a seamless progression. "Once the Court took a first crack at censorship, it set off a circular, self-nourishing process of liberalization. Each new decision produced a change in public attitudes. The new state of opinion encouraged the court to take a further step, which in turn brought more public enlightenment, which . . ." Lewis trailed off, suggesting that the self-perpetuating process had given birth to endless progress.[2]

Lewis contended that there were "strong policy arguments for dropping all governmental censorship, even of hard-core pornography. The mere existence of censors produces trouble because they are likely to be ignorant, even paranoid types, secretly fascinated by the smut they condemn." Even a conservative authority like C. S. Lewis supported a repeal of censorship because the process made "a travesty" out of the judicial system. Judge Thurman Arnold agreed, citing in a brief: "The spectacle of a judge poring over the picture of some nude, trying to ascertain prurient interests, and then attempting to write an opinion which explains the difference between the nude and some other nude, has elements of low comedy."[3]

True, a new culture had emerged, but it was one that existed uncomfortably between Susan Sontag's new sensibility and the pornographic imagination. Prevailing opinion accepted that movies were art and therefore should not be subject to the kind of censorship carried out by the web of control. However, it remained unclear whether a culture liberated from censors meant a culture liberated from taste as well. In April 1965, *Time* magazine provided insight into this emerging new sensibility in a long think piece, "The New Pornography." The editors pointed out that the artistic fringe of New York City was beginning to influence the American mainstream. Controversial artists (including Jack Smith and Andy Warhol) were "obviously trying to determine just how far things can be pushed before anyone will actually admit to being shocked." The magazine's editors acknowledged that although many outside New York would find these trends "unnecessary or unseemly, or just unpleasant," it was nevertheless the case that "what young and old may now read or see is part of the anti-Puritan revolution in American morals."[4]

But many American intellectuals were not willing to cheer on this revolution. William Phillips, editor of the modernist *Partisan Review*, objected to what he saw as a corruption of art. He was critical of these "new immoralists," arguing that novelists Jean Genet and William Burroughs did not grace the same literary terrain as Jonathan Swift and James Joyce, who had pushed the boundaries of taste for reasons of politics and aesthetics. What the new immoralists had going for them was merely a cultural trend, Phillips explained, "to embrace what is assumed to be beyond the pale." Such a stand was "taken as a sign of true sophistication." To him, it was "not simply a change in sensibility"; rather, "it amount[ed] to a sensibility of chaos."[5]

This situation produced, if not chaos, then at least a good deal of confusion. Among the most curious examples of this conflicted sensibility was the way the venerable *New York Times* dealt with the rise of obscenity in the arts. On the same editorial page in March 1966, the *Times* ran two pieces that captured the paradox of the new sensibility. In an editorial entitled "The Obscenity Cases," the editors commented on the recent Supreme Court decision in the Ralph Ginzburg case. They gave their unequivocal support for the decision: the justices had "shown wisdom and moral courage in the subtle and arduous task of upholding the law against obscenity while still protecting liberty of expression." In affirming the conviction of a porn peddler who had sent catalogs advertising his material to consumers, the *Times* believed, the justices had fairly evaluated the defendant's intent. Ginzburg, the editors concluded, "was strictly an entrepreneur in a disreputable business who took his chances on the borderline of the law and lost." Ginzburg was not, they asserted, a heroic figure like other martyrs for the First Amendment—in other words, he was not James Joyce, an icon of free speech struggles to the intellectual elite. "There was no intention 35 years ago at the time of the 'Ulysses' decision to lower the barricades against pornographic trash. But so swiftly has the revolution in law and public opinion moved that freedom for the creative writer and publisher has turned into license for the merchants of pornography." Society not only had the right to "curb this 'sordid business of pandering,'" the *Times* declared, it would illustrate a progressive streak if it did so.[6]

Russell Baker was not so encouraged by the Court's decision. To him, the ruling only complicated a situation that was already too confusing. In an essay that occupied the space next to the editorial, Baker proposed another test in lieu of the one employed by the Court. He recommended returning to an age-old way to determine whether something was obscene: if a person was embarrassed by the act of acquiring the book, seeing the movie, or paying for the magazine, he contended, "it is almost certainly pure smut." Echoing the tone taken by his colleague Anthony Lewis and writing with his characteristic wit, Baker offered that it was "not pleasant to have to add to the Supreme Court's burdens by calling attention to its utter innocence in the smut field. The plain fact, however, is that the rest of us out here . . . have never had the slightest difficulty determining what is and what is not obscene. Since practically all of us are better equipped than the Supreme Court to make the distinction, the court might save itself further embarrassment by henceforth leaving it up to us."[7]

Taken together, the two editorials illustrated an odd kind of aesthetic equivocation. On the one hand, the editors found it valid to protect obscenity when it was artistic, but not when it was commercial. Baker decided that shame rather than censors or courts could better serve a community. These two positions suggested that if an obscene artist produced material for an audience unencumbered by a sense of decency, then that artist could do just about anything he or she wanted to and be protected. Here was a way to merge the new sensibility with the pornographic imagination. As long as obscenity was produced in the name of art, laws and taste should bend to accept the product. Perhaps such an approach could work among the more obscure arts, but this was a dangerous notion when applied to America's greatest mass art, the movies.

No single figure in New York's movie culture illustrated the implications of this new atmosphere better than pop artist Andy Warhol. Warhol had been making films since the early 1960s along with his silk-screen portraits and sculptures made out of found objects. His art had made him a prominent figure in New York's avant-garde community, and his nonchalant dismissal of traditional standards of modernism made him an icon of the new sensibility championed by Susan Sontag. Warhol also reveled in making art out of transgressing sexual mores. Thus, his work created a cultural conundrum: he was seen as either a heroic artist or a provocateur of the smutty vanguard.

In April 1966, Joel J. Tyler, the city's license commissioner, took action against Jonas Mekas and Film-Makers' Cinematheque for showing films, including Warhol's *My Hustler* (a gay sexploitation film), that contained "sexual immorality, lewdness, perversion and homosexuality." Tyler ordered a summons served to the operators of the theater who rented out space to Mekas for shows that ran from 6:00 P.M. to midnight seven nights a week. Vincent Canby, a relatively new film critic at the *New York Times*, reported this incident. Canby had established his credentials as a supporter of the city's avant-garde by criticizing Tyler for having a "dim view" of "fetish footage." Tyler had failed to appreciate transgressive art.[8]

The case ended in frustration for Tyler, however, when his office "admitted that it did not have the power to investigate the content of films in determining whether to grant, review or revoke licenses." The courts had turned against the old guard once again, ruling that the city's license commissioner no longer had the power to seize films; he had the power only to regulate the places that exhibited them. The New York branch of the ACLU rejoiced: "This seems to take the license department out of the business of film censorship." New York City had been saved from the whims of the dreaded license commissioner, and Canby and other critics were free to deal with such films on their own terms. To Canby, the implications of such cases extended beyond the confines of Manhattan. "To observers, it is apparent that the movies, once the mass medium of entertainment, are going through a revolution that could remove all the old taboos concerning subject matter and treatment." True enough. But what would happen to that mass appeal of movies if they became, as Canby suggested, the leading edge of such a revolution?[9]

Future *Village Voice* rock critic Bob Christgua found out. In the fall of 1966, he tried to impress a date by taking her to the hottest film in New York City, Warhol's *The Chelsea Girls*. He failed. The film had opened that September at the Film-Makers' Cinematheque and was officially distributed by Mekas's Film-Makers' Distribution Center. Thus, it was a Mekas production, replete with all the promise of controversy and artistic pretenses. The first time Christgua attempted to get tickets, the show, which ran at least three and one-half hours, was sold out. The second time he noticed too late that he needed to get reservations to secure seats in the small, dimly lit theater located "in the bowels of the Wurlitzer Building." The third time, unfortunately, was not the charm for Christgua, either; he and his date made it to the theater, had reserved seats, but because the lobby was so loud he failed to hear the general call to enter the auditorium. Christgua, frustrated and furious, turned to the *Village Voice* to vent. In an angry letter to the paper, he lodged his complaint in a way that hinted at a much deeper problem emerging within New York City's movie culture. Jonas Mekas was to blame, Christgua thought. "His inability to handle large numbers of people is," he contended, "symptomatic of his contempt for them. It should surprise no one that the same otherworldly disdain mars the work of so many of the film-makers he heralds." The new sensibility showed signs of turning into an age of hubris.[10]

Christgua's letter was an expression of protest, but not against censors. New York's movie culture had become devoid of a certain type of thought. The struggle against oppositional ideas had come to an end. Rather than fighting against a censoring attitude, the new heroes of New York City movie culture embraced a "new sensibility" that rejoiced in the ability to see worth in all cultural expression. But this brave new world contained a strange irony: there was no need to distinguish between a movie such as Jack Smith's campy *Flaming Creatures*, which was made for a few friends, and Andy Warhol's raunchy films, which were intended to take advantage of popular appetites for sex. In the past, *The Chelsea Girls* would have been banned and therefore would have earned some significance by sparking a discussion of why it was forbidden. Instead, the film became important because it held the allure of promiscuity. It challenged nothing—except, perhaps, one's tolerance for banality.

The Chelsea Girls became popular not because it was the cinematic vanguard or because it was good, but because it represented little more than the leading edge of adult films made for "mature" audiences. In other words, it was popular because it had sex in it. To be fair to Warhol, he never expected the experience to be much more than a filmed romp at the Chelsea Hotel. The poster for the movie made that clear: an image of a naked woman was the centerpiece, and her midsection, from her breasts to her crotch, were the tiny hotel rooms in which the action took place. This was Warhol's contribution to film art; he knew what moviegoers wanted to see.

The Chelsea Girls was a tipping point. While it was one of a slew of films that by the mid-1960s exploited sex for commercial gain, Warhol's films were more than silly skin flicks or obscure "naturalist" documentaries. They were the products of a respected artist—and, therefore, represented to many observers a harbinger of decline. The titles of Warhol's films tell the story: His early films celebrated the ability to invert moviegoing—*Kiss, Haircut, Empire,* and *Sleep* were hours long with no traditional plot, action, actors, dramatic arc, or ending. The audiences sat through them almost literally exposing their expectations of what movies were supposed to do, and failing to have those expectations met. There was a relevance to that experience because it forced critics and moviegoers to consider what made going to a movie worthwhile. But beginning in the mid-1960s, Warhol and his disciples produced *Blow-Job, The Chelsea Girls, My Hustler, I, a Man,* and *Fuck* (later retitled *Blue Movie*).[11]

Popular and critical reception of *The Chelsea Girls* marked the end of ideology in New York's movie culture. It became clear that there was only one way left to think about movies—as abstractions. The struggle over movies as a popular experience—one with obligations to moviegoers as well as to art—ended. At its height, such a fight had determined the scope of debate over movies in New York and had helped create an environment in which fundamental issues regarding movie culture could be discussed, even if left unresolved. It took a supremely ironic artist like Andy Warhol to reveal that censors had been necessary as a source of opposition. Without censorship, *The Chelsea Girls* illustrated the sad dimensions of an emerging culture of crassness. No doubt, the desire to catch a glimpse of flesh was a product of the censoring attitude, but that a film as mundane, disjointed, and, frankly, unsatisfying as Warhol's attracted thousands of New Yorkers illustrated something fundamental about popular taste.

The Chelsea Girls had its premiere in September 1966. In its initial screenings, the film seemed little more than a macabre slice of bohemian life. Warhol had fixed a camera to a tripod, allowing the action to take place across, rather than solely within, a field of vision. That meant he sometimes captured his "actors" directly and sometimes the "action" happened on the margins or completely off the screen. The result was also a surprisingly tantalizing glimpse of underground New York, a world inhabited by creatures far more exotic that those in Jack Smith's films because they were playing themselves—living at the infamous Chelsea Hotel, taking drugs and having sex in a world that, as the film suggested, seemed enticingly foreign. In the *New York Times*, Elenore Lester explained that upon returning to New York from a tour with the alternative rock band Velvet Underground, Warhol had raised $1,500 for film stock and made *The Chelsea Girls*. It had no script, no theme—just an idea to film his friends and some others "doing different things." "The film was seen as a searing version of hell," Lester wrote, "symptomatic of the corruption of the Great Society, from godlessness to white power, the profit system and napalm."[12]

Exhibition of the film became as experimental as the film itself: Warhol decided not to cut any footage from the twelve reels his camera had captured and instead to project all twelve on a split screen with different, though unrelated, reels running at roughly the same time. He gave few instructions to projectionists, which meant that moviegoers would have a unique experience every time they entered the theater. Its soundtrack only occasionally corresponded to the scenes of one of the reels, and creative employment of lenses, gels, and glass changed the image projection. Audiences knew they were part of something that went well beyond anything that was controversial, confrontational, and censorable.

In *Midnight Movies*, J. Hoberman and Jonathan Rosenbaum report that "from October 1966 through May 1967, there was scarcely a week when *The Chelsea Girls* was not playing somewhere in Manhattan." Such success was modest compared to Hollywood products but extraordinary for underground cinema. Warhol admitted: "For all anyone knew yet, the people filling the theaters for *Chelsea Girls* might be there purely for the nudity. So the success of *Chelsea Girls* didn't necessarily mean that other underground movies would make it—it didn't even mean that our *own* movies would make it." Warhol chronicler Steve Watson concurs: "*The Chelsea Girls* brought a previously invisible subculture into focus for a broader American public. The reviews reflected the popular media's vision of the burgeoning Sixties revolution." As the vanguard of this revolution, Mekas promoted *The Chelsea Girls* in the hope that Warhol would subvert mainstream moviegoing just as he had already destroyed the staid conventions of the art world. Warhol admitted, "*Chelsea Girls* was the movie that made everyone sit up and notice what we were doing in films (and a lot of times that meant sit up, stand up, and walk out)."[13]

The Chelsea Girls had indeed broken new ground, grossing $19,451 in a two-week stint when it emerged, literally, from underground to a first-run theater, the Cinema Rendezvous, in December 1966. Over the course of its first nineteen weeks in New York, the movie earned over $150,000. Turning a profit was almost unheard of for the cinematic avant-garde; Mekas and his brethren were far more accustomed to losing money. Vincent Canby called it the *Sound of Music* of the underground. After three sold-out performances at the Film-Makers' Cinematheque in September, *The Chelsea Girls* became, he observed, the "first underground production to make the move to a conventional midtown Manhattan art theater."[14]

It was Warhol's "most ambitious, most important" work to date, Mekas gushed in a piece of self-promotion in his *Voice* column. He compared Warhol to D. W. Griffith and even threw in James Joyce to give his rave more gravitas. He pleaded: "Forgive me this sacrilegious comparison—really it is the first time that I dare mention Joyce in connection with cinema. This is the first time that I see in cinema an interesting solution of narrative techniques that enable cinema to present life in the complexity and richness achieved by modern literature." Then, not stopping, he also invoked Victor Hugo. Mekas reveled in the reality of the action—real drugs, real addicts, real rages, and real slaps.[15]

Anticipating and probably hoping that the movie would generate controversy, Mekas dismissed any condemnation as evidence of ignorance. "Most of the critics and viewers do not realize that the artist no matter what he is showing, is mirroring or forecasting also our own lives." Mekas's description of Warhol's achievement would become almost as influential as the film itself. Some reviewers mocked his characterization of Warhol; others took it as evidence of the inordinate influence of the pop artist. "It's our godless civilization approaching the zero point," Mekas wrote. "The terror and hardness that we see in

Chelsea Girls is the same terror and hardness that is burning Vietnam; and it the essence and blood of our culture, our way of living: This is the Great Society."[16]

Jonas Mekas had fought hard to promote the underground, and he pinned a great deal of hope on Andy Warhol. Many in the underground community looked at Warhol as a creature apart from them, and many of the original group that gathered in the Film-Makers' Co-op found little use for him. But Mekas was different.[17]

Discussing Warhol's *Sleep*, an eight-hour film of a man sleeping, Mekas wrote, "As simple as it is, it is a movement forward that carries others with it. Therefore it is beautiful like anything that is alive." He had been on hand to witness Warhol's filming of *Empire*, another endless exposition on an inanimate object, the Empire State Building. After spending the night on location, Mekas confidently declared: "My guess is that *Empire* will become the *Birth of a Nation* of the New Bag Cinema."[18]

There were other reasons, though, that Mekas looked to Warhol. The New American Cinema had reached a breaking point around the time that *The Chelsea Girls* premiered. Hoberman and Rosenbaum offer some insight into that atmosphere. Mekas's legal troubles in 1964 had almost ended the underground, the authors note. "The moment of 'Baudelairean Cinema' was waning. . . . Smith was unable to complete *Normal Love*. . . . [Ken] Jacobs's subsequent movies were to be less outrageous and more concerned with issues of film form, while [Ron] Rice took off for Mexico, where he died of pneumonia in December 1964. Under the circumstances, the major force in underground movies became Andy Warhol." He broke onto the scene, the authors explain, just as the public at large was learning about the underground. "Virtually every magazine in the country—from the *Saturday Evening Post* to *Playboy*—had run one sort of article or another on the phenomenon; the Museum of Modern Art had organized a symposium on the New American Cinema; and, in addition to the nomadic Film-Makers' Cinematheque, two East Village venues—the Bridge . . . and the Gate, around the corner on Second Avenue—were regularly screening underground films."[19]

Mekas chose Warhol as the filmmaker best able to make the underground matter. In his earliest films, Warhol had raised banality to new heights, and because he did this within a motion picture world obsessed with clarity of message and narrative arc, it was hard not to imagine that Warhol had taken avant-garde filmmaking to an end that was neither logical nor inevitable but imaginative. And Warhol brought something much more important to the underground—his reputation and fame. Mekas and a small team composed of some members of the Film-Makers' Co-op, including Shirley Clarke and Lionel Rogosin, had created the Film-Makers' Distribution Center to raise money for their other projects. They clearly hoped that one of Warhol's films would show the way to cinema nirvana, a place where financial solvency and artistic integrity flourished together. The film that this group believed merged the multiple streams of Warhol's talents and Mekas's aspirations was *The Chelsea Girls*.

Most mainstream critics reacted as Mekas had predicted. Art critic John Gruen, writing in the *New York World Journal Tribune*, provided a decidedly mixed review. "For all its self-indulgent pre-occupation with cinema voyeurism on a marathon scale," he believed that *The Chelsea Girls* was, "nevertheless, something of a landmark in underground film-making." He did take note, though, that "the danger of anyone becoming overly stimulated by what's on the screen is literally nil. Apathy reigns supreme," he concluded. "And that, in fact, is what Warhol means to tell us. And oh, do we believe him!" *New York Post* critic Archer Winsten seemed to sigh, "It has the usual components: perversion, degradation, seeming influence of narcotics, suggestion of depraved gatherings, frank views of an uncircumcised lad, whips, sadism, masochism and acres of sheer unintelligibility." Winsten had been among the most vocal champions of New York's underground cinema. But when it came to Warhol, his patience had run out. "What can be said positively," he concluded, "is that Andy has again reached stupefying heights of boredom." Jack Kroll of *Newsweek* found *The Chelsea Girls* another example of vacuous society. "The fact is that in today's splintered world, Warhol's split-screen people are just as meaningful as Jack Gelber's garrulous junkies, Edward Albee's spiteful comedians, John Updike's poetic suburbanites." Thus, Kroll imagined that the film "is one of those semidocuments that seem to be the most pointed art forms of the day. It is as if there had been cameras concealed in the fleshpots of Caligula's Rome": "They [underground filmmakers] are monitoring, processing and manhandling the rising tidal wave of events and images into works of art which, perhaps more powerfully than any others, attempt to make sense and structure out of an age of fragmented reality, dubious morality, and no-cal spirituality. Not that everything they do is good. But the percentage compares favorably with the percentage of good films made in Hollywood, good programs on television, good games in the major leagues and good bread in the supermarket." To Kroll, Warhol's work revealed that the avant-garde suffered from the same sickness of mediocrity that afflicted the mainstream. In the *Daily News*, columnists Lawrence Witchel and Ernest Leogrande told readers: "Through the smoke and babble of an arty New York cocktail party the other evening, a voice was heard to proclaim: 'Fornication is obscenity, lovemaking is art!' Don't confuse this warning with the 'blue' movies offered at stag affairs or the nudie flicks shown on the nation's 42nd Streets. These are movies which claim to be art, an answer to Hollywood product which their makers scorn, or pretend to scorn." The authors warned America to brace for the emergence of the underground.[20]

Rosalyn Regelson asked the most obvious question, "Where Are 'the Chelsea Girls' Taking Us?" Part of the tantalizing quality of foreign films, she argued, was the suggestion of things they might reveal — from sexy scenes to dead-end marriages. "The sudden popular success of several Underground films indicates a major psychic shift may be in process." She noted that at the 1966 New York Film Festival "distributors laughed off the idea presented by Jonas Mekas . . . that Underground films might be distributed through commercial channels." But all this changed in 1967 as the underground invaded the mainstream. Warhol's films did so most conspicuously by running for weeks at art theaters in New York and other places both in the United States and abroad. The Hudson Theater even changed its programs to show only Warhol pictures following the success of *My Hustler*. Regelson added that two theaters in the Village were opening to show avant-garde films exclusively; other theaters were bringing in 16 mm projectors, and even Mekas's Film-Makers' Cinematheque was getting a promotion by moving to a venue on 42nd Street. It was a replay of the foreign film invasion of the late 1940s, except this time the films, Regelson commented, "gradually wear down the viewer's stepped-up Western time-sense, seducing him into a suspension of his normal-value system." Thus, "Hollywood's tinsel titillation and the art house film's hard bedrock fornication are replaced by a new sexual mythology, a cool, low-keyed playful polymorphism." However, Regelson was skeptical, thinking that Hollywood would merely plug in themes used in underground films and thereby miss the "filmic poetry which the offbeat sexual mystique provides."[21]

Richard Roud, a British film critic and the director of film selection for the New York Film Festival, wondered if it was only the social context, rather than art, that mattered in the underground's breakthrough. "There *are* no censors any more," he asserted in *Sight and Sound*. "And it would seem that the Lindsay administration has given orders not to harass the avant-garde." Such freedom allowed films like *The Chelsea Girls* to capitalize on a certain popular understanding—"the success of these films," Roud believed, "depended on the greater public's identification of 'underground' with 'sex.'" For proof of this, he pointed to advertising campaigns "launched by one of the old-time exploitation houses for their latest offering." It wasn't that the avant-garde had transcended the older taboos, but that theaters making money off sex films merely exploited the benighted avant-garde. For a film critic of Roud's caliber, few developments were more offensive.[22]

"Ironically," Calvin Tomkins explained in the *New Yorker*, "the general relaxation of censorship that had come about since the 'Flaming Creatures' scandals (and which many people attributed in part to the impassioned anti-censorship battles of Mekas and a few others) now seemed to be working against the film underground. Several of the theatres that had agreed to book the Filmmakers' Distribution Center's films had subsequently become outlets for the sexploitation movies that were starting to flood the market." Commercial cinema was catching up by becoming more explicitly sexual, and the use of avant-garde techniques was popping up in everything from commercials to Hollywood movies.[23]

All Warhol had done was take full advantage of the more permissive environment. To Stephen Koch, the violation here was not social or political—as it had been for other controversial films—but aesthetic. "Warhol's sexualized and theatricalized eros had informed all his early work," Koch contends. "But, when general cultural permission was given for the pornographic spectacle, something emerged from Warhol—a violation of his own artistic sensibility, which is far more shocking and repellent than any imaginable violation of sexual taboo." Koch calls what followed *The Chelsea Girls* a period of "degradation" when Warhol lost "his visual intelligence and his taste." The coolness and detachment with which Warhol had treated his subjects—and, more important, his audience—seemed to transform into arrogance. Was it the culture that had changed, though, or the films? Koch suggests it was Warhol. "I can hardly imagine that any director has ever responded to his audience's loyalty with such contempt. And that contempt must surely have involved self-loathing as well, as if Warhol had come to agree with his most hostile critics when they claimed that he was a mere fraud who could put any junk he chose before his mindless audience and expect adulation for it."[24]

In May 1966, Bosley Crowther began a public evaluation of the damage done by Andy Warhol. "I've always said one unintentional reason for the term [underground] is that it embraces films that are like words scribbled on the subway walls." But he also pointed out that the term was a strange catchall for "interesting experimental films—or just plain unusual movies." He observed that the term could be used to cover "a multitude of cinematic sins." "Well, it all goes to show there are no boundaries or restraints for the 'underground,'" Crowther lamented. "Think of this when you next hear the term used. Already it has reached way uptown."[25]

After the move of *The Chelsea Girls* to the posh Cinema Rendezvous on West 57th Street, Crowther scolded the film's supporters: "It has come time to wag a warning finger at Andy Warhol and his underground friends and tell them politely but firmly that they are pushing a reckless thing too far." There was no problem, he argued, if the underground remained "underground." But once Warhol's film moved into the Rendezvous, Crowther thought it "time for permissive adults to stop winking at their too-precocious pranks and start calling a lot of their cut-ups—especially this one—exactly what they are." It was not a puritan sensibility that propelled such criticism but a fear that a younger generation of filmmakers would consider Warhol a model and begin producing similarly hopeless works. Crowther dismissed the critical acclaim the film received. "At best," he wrote, "[it] shows the squalor of a few unfortunate people—and not very artfully at that." He argued that Warhol compared unfavorably with every other good avant-garde filmmaker—and complimented Cinema 16 as a respectable venue for the "best" avant-garde films. Crowther illustrated, clearly, that he had little patience for the cheap sexual thrills.[26]

While no friend of Crowther, Amos Vogel was also deeply suspicious of the effect Warhol had on avant-garde film. As *The Chelsea Girls* made its popular run, Vogel was on the front lines of a debate over excluding Warhol and his friends from the New York Film Festival. In 1963, Vogel became the program director for Lincoln Center's annual film festival. He saw his job there, as he had when he ran Cinema 16, as one concerned primarily with the cultivation of taste among New York's moviegoers. Warhol's latest film, Vogel thought, added nothing of value to the discussion of film as art. Mekas, of course, excoriated Vogel for acting like a gatekeeper in New York's movie culture.

Yet what many in the underground did not know was that Vogel had been determined to open the 1966 festival to the avant-garde—just not to Warhol. In a memo sent to his immediate superior, Schuyler Chapin, in April 1966, he argued for the purchase of a 16 mm projector for Philharmonic Hall, the main exhibition space for films. In his days with Cinema 16, Vogel had screened hundreds of 16 mm films with great success. He told Chapin in no uncertain terms: "The Film Festival has justly been criticized by critics and filmmakers for not presenting 16 mm film by American independent filmmakers. As you know, most of the significant work in this significant field of American film activity is done in 16 mm and its absence from the Film Festival—especially when our presentation of films by the American majors is necessarily limited in any case—lays us open to charges of neglecting the cinema in our own country, while encouraging directors from abroad." Far from avoiding or dismissing underground cinema, Vogel attempted to prepare the festival for it. In doing so, though, Vogel hoped not to placate Mekas and others of the New American Cinema but to encourage their integration into a serious cinematic atmosphere. Moreover, critics of the festival had focused on the lopsided treatment of foreign films, suggesting that it differed little from a comparable two-week selection of the multitude of revival and art house theaters around Manhattan. Thus, inclusion of 16 mm films added a distinctive element to Lincoln Center's festival.[27]

Chapin and the other administrators met Vogel halfway. Rather than devote any time in Philharmonic Hall to the underground, which they read as "bad and possibly scandalous," the festival organizers relegated 16 mm projections to the two-hundred-seat auditorium of the Library and Museum of the Performing Arts at Lincoln Center. Vogel scheduled a series of twenty-seven cinematic events in the hope that exposing festivalgoers to films, the filmmakers, and discussions with "experts" would demonstrate the seriousness of his cause. In an interview Chapin gave to promote the festival and events such as this, he revealed a somewhat conflicted view of the underground. When asked if the 1966 festival would include avant-garde and underground films, Chapin replied: "Yes it will. We'll have a due quota of people coming out of basements with questions or answers—mostly answers, I guess, because nobody seems to be able to tell me very much. On the other hand, we will have some of the most skillful and recognized American independent film makers." He could name only one.[28]

Vogel organized a series of events around what he called the "independent cinema," in order to highlight work being done at the margins. One of those events brought together the critics from the city's avant-garde community. Entitled "What Are the New Critics Saying?" the session became noteworthy for its exasperating display of egotism, making the establishment's distaste for the underground seem quite sensible. The panelists proceeded to denigrate almost every film critic in the city, aiming especially violent pronouncements against Bosley Crowther. Toby Mussman, critic at large for the lightly circulated *East Village Other*, declared: "Crowther stands for the worst possible sort of criticism," because he was willing "to represent only an established point of view—one whose paths were blazed in previous years by more intelligent and more daring individuals." In an inversion of logic indicative of Mussman's entire argument, he seemed to suggest that Crowther was at once both an example of an intelligent critic and an example of a failure. "He represents standards which had to fight against other Bosley Crowthers in order to become understood and accepted, and in so doing have lost some of their original intuitive brilliance. Crowther, therefore, can only represent a narrow and shallow vision." Mussman offered a second, more curious reason for dismissing Crowther: he acted like a critic. "He lacks the integrity when in his daily reviews he assumes the position of a judge, telling his readers what they will and will not like, while all the while refusing to acknowledge the degree of importance he has given in making the judgements to his own personal prejudices." Mussman's observation captured an especially disturbing trend in New York movie culture, the growing disenchantment with authority of any kind. Opposing censors who indiscriminately hacked away at movies was a defensible position; opposing critics who evaluated movies based on a notion of taste was simply immature.[29]

Mussman and his colleagues showed their disdain for the concept of oppositional ideas by opposing critics who merely did their jobs. P. Adams Sitney, a frequent contributor to Mekas's *Film Culture,* exemplified that attitude: "I can see absolutely no reason for a man to sit down and presume to explain what's wrong with something. . . . I think anything I'd say against a person today is just worthless, because it doesn't do any good to speak against them." Sheldon Renan added: "I attacked all those critics or reviewers because I think they simply don't know anything about film." He complimented Crowther on having a lot of good things to say about a movie that he liked, but added, "[he] just didn't have any understanding or involvement whatsoever. . . . They use film as a springboard, or they just go ahead and write because they have to fill up their space." Mussman contributed more wisdom by calling Crowther and any other critic "dishonest" when they "sit up every day after seeing a movie once and judge, decide." He then turned on the audience, wagging a finger at those who read such critics.[30]

At this point the moderator, Parker Tyler, showed his impatience with such aimless griping. Tyler was considerably older than any of the critics on the panel, but his credentials were unassailable because he was among the first serious critics in the city to write intelligently about the avant-garde. At the same time, though, he was far from an apologist for the New American Cinema. Obviously tiring of weak arguments, Tyler asked: "Do you think it's ever necessary to point out what's wrong with something when it's on the whole very good? Do you think it's pointing out what minor faults it may have?" Renan wondered if the panelists should risk being specific—picking a certain film. "No, no," Tyler shot back, "you have to be general. You can think in terms of generalization, can't you?" The young critics were at a total loss to answer Tyler—they stumbled over words such as "essence" and "propaganda" and "mistakes" in their collective attempt to explain away the obligation any of them had to a critical line. If this was the future of New York's movie culture, there was little to look forward to.[31]

Then, near the end of the session, a member of the audience stood up. Harold Samuelson spoke as a member of the "old" critical establishment. "I don't see any of you who show further understanding of what the motion picture medium is (which is of course all I can talk about) than either Mr. Crowther or Miss [Judith] Crist," he declared. Panelist Renan responded: "You, sir, have nothing worth the price of beans." The discussion went this way for a few minutes until Parker Tyler attempted to pull it back by providing some historical context: "So, if no progress has been made," he offered, "at least everybody's sticking to his flag, which is the least you can ask for, no?" Actually, no. Not if that flag represented the absence of critical thought. In fact, that was the tragedy of the evening: Progress should have been made now that censorship was all but dead. Instead, these new critics attacked the very essence of movie culture—serious thought about what movies should be. Crowther was simply a convenient target, someone many in and outside the avant-garde regarded as part of the establishment. Fair enough, replied Samuelson, but he wanted to add "one word in defense of Bosley Crowther." Before Mussman could interrupt him with an apology for ever bringing up Crowther's name, Samuelson declared: "Bosley Crowther happens to be one of the few critics in New York who if he feels concerned, which is very often, bothers to go and see a film a second time before he writes about it." Another member of the audience shouted that Crowther wrote exclusively about Hollywood and European cinema and neglected the underground—"you're not likely to catch him dead at the Cinematheque." In the transcript of this exchange published in *Film Culture*, an editorial comment appears, which most likely came from Mekas. He noted: "I am very sorry, but I have to report here that Mr. Bosley Crowther has attended more screenings at the Cinematheque than any other daily or weekly reviewer I know."[32]

Reading the transcript of this session, I am struck by the inability or, perhaps, the unwillingness of the younger critics—the self-proclaimed cinematic rebels of the underground—to engage any real issues. Their arguments threw up much smoke but had very little intellectual fire. Amos Vogel not only understood this but believed it time to uncover this sham once and for all. A few months after the 1966 New York Film Festival, Vogel went on the attack. In a piece entitled "The Thirteen Confusions" published in the *Evergreen Review* (a journal with a reputation for taking chances, especially with sexually provocative essays and photographs), he argued that the underground had committed the "crime of crimes, it has become fashionable." It was suffering from "over-attention without understanding, over-acceptance without discrimination." Vogel had identified the paradox of the NAC—it was succumbing to the ills of freedom. Without resistance from mainstream movie culture or the law, the underground had been allowed to move in whatever direction it wanted. That underground films had become better known than ever before was, Vogel conceded, "the undeniable achievement of Jonas Mekas." Vogel, too, had a share of that success, but as a partisan in the larger battle to improve New York movie culture, he believed it was time to launch an "informed critique of the American avant-garde (and more specifically, the ideology and style of the New American Cinema tendency within it)," for such "an act [illustrated] the highest and most necessary loyalty to the movement." "The time has come," Vogel declared, "to rescue it from the blind rejection of commercial reviewers and the blind acceptance of its own apostles; both posing as critics and neither subjecting it to dispassionate, informed analysis."[33]

Vogel differed from other critics writing in newspapers because he had created a coherent and successful way to expose audiences to avant-garde cinema. From Cinema 16 to the New York Film Festival, Vogel's ideas of exposing moviegoers to distinct cinematic experiences had created a new type of audience for movies. He had hoped to get Mekas and the "prophets" of the New American Cinema to recognize that there were natural limits to their movement. Foremost among such revelations had to be, Vogel contended, that the NAC was "an economic and not an aesthetic unit." If Mekas had acknowledged such an insight, his connection to Warhol and the distribution of *The Chelsea Girls* could not have been played as accomplishment for art. It was commercial, not spiritual. By rejecting that conflict, Vogel believed, Mekas and his supporters were becoming "Commissars of Film Culture," able to rationalize whatever the NAC produced and denounce everything else. Mekas had declared during MoMA's recent "New Cinema" program that "old cinema, even when it is successful, is horrible; New Cinema, even when it fails, is beautiful." Vogel shot back, "The creations of . . . so-called 'commercial' directors can be disregarded only by hopeless dogmatists."[34]

Disenchanted with the NAC's philosophical approach and commercial practice, Vogel argued that "so many current efforts . . . confuse freedom with formlessness. Thematic liberation is no guarantee of quality. Nor is the use of five simultaneously-operating projectors, extreme nudity, unexceptionable anti-Vietnam sentiments, hand-held cameras, portrayals of transvestism." He leveled sharp criticism at the indiscriminate selection process of the NAC. As in the past, Vogel revealed his respect for critical taste and the audience: "Sooner or later," he warned, "the audience refuses to accept the frequent ratio of five minutes of promising footage to two hours of tedium. It is time for the NAC to admit that there is such a thing as bad avant-garde film. Ultimately, there is only good art and bad art. . . . Our real interest in avant-garde art resides not in its being avant-garde, but in its implicit promise of quality as against the exhaustion of the commercial cinema." Vogel saw clearly that the notoriety of avant-garde film rested on its infamy rather its quality and radicalism. "The avant-garde's aggressively antiestablishment stance expresses itself frequently in well-advertised taboo subjects. . . . Large scale attention by the mass media is no guarantee of achievement." The exemplar of such "success" was Warhol's experience with *The Chelsea Girls*—his success, Vogel cautioned, did not reflect the commercial potential of the underground. "The reviews and word-of-mouth publicity regarding this film's presumed depravity and sexual daring automatically provide a ready-made audience for it. No pejorative comment is intended," he explained; rather, "the saleability of sex in a sexually repressed society is inevitable." Vogel suggested that the NAC had deceived itself and in that way let down the legacy of the avant-garde and the audience that potentially was available for it. Instead, "what the American avant-garde is confronted with is sectarianism parading as freedom, flattery as criticism, sterile eclecticism as artistic philosophy, anti-intellectual know-nothingness as liberation."[35]

Vogel's critique illustrated the kind of force that New York's movie culture needed but was beginning to lose. And while many of his targets felt his attack was personal—retribution for being shunned by the NAC—it wasn't. Vogel made a larger point, one that he hoped to rectify as director of the New York Film Festival. He believed that the city's movie culture needed true alternatives to mainstream trends and institutions. Led astray by Warhol's commercial success and stunted by its own dogmatism, the avant-garde seemed compromised by egotism and naïveté. In the past, controversies that surrounded films had raised fundamental questions regarding the artistic and intellectual dimensions of movie culture. The stir caused by *The Chelsea Girls* reduced all controversy to sex—how much could be shown before a film would be considered legally obscene. Vogel justifiably feared that movie culture would be debased by trends that made moviegoing deceptively heroic. By the late 1960s, many in New York's movie culture seemed unable to tell the difference between the latest passing cause and real thought. Perhaps they just enjoyed the sex too much.

The *Evergreen Review* solicited responses to Vogel's critique. Not surprisingly, Dan Talbot, owner of the New Yorker Theater, found Vogel too uptight. Unlike Vogel, Talbot was not really interested in operating principles or ideologies. He could forgive the failings of New York's underground because he thought most of movie culture was a sham anyway. "Audience capacity for bullshit in America is awesomely big," he declared. His attitude was Warholian cool: "I'm perfectly willing to take my chances at any underground hall," he said. "It's simple enough to walk out on *drek*. That's what our whole country is all about once you leave the front door in our society. There just aren't that many options. But, please," he added for Vogel's benefit, "don't program me."[36]

Underground filmmaker Gregory Markopoulos thought Vogel's efforts had "little or no foundation." Markopoulos offered the same argument made by his comrades at the 1966 New York Film Festival. No one—not critics, film distributors, or old guard avant-garde—had the right or the ability to distinguish good films from bad. He had decided that critics "know very little about the medium," because "[they] have hardly ever inspected a foot of celluloid in a viewer, let alone understood the vital intricacies, the chaos that is film creation." Parker Tyler once again provided a check to this mushy logic, arguing that NAC "passion" was "the arch excuse for every possible offense against film form, against grace and precision of style, against significant and mature reference to human experience."[37]

Tyler deflated the pretentious nature of the underground's moral stance. "Automatically, the NAC ideology translates aesthetic revolution into stepped-up 'moral outrage' as if the main object of assault should be, not 'bad' filmmaking or 'commercial' filmmaking, but the film industry's old Hays Code psychology of prudish suppression of subject matter." Mekas and others had come late to this courageous struggle—commercial films had already tested the bounds—and European films "to date have displayed much more credible performances in . . . erotic candor than the equivalents the NAC has been able to muster." The underground had not merely failed to keep pace with changing morality, it struggled to maintain any artistic edge as well. To Tyler, New York's avant-garde had reached its intellectual limits. Its practitioners were at one time visual pioneers, but its techniques had been absorbed and commodified by everyone from advertising agencies to Andy Warhol. The next step was to chase sexual sensationalism. "Titillation," Tyler wrote, "is titillation, no matter how you cut your film." He concluded, "Let the avant-garde become the analysts of our mass fantasies. Or let them go to the analysts."[38]

Both Vogel and Tyler had been involved in the cinematic avant-garde when it had acted as a source of oppositional ideas in New York's movie culture. And while neither was a supporter of censorship or the censoring disposition, they were both deeply disappointed by the carelessness with which the NAC pursued easy money and notoriety through sex. More important, both also mourned the realization that Warhol's ironic coolness and Mekas's cheerleading had squandered hard-won opportunities to create a genuine alternative movie culture. Vogel sought to keep his hopes alive in the New York Film Festival—a prospect that ultimately disappointed him. Tyler's situation was more difficult because he hoped to regain control of a movement that he had helped create.

In 1969, Tyler published a profoundly pessimistic assessment of the influence Mekas and Warhol had had on the underground. In a book-length study entitled *Underground Film,* Tyler attempted to move beyond the petty disputes and personal fights that had animated the kind of discussions seen at the 1966 New York Film Festival. Mekas was unimpressed; he belittled Tyler's sophisticated argument in a *Village Voice* column in which he merely listed the negative terms Tyler had used to describe the underground. But Mekas's response reflected Tyler's larger point probably better than Tyler could have hoped. Eschewing intellectual context and aesthetics all together, Mekas responded like a wounded teenager, thereby reinforcing Tyler's claim that the underground had bottomed out in "childish self-indulgence."[39]

Film historian Greg Taylor has noted that Tyler's critique was "ironic" because it was Tyler (and his cultist critic colleague Manny Farber) who had pioneered vanguard criticism, turning forgettable culture into art. "Challenging the notion that aesthetic value is fixed and inherent, they suggested quite the opposite—that it is variable, contextual, and even spectator-driven," Taylor writes. "Here they were fulfilling the vanguard agenda, reclaiming art as a pragmatic, transformative activity. Art was something you as a modern spectator did with the world around you; the artwork might look nonart at first glance, but that was only because its underlying aesthetic qualities had not been revealed." Using such logic enabled Tyler and subsequent generations' pop connoisseurs, from critics such as Andrew Sarris and Pauline Kael to film studies professors, to enjoy a mass conspiracy with moviegoers against more traditional views of art and culture. What shocked Tyler and nagged critics such as Kael was the unsophisticated co-optation of this approach.[40]

For Taylor, vanguard criticism hadn't been corrupted; the seeds of its own misapplication lay within it. "In truth," he asserts, "Mekas's vanguard stance *was* radical. In being easy to emulate—and thus more accessible to the public—it was perhaps ultimately more radical than Tyler's high-flown transmutation had ever been." In other words, how could Tyler object to the subversion of standards when he himself had performed a kind of stylish—campy—assault on an older order? Yet there something troublesome in that observation—Taylor's logic suggests that it is ultimately impossible to appreciate mass culture in any serious way without sliding toward a world devoid of aesthetic judgment. Must the subversion of older standards lead to an inversion of standards and therefore the abandonment of standards?[41]

I think Tyler suggested a way to avoid such a conclusion, but it required a measure of humility, and perhaps that was Tyler's greatest mistake, to overestimate what mass culture does to all who are involved in its serious evaluation. He mourned the loss of restraint and authority in the avant-garde because, he argued, it had succumbed to "wish-fulfillment psychology masquerading as a system of aesthetic values." Thus, the darlings of the underground, from Brakhage to Warhol, were almost beside the point to Mekas because for him value lay in the ability to show anything rather than in what was being shown. To illustrate his point, Tyler recalled the scene in *The Bicycle Thief* that had created a stir because it depicted a little boy urinating against a wall. He compared that to a scene in a film by the Kuchar brothers, the underground's prolific jokesters, in which one of the brothers urinates at the side of the road so that the camera can capture it in all its crude detail. "It remains," Tyler suggested, "one of those sublime Underground gratuities for which the audiences at the New York Film-Makers' Cinematheque so patiently stay in their seats." Indeed, the audience shared some responsibility for making such stuff heroically transgressive. Like Sontag, Tyler promoted a kind of poetry of transgression. But what he couldn't tolerate was an ideology in which "any juvenile sort of buffoonery . . . equals 'poetry,' and there are no shades or grades of buffoonery, aesthetic or otherwise; there are only fond epithets uttered in a vacuum, fond superlatives, fond fondling."[42]

At the end of *Underground Film*, Tyler asked a simple question: was the most radical phase of underground filmmaking, represented by Warhol and other fetish filmmakers, a "symptom of a historical movement *to end all history?*" He posed this question to get at a more profound problem that this radical phase had created: it had become impossible to decide "what to *keep* [and] what to *discard*." "In fetish-footage psychology—the very heart of Underground Film—all conscious arrangements for the future are too logical, too explicit, too 'conservative.' Why conservative?" he asked. "Because of the idea of historical continuity, which means the responsibility of relating end to means, effect to cause, result to intention." Giving up such evaluative tools allowed for the mass conspiracy among the audience, for it abandoned any hope of creating coherency among a community and allowed individual audience members to experience their reception of films as if nothing else other than their own private taste mattered. "To insist on responsibility, from the widest Underground standpoint, is to betray the very life blood of the avant-garde, whose prevalent aim is to exist without being measured or weighed by anything but its own self-approval. Underground Film and Pop Art represent the only elites in human history which insist on the privileges of an elite without any visible means of earning or sustaining those privileges; that is, without any values that can be measured, or even, properly speaking, named except by its own labels." He concluded: "I prefer *history* for the film only because I prefer *consciousness* for the film. Therefore I am for Underground Film only as I am for its historic avant-garde values as these exist and can be verified in a total continuity of aesthetic values. Fetish footage is a dead end . . . or rather, a trailing filament of the visual void." Here is the final statement on a corrupted version of the new sensibility, for it made clear that freedom from older critical traditions was reduced to a notion of freedom to be without—without a past, a set of aesthetic standards, a point—rather than a freedom to become. In such an ego-driven atmosphere, how would one deal with a controversial movie? To rephrase the famous opening line of Pauline Kael's long review of *Bonnie and Clyde,* how could one criticize a cool film in this country without being jumped on? Bosley Crowther found out you couldn't.[43]

7

Did *Bonnie and Clyde* Kill Bosley Crowther?

BY THE LATE 1960s, Bosley Crowther began to understand what made Andy Warhol popular. The ironic detachment from social concerns and aesthetic standards that had disappointed Vogel and Tyler had gone mainstream. It struck Crowther as a sensibility that had contempt for anything serious and for anyone who wanted to be serious. Crowther was most disappointed by the fact that the hard-earned freedom that had emerged by the mid-1960s seemed to lead to a decline in taste among the public. Rather than demand better films that could explore difficult subjects in mature ways, moviegoers seemed to relish the exploitation of this new freedom as if it were a constitutional right. Crowther wondered just where this heroic view of movie frankness was leading movie culture.

Crowther was not a prude. He had defended movies that many of his middle-class readers found offensive because he believed that movies could challenge moviegoers as well as entertain them. That was why Crowther cheered when films such as *Tea and Sympathy* and *The Man with the Golden Arm* received PCA seals—both broached taboo subjects (homosexuality and drug addiction, respectively) but did so intelligently. And that is also why he became enraged when valid movies, such as Ingmar Bergman's *Virgin Spring*, were denied a license by New York State. Because of a depiction of rape, Bergman's film had violated one of the state board's rules. Crowther snorted: "What amounts to a valid and artistically brilliant scene has been denied to New York viewers . . . on the stupid pretext that it is 'obscene.'" What Crowther

177

found obscene was the fact that the state censors charged money to dispense their criticism under the guise of protecting the public. He barked: "The anti-censor is not pro-obscenity. He is pro the democratic system. Think about that. How many censors do?"[1]

Crowther even defended the black female independent filmmaker Shirley Clarke against state censors who denied her film *The Connection* a license because she used too many four-letter words too many times. He also made a case in favor of avant-garde filmmaker Hans Richter, because his film *8x8* was the sort of material that New York's censors rejected. "No one says the screen should be exempt from the laws of decency," Crowther argued, "but we do say—and say with insistence—that all efforts to withhold from films the Constitutional right of saying or showing things and taking their chances in the court of public opinion should be fought vigorously." The critic that many considered frumpy by the late 1960s was also the man who called the Supreme Court decision in the case involving the movie version of *Lady Chatterley's Lover* a "Victory for Ideas." Crowther rather gleefully reported that the only category still off-limits legally for movies was obscenity; "everything else," he declared, "is okay." Yet, he reasoned, "this anxiety—and the equally reckless notion that anyone who is opposed to censorship, or the pre-release suppression of pictures on the arbitrary decision of a censor, is an advocate of sin—reflects sheer emotionalism and little knowledge of the commerce of films. The sooner this fact is realized, the better for the peace of mind of everyone." He once again admitted that some people want obscene material and patronize theaters that show it but hoped that authorities that governed movie culture would trust the majority of moviegoers who, Crowther argued, have "sufficient sensibilities and taste to render them unsympathetic to downright offensive films." The bottom line for Crowther was not freedom from restrictions but the freedom to determine limits and to explore the art of film within them. "It is the protection of ideas in a free society that the court plainly feels more important than the protection of somebody's interpretation of 'morals.' And this protection should now liberate filmmakers from petty subterfuges and restraints."[2]

What, though, were the consequences of such freedom? Wasn't it fair to ask that question as well? The editors of the Catholic journal *America* wondered: when critics became "the first to welcome an ever-growing candor and frankness, who is to hold the ramparts against cultural vulgarity and frankness?" For Crowther, that role had always rested with parents and guardians like the Catholic Church. He advocated the freedom of filmmakers to make mature movies for American adults—not children—to see. He explained that while "there are plenty of good reasons for criticizing the cheapness and gross salacity of many films . . . there is one good way for the American public to show its disinterest and distaste for them (if it actually does). That is to stay away from them of its own free will and accord." The editors at *America* found such logic dangerously optimistic and idealistic because it was based on the assumption that moviegoers would actively seek out information with which to make educated (and "moral") decisions regarding the movies. "One wonders," the editors mused, "whether Mr. Crowther and those who share his view really want their approach taken seriously."[3]

Such concerns were not frivolous, and Crowther knew it. He had always coupled his championship of freedom with recognition of the need for responsible filmmaking and discriminating moviegoing. And he backed up that position with his pen. The decade and a half between the *Miracle* case and the appearance of downright obscene movies tested Crowther's faith in filmmakers and, more important, the public. Before it became trendy to embrace European film theories, Crowther had promoted a view of sex and violence that was closer to the continental line than what many moviegoers—and certainly censors—were willing to tolerate. In his columns one finds a clear predilection for "mature" and "adult" material but a weaker stomach for violence. In other words, he didn't mind themes such as seduction and adultery but was alienated by, as he said, the "violence and senseless sadism and calculated brutality [that] have been conspicuously present in our movies since World War II."[4]

Crowther judged the content of most movies by a simple gauge: "It is the merely pointless, the untrue and the willfully sensational we can fairly damn." He also hoped movies would probe reality and that great buzzword of postwar culture, "truth." "What do we expect the medium of motion pictures to convey?" Crowther asked. "Do we allow that motion pictures should be free to contemplate life as it is, which means aspects of it that may be seamy, such as infidelity, prostitution and treachery, as well as aspects of fine and noble nature, such as devotion, courage and self-sacrifice? Or do we expect motion pictures to be

only about the good and cheerful things—about absent-minded professors, Swiss families and Dalmatian dogs?"⁵

Crowther believed that movies had limits that should not be
breached because the health of society depended on a certain amount
of restraint from both filmmakers and moviegoers. A clear illustration
of this concern was Crowther's reaction to *Blackboard Jungle*, a film
that was part social message and part social shocker. The movie featured rock-and-roll music, including Bill Haley and the Comets' rock
anthem "Rock Around the Clock," and a cast that included a young
Sidney Poitier. It depicts a technical school trapped in a social conundrum: the students are vicious sociopaths who take great pleasure in de-
stroying the liberal ideals of weak teachers and eliciting medieval forms
of punishment from the disciplinarians. The film, Crowther recounted, "gives a blood-curdling, nightmarish picture of monstrous disorder
in a public school. And it leaves one wondering wildly whether such
out-of-hand horrors can be." His reaction echoed the general response
by other critics; some even suggested that the film would directly incite
juvenile delinquency. Crowther, in concert with other critics of the
movie, wondered about the damage such a film could do—calling it
"social dynamite." Letters poured in to the *Times* telling Crowther that
the movie was accurate. Most came from teachers and parents who
said that the situation was bad, but that the states and cities in which
these schools were located cared little about the kids in them. Principals and students and others involved with such schools also wrote in
to commend Crowther for questioning the accuracy of the story. The
Vocational High School Principals' Association even gave Crowther a
special award for his article on the movie.⁶

Dore Schary, president of MGM and a longtime friend of Crowther,
made a most insightful observation of the controversy. He wrote a long
letter to his favorite movie critic pointing out that he could accept criticism "on artistic grounds" but could not understand why Crowther
would question his studio's veracity by claiming it had "stacked"
the film. Crowther replied that if the depiction was accurate, "then
you've made a tremendous picture—a shattering and historic document. But," he cautioned, "if it isn't, then I think you have done a
disservice not only to our students, teachers and school systems but to
American society." Where, one might reasonably ask, was the critic
who believed truth could be found in the freedom to explore real-

ity? Moreover, what was a movie critic doing defending the honor of American society?[7]

Given some time to reflect on his reaction to *Blackboard Jungle,* Crowther moderated his view. A few months later, the critic wrote a piece on the refusal of Clare Boothe Luce, then U.S. ambassador to Italy, to attend a screening of the film at the Venice Film Festival. Crowther suggested that her act was tantamount to censorship and that it projected an overly cautious attitude, as if "our films should be in the nature of unblemished mirrors of the favorable aspects of American life." Crowther had defended the right of American filmmakers in a way that hinted at a conflict deeply internal to the critic himself.[8]

In 1958, Crowther was asked to explain his review of *Blackboard Jungle* in an interview conducted by Columbia University's Oral History Project. He revealed that his criticism was the product of tension between two currents: aesthetic and social concerns. He recounted that as a boy he had witnessed the reaction to D. W. Griffith's *The Birth of a Nation* by people in his hometown of Winston-Salem, North Carolina. Even though the city was 50 percent black, "there were very, very few Negroes that could be seen within blocks of the theater." As Crowther remembered it, "if the people coming out [of the theater] did no more than abuse the Negroes they saw in the street it was fortunate. Actually, a lot of people would throw rocks at them and do things of that sort. It was an unpleasant, a mischievous sort of thing." Reflecting on the popular reactions to such films, Crowther reasoned: "It seems to me that the significance of an occurrence of this sort in a community such as that one had to be taken as the reflection, an indication, of what power motion pictures have upon the mass mind." Likewise, in regard to the provocation of *Blackboard Jungle,* he worried, "You question simply how much more good does it do than harm, or how much more harm does it do than good, and try to weigh them and say, well, this is something that's good for society or it's unfortunate for society. I don't like to be harping too much on this particular consideration, but it certainly is one that I don't feel anyone should overlook, and particularly the critic."[9]

The tone of that last comment illustrated Crowther's recognition that his sentiment was controversial because it sounded like the rationale employed by censors. Yet Crowther worked to strike a balance between the latitude artists needed in order to explore controversial subjects and the capacity the mass audience had to understand in some constructive way what a controversial movie—even one that was offensive—had to offer. In 1962, he offered an example of this approach in a pamphlet on movie censorship for the Public Affairs Committee, an organization that addressed important social issues with the intention of enlightening the public and improving its welfare. To illustrate the dilemma that movies created, Crowther recounted the experience of a friend who had taken her daughter to see *Two Women*. She found the story line shocking—a depiction of the rape of a mother and her daughter. She also expressed her outrage that such a heinous act could be shown on the big screen. "Here," Crowther observed, "was a typical example of the lack of understanding of the majority of people today about what is happening in the realm of motion pictures." Movies had become more realistic. Moviegoers, in turn, had grown increasingly accustomed to cinematic realism. Thus, the relationship between the cinema and its audience was more sophisticated, allowing filmmakers to explore topics previously forbidden. Yet Crowther was also sympathetic to moviegoers who hoped that movies would continue to exist within a certain prescribed and controlled environment. "It is understandable, too," he added, "regardless of whether one is aware of change, that there should still be some serious critical questioning of the responsibilities exercised in the field of films. For despite the 'maturing' of the medium, there are still many liberties taken in its commercial creation and merchandising that need to be better controlled to qualify it fully for its new cultural status." Indeed, Crowther was no apologist for Hollywood or defender of an abstract concept of movies as free speech. To him, motion pictures remained commercial ventures that always had the potential to be artistic. But the only way that movies could be art was if filmmakers and moviegoers acted like responsible adults. In the years to come, that expectation proved to be an unfortunate failure.[10]

Movies created a public culture that was serious business both culturally and commercially. And that was the dilemma Crowther grappled with. Movies did not exist in an artistic vacuum, and audience reaction did not resonate among a tiny community. Movies were a mass art with an enormous following. They were simply not the same thing as a painting hanging in a museum or even a novel with a large readership. Movies had become, during Crowther's career as a critic, the most significant fleeting experience in American culture. While the fate of Western civilization did not depend on the quality of movies, the quality of public life was undoubtedly influenced by popular reception of them. That was why Crowther believed criticism played a vital role not merely as an assessment of movies as art but as a check on popular taste. In the latter half of the 1960s, however, Crowther seemed to many of his detractors incapable of discussing the art, rather than the influence, of movies.

In June 1964, Crowther opined in the Sunday *Times* about a movie entitled *Lady in a Cage*. The movie is largely forgotten today but had particular resonance for Crowther and other New Yorkers in the early 1960s. It is a story about a disabled woman who, trapped in an old-fashioned, iron-gated elevator in her apartment house, is repeatedly brutalized by a gang of young men over the course of a weekend. Crowther found it to be a "reprehensible film." It was, he felt, an awful reminder of one of the most unspeakable crimes in recent city history: the daylight murder of Kitty Genovese, an act witnessed by many but stopped by none. "What is irresponsible about it—what is downright dangerous, indeed," Crowther declared, "is that [the movie] tends to become a sheer projection of sadism and violence for violence's sake." The writer and director of the film responded with a long letter rationalizing his attempt to force audience members to confront their sympathies with brutal villains, and proposing that American society could never overcome its basic sadistic tendencies until the people who constitute it understood that such tendencies exist. Anticipating that kind of response, Crowther argued that the "critic must speak out boldly and let his anxieties fall where they may"—even if that meant, Crowther suggested, alienating his readers. By the end of 1964, Crowther had even permitted himself a word in support of the Legion of Decency: "I'd say the Legion of Decency has good reason to file a loud complaint against the evidences of deterioration or what it calls a slide of movies towards 'moral brinkmanship.'"[11]

Crowther had hoped that in the absence of moral guardians moviemaking might actually rise to meet the rather sophisticated tastes of moviegoers. He was to be let down by both filmmakers and viewers. In an aptly entitled piece, "The Heat Is on Films," Crowther suggested that another kind of pressure should take the place of censors: the weight of responsibility. He worried, though, that the "flow of films of a cheap and sordid nature" threatened gains made against censorship and hastened the rise of new repressive regimes of control. In a world without the old limitations, Crowther told moviemakers and moviegoers, "the moral integrity of a picture, like its artistic quality, is inevitably controlled by the people who make it. And it is up to them to assume responsibility." He advocated "active education and elevation of public taste." He called for "more solid critical guidance." And he argued, "It is absurd that this mature and mighty medium should be entirely down-graded and exposed to public scorn because of a run of cheap, stupid and easily avoidable mistakes."[12]

There was a cruel irony to Crowther's situation. He had been an ally of filmmakers and moviegoers by taking a bold stand against restrictions that belittled their talent and their judgment, respectively. However, in the postcensor movie world, Crowther had to face a much tougher beast, the vagaries of postcensor taste. He did not stand by passively and accept what he viewed as a flippant attitude toward serious problems, or the cheap use of mature subjects for either commercial gain or, in the case of underground films, atmosphere.

He scoffed at early efforts from Arthur Penn and Tony Richardson, saying of their films *Mickey One* and *The Loved One*, "Never in Hollywood's history have two films more likely to offend the middlebrow tastes and sensibilities of the people who run the show out there been not only bought and paid for but given the go-ahead by them, simply because the films' makers said this was how they wanted their films to be." The problem, it seemed, was not simply making a bad film; it was that Penn and Richardson had made bad films at a time when they didn't have any excuses—such as a code, censor, or Catholics—to blame for such poor content. They had squandered opportunities and, perhaps even worse, had almost rubbed the faces of moviegoers (and critics) in their hubris.[13]

Crowther was especially sensitive, as were many liberals of his generation, to the web of obligations and responsibilities that held civil society together and was necessary to advance it. It was a great disappointment to him to find that after fighting so long and hard for freedom on both sides of the screen, both filmmakers and moviegoers were happy to reduce the artistic level of motion pictures to what was banal and crude. All movie critics had to play a game with these two sides of the screen—attempting to coax the production of better films and educating the public to appreciate it when it got to see those better films. Considering his protracted public discussions with moviegoers, Crowther clearly took his responsibility very seriously. When he was fighting for greater freedom to make and see more mature films, he probably seemed quite heroic. However, his stance on movie violence made his criticism seem anachronistic.

"Something is happening in the movies that has me alarmed and disturbed," he wrote in a diatribe against *The Dirty Dozen*. "Movie-makers and movie-goers are agreeing that killing is fun." Crowther was, again, not so misguided as to believe that all violence was bad; he understood, accepted, and liked his fair share of cinematic mayhem. No, "this is killing of the sort," he reasoned, "that social misfits and sexual perverts are most likely to do. And the eerie thing is that movie-goers are gleefully lapping it up." He singled out *The Dirty Dozen*, initially, because he believed it was "a blatant and obvious appeal to the latent aggressiveness and sadism in undiscriminating viewers. And I would guess that the people who are seeing it . . . are taking it for kicks and thrills and are coming away from it palpitating with a vicarious sense of enjoyment in war."[14]

Crowther's critical observations of popular taste elicited mail that made him consider retirement. Readers told him that in a violent world, violent movies made sense, that violent heroes could have existential meaning to a public that craved something beyond liberal platitudes and bureaucratic procedures. Crowther's reply illustrated that he was indeed growing incongruous with his era. "It is the fallacious idea," he shot back, "that violent movies are playing an important cultural role as ironic reflection." Where was the irony? Crowther asked. How was it ironic to glorify violence on the big screen? Where was the critique of America as a violent society? Today, Crowther's position on film violence might sound prescient rather than anachronistic, but in the late 1960s Crowther had become the odd man out among his fellow critics. Many of his colleagues began to whisper that Crowther considered himself some kind of new censor. That was a baseless charge, though Crowther was clearly guilty of expressing a sincerity in his concern for movie culture that made him appear simple. Referring to the care filmmakers took in portraying detailed scenes of bloodshed and killing, Crowther pleaded, "I feel again and again the penetration of an antisocial venom into my own flesh and I dread how widely such deliberate exploitation of the public's susceptibilities is poisoning and deadening our fiber and strength." Whereas once he found the problem to be a movie culture controlled for the protection of the public, Crowther had come to believe that civilized society now had to protect itself from a public disturbingly impressed by cinematic violence.[15]

Letters to the *Times* poured in. Many expressed support for Crowther's stance against the rising tide of violence, and many of those letters came from parents and religious officials. Letters in disagreement with Crowther heckled the critic through the summer and fall of 1967, making it the most difficult period of his career. One reader said of Crowther, "Instead of criticizing the movie for its worth as a dramatic entity, he moralizes and moralizes." When his concerns began to annoy his readers, they told him all they wanted was a simple suggestion of whether the movie was good or bad in "cinematic" terms. A second criticism struck at something a bit deeper. All critics had their pet proclivities; Crowther's was his social concern—he was a social critic. But another reader argued that it was Crowther's politics, rather than his approach or taste, that were outright wrong. In the same pan of *The Dirty Dozen*, Crowther had attacked Sergio Leone's neo-westerns as hollow and grotesquely violent replicas of Hollywood classics from John Ford and Fred Zinnemann. In response, reader Marvin Fein suggested, "It appears to me to be more moral to accept Leone's view that murder in a frontier society was not done in an honorable fashion than to accept Zinnemann's and Ford's view that murder can be justified if done by an honorable person. It is precisely that delusion that makes some madmen feel the taking of a life can somehow be justified." The reader went on to ask if Crowther could imagine Jack Ruby "thinking himself more as a Gary Cooper than a Clint Eastwood."[16]

This reader had identified the fatal disconnection in Crowther's relationship with his public. He did not understand that his audience looked at society and its institutions and even its ethics through the lenses of irony and cynicism. How could such people have faith in a critic of Crowther's ilk when they no longer trusted the government and were told to dismiss those over the age of thirty? Without a basic trust in Crowther's ability to lead, his readers lost faith in him. Once he had fought to free the screen for these people; now he fought to free himself from an attitude he thought was poisonous and ultimately ruinous for movie culture.

The tension that was building between Crowther and his readers reached its climax in the late summer of 1967 when the movie *Bonnie and Clyde* premiered at the World's Fair in Montreal. Over the course of two weeks, Crowther wrote three reviews of the film, each one addressing the thing that bothered him most about the film—audience reaction to the film's violence. In the first, he thundered from Montreal: "It whips through the saga of the cheapjack bandits as though it were funny instead of sordid and grim." But it wasn't just that the film seemed cynical in its treatment of violence, it was how the audience received that violence that made Crowther cringe. "Just to show how delirious these festival audiences can be," he wrote, "it [*Bonnie and Clyde*] was wildly received with gales of laughter and given a terminal burst of applause." He also observed other Americans—presumably critics—"wagging their heads in dismay and exasperation that so callous and callow a film should represent their country in these critical times. It seems," Crowther editorialized, "but another indulgence of a restless and reckless taste, and an embarrassing addition to an excess of violence on the screen."[17]

When the film hit New York, Crowther blasted the industry for exploiting that trend. He reminded his readers that the movie had been made to capitalize on the popularity of glamorizing villains and romanticizing violence. Crowther took issue with the publicity campaign mounted by Warner Bros. that promoted the film's historical accuracy. "It is nothing of the sort," he objected. "It is a cheap piece of bald-faced slapstick comedy that treats the hideous depredation of that sleazy, moronic pair as though they were as full of fun and frolic as the jazz-age cut-ups in 'Thoroughly Modern Millie.'" But it was the way the filmmakers used violence to sensationalize the action that offended him most. "Such ridiculous, camp-tinctured travesties . . . might be passed off as candidly commercial movie comedy . . . if the film weren't reddened with blotches of violence of the most grisly sort. This blending of farce with brutal killings is as pointless as it is lacking in taste, since it makes no valid commentary upon the already travestised truth."[18]

When asked to respond to such charges, director Arthur Penn was as coy about the use of violence in his film as Elia Kazan had been about sex in *Baby Doll*. "The filmmaker's only responsibility is to be truthful," he told Vincent Canby, Crowther's colleague at the *Times*. "There's no question that some people may be stimulated by violence, but some people are also turned on by music. The important question is whether the work itself is good or bad art. In bad art, I suppose, violence can seem isolated and arbitrary, but even so, you can't censor bad art." Penn played both sides of the history issue: he argued that violence was absolutely necessary for verisimilitude in films about crime, and at the same time that he and screenwriters had to romanticize the characters because they were "dealing with the mythic aspects of their lives."[19]

In an interview almost a year later, after *Bonnie and Clyde* had won critical acclaim and been idolized by the younger generation, Penn began to embrace a kind of cinematic populism to rationalize the violence. "We used laughter to get the audience to feel like a member of the gang, to have the feeling of adventure, a feeling of playing together." This device, he explained, drew the audience into the story before it turned more serious, melancholy, and troubled. By then, the audience was "caught in the film as a member of the gang and [would] have to go along."[20]

Penn was right. The audience responded to the characters because they identified with them. One person suggested that Bonnie and Clyde "did all the normal American things . . . and the violence which was their stock in trade is also an integral part of the American scene." Thus, the film was a projection of a sick society rather than the reflection of that sickness. But if society *was* the enemy, Crowther noted incredulously, then "this is certainly a complex thesis to support on evidence as unsubstantial and disreputable as the careers of a couple of fanciful crooks." Warner Bros. answered that charge with a bit of marketing cynicism. On posters for the movie, there was a simple exclamation under a stylized picture of Faye Dunaway's Bonnie and Warren Beatty's Clyde that read: "They're young . . . they're in love . . . and they kill people."[21]

How could Crowther the humanist respond to that? He couldn't, and letters from the public illustrated why. A postcard from one reader told Crowther that none of his friends even bothered to read him anymore and that he would like to see Crowther replaced by "a reviewer more atuned [sic] to the taste of New York moviegoers—someone with just a little fresher point of view." Another mocked Crowther as the "Reverend Davidson" of film critics. Joyce Mack implored Crowther to understand the appeal of *Bonnie and Clyde* to younger people: "I don't know whether the script of this movie is historically correct," she admitted. "It is a horror film where we in the audience are forced to watch two people who we deeply care about, destroy themselves." Actor Orson Bean told Crowther that he had gone to see the movie for himself after growing curious about why the critic had received such violent letters in opposition to his views. With lines around the block to get in and the audience going "crazy" in the theater, Bean concluded, "Now I realize why Bosley Crowther feels so defensive. Soon everyone will know that his reviews can't be trusted." Crowther probably chuckled at that, remembering how many Catholics had thought the same thing a few years earlier. Unlike debates over censorship and the Legion of Decency, differences over *Bonnie and Clyde* quickly became rather pointless and petty. "Having decided that violence in the movies hardens us to violence in life and hurts the cause of a peaceful existence," Bean added, "Mr. Crowther has served notice on Hollywood that he will no longer favorably review a picture with 'too much violence' in it. More and more it seems that a liberal is someone who will fight to the death for your right to agree with him." Had Bean confused the issue here? Crowther was not looking for agreement; he was offering criticism. But in return, letters in opposition to Crowther merely pointed out his inability to be "with it."[22]

The star of *Bonnie and Clyde*, Warren Beatty, also seemed bewildered by the world of criticism. "What really hurts," Beatty told critic Roger Ebert, "is that one lousy review in the *New York Times*. Bosley Crowther says your movie is a glorification of violence, a cheap display of sentimental claptrap, and that's that. *The New York Times* has spoken, hallelujah. . . . Because Crowther writes for the *New York Times* he has influence all out of proportion to his importance. Out in the bush leagues, the theater owners, they read the *Times*. For them, Crowther is God. Everybody in the world can like a movie, and if Crowther doesn't, he kills it." Beatty's lament was partly correct; Crowther's reviews had in the past carried some potential economic power. But his influence did not come solely from his position at the *Times*; it came from a career spent cultivating a reputation as an honest, thoughtful movie critic. Beatty overstated Crowther's influence in 1967. *Bonnie and Clyde* not only enjoyed a lucrative second run in the spring of 1968 but also was responsible for illustrating beyond any doubt that Crowther's appeal had become obsolete. The victim was not poor Warren Beatty, who could lick his wounds all the way to the bank, but Bosley Crowther. Crowther didn't kill the film; *Bonnie and Clyde* killed Bosley Crowther.[23]

If public reaction seemed severe, it was merely a prelude to the sentiment of Crowther's colleagues. New York's numerous film critics unleashed an unprecedented barrage of critical barbs and personal putdowns against him. Crowther had been a consistent target in the past mostly because, as Beatty had alluded to, he was perceived as an influential critic and thus a standard-bearer against which to rebel. But this situation was different. Never before had a community of film critics singled one out for a public lashing.

In a long piece on the film for the literary journal *Hudson Review* in the spring of 1968, Charles Samuels addressed the personal attacks against Crowther. Samuels recognized that it was no surprise that Crowther was once again "out of step," hinting that at the *Times* Crowther had not been keeping up with the times. Nevertheless, he pointed out that the "anger" Crowther's views had elicited revealed just "how precious a possession the film's attitude had become." This was more than simply a disagreement over a film or even the limits of movie brutality. One's reaction to the film served as a referendum on where one stood in American culture. Crowther's stance suggested that he was blind to the ability of popular expressions to be energetic critiques of corrupt authority. Here was an example of art giving voice to the people, creating, as J. Hoberman has recently argued, "a movie that might speak for, as well as to, its audience. Like political demagogues or world-historical individuals, such movies might articulate ideas that an imagined community had only felt. These movies might even reconstitute the imagined community." By panning *Bonnie and Clyde,* Crowther seemed to have indicted this community. It was an action that made him unwelcome in his own world.[24]

New Yorker critic Penelope Gilliat commented that a critic must have "wood shavings" for brains to claim that *Bonnie and Clyde* glamorized violence. Auteur critic Andrew Sarris declared that Crowther's "crusade" made the "100-Years-War look like a border dispute." Even Moira Walsh at the Catholic periodical *America* wrote that Crowther had missed an opportunity to explain to the audience how to distinguish between artistic violence and gratuitous violence.[25]

Samuels wondered "why so many reputable critics condone violence lacking expressive purpose and why customers are willing to pay for a movie both repulsive in its bloodshed and disorienting in its tonal shifts." Was it that the movie was part of the vogue of the ridiculous, a riff on gangster films—ironic, detached, and ridiculous? In contemporary parlance, Samuels noted that *Bonnie and Clyde* was up-to-date. "Not because of its technique," he contended, "but because of an attitude which persuades the viewer to swallow its violence: the attitude . . . that society and normality are frauds." And that attitude had "become a contemporary article of faith." The implications of it disturbed Samuels as they had Crowther, because they both believed that the film's popularity was based in large part on a collective egoism. The underlying attraction of the film was a notion that "the crooks are superior to society." Here was a way for those in the audience to take the film with them after they left the theater. That was what made the popularity of the film significant. "Whereas the audience probably identifies with Bonnie and Clyde as surrogate social victims, serious reviewers identify them as surrogate social problems. No wonder, despite the bloodshed, that everyone is happy."[26]

Bonnie and Clyde had insinuated itself into the mass-mediated national psyche. Hoberman writes that it "signaled a new complicity, a willingness to go with the flow, a sense of crime as a game ruined by grown-up society's tedious insistence that acts had consequences." It was a movie that had "partisans," not just fans. Charles Moskowitz, the theater critic for the *Village Voice*, wrote in December 1967, "If you are a bonnie-and-clyder, you are pro-camp and anti-Ugly; pro-permissiveness and anti-authoritarian; an advocate of the easy, improvised approach to life rather than a Five Year Planner." Perhaps Sarris was correct: this was a war. It wasn't one that Crowther started, but it was one that he wouldn't survive. And Pauline Kael made sure of that.[27]

In the opening sentence of her unusually long review for the *New Yorker*, Kael quipped: "How do you make a good movie in this country without being jumped on?" The implication was clear: Crowther had become dangerous to movie culture. Not only did he fail to recognize a great film, she suggested, but his tone was reminiscent of censors', decrying the movie as morally harmful. Kael's review added mightily to the burying of Crowther by implicating him as a part of a drift toward reactionary politics: "The whole point of *Bonnie and Clyde* is to rub our noses in [the violence], to make us pay our dues for laughing," she lectured. "The dirty reality of death—not suggestions but blood and holes—is necessary." Why? Because a sophisticated reading of contemporary society demanded it. "Tasteful suggestions of violence would at this point be a more grotesque form of comedy than *Bonnie and Clyde* attempts," Kael asserted. "*Bonnie and Clyde* needs violence; violence is its meaning." Kael waxed rather righteous on the use of violence in the movies, declaring that filmmakers have the "freedom" to use violence, whether or not a movie is a work of art. "Too many people—including some movie reviewers—want the law to take over the job of movie criticism; perhaps what they really want is for their own criticism to have the force of law."[28]

That comment was disingenuous of Kael. It was Kael rather than Crowther who held the power at that moment. Her opinion was so weighty it convinced another critic, Joseph Morgenstern of the popular political weekly *Newsweek,* to issue an unprecedented retraction—after panning *Bonnie and Clyde* a week earlier, Morgenstern suddenly found it impressive. Morgenstern had listened to Kael, had received the wisdom, and made his confession. It was an instance of critical retrenchment.[29]

Crowther thought he was doing his duty by calling attention to the numbing effect of movie violence on moviegoers. But to Kael, that was mushy middle-class liberalism. It was the kind of thought that in the past had made it impossible for mass art to provoke audiences. As Kael pointed out: "The fact that it is generally *only* good movies that provoke attacks by many people suggests that the innocuousness of our movies is accepted with such complacence that when an American movie reaches people, when it makes them react, some of them think there must be something the matter with it—perhaps a law should be passed against it."[30]

Fair enough. Crowther could seem patronizing. But he and Kael both felt protective of moviegoers. Crowther wanted to shield them from their own worst impulses that were only too easily exploited by the movie industry. Kael wanted to affirm the best of those impulses by making them part of a critical embrace of movies as a mass art. She rejoiced in the fact that the audience was "alive" to *Bonnie and Clyde.* To her the movie elicited the best kind of response: immediate, unfiltered, passionate. It belonged to the audience, not to the critics or to the industry, because moviegoers had celebrated it spontaneously.

"Once something enters mass culture, it travels fast," Kael explained. "In the spoofs of the last few years, everything is gross, ridiculous, insane; to make sense would be to risk being square."[31]

What did it mean, though, to be out of touch with a movie that had generated a mass following? In the radical magazine *Ramparts*, writer Peter Collier offered a different take on the meaning of *Bonnie and Clyde*. "They deny the law without affirming a higher one," he said of Penn's creatures. "Their celluloid lives make no real criticism of the status quo that supposedly oppresses them. It is a myth of pop nihilism; it is Andy Warhol's serial put-ons packaged in a dramatic context with all of Hollywood's savvy behind it." Collier, like Crowther, nailed Penn on his historical ineptness, not because the film was untrue to some false god of truth, but because the film made a mockery out of something that was important: "The setting [the Depression] is used in much the same way that the world of advertising uses backgrounds: to create more or less subliminal presumptions in favor of what they're trying to sell." In this case the sales pitch was for the glamorous nature of a rebellious youth. And yet one could not dismiss the film as a failure, Collier argued, because it had life as a cultural signpost—while transitory as art, it was invested with significance nonetheless. To most people who watched *Bonnie and Clyde*, it was a taste of violence and rebelliousness that drew them to the theaters because they would never, as upstanding members of American society, actually be part of the real thing. Collier conceded that the film undoubtedly spoke to aspects of a generation that was attempting to make something out of its new freedom, but the ease with which many embraced this film should have tipped them off to the con being run. "From some parts of the cult come angry voices saying that this inevitably occurs to that which is potentially pure in our corrupt world. So it does. But it isn't that much of a perversion of the role Bonnie and Clyde played in the film. They were an advertiser's dream the minute they were reborn."[32]

In a recent interview, David Newman, half of the screenwriting duo that wrote *Bonnie and Clyde*, somewhat unwittingly revealed just how precious the filmic moment had become. He and cowriter Robert Benton met Crowther at the New York Film Critics Awards, where Newman and Benton had won the award for best screenplay. Crowther congratulated them both and spoke politely for a while until his wife joined them, at which point Crowther turned to her and said, "Dear, these are the fellows who wrote *Bonnie and Clyde*. They're not so bad after all." Newman was indignant about such a backhanded remark. But why? Didn't he understand that he should have taken pride in being an object of Crowther's derision? He couldn't understand that because, it was clear, he wanted and enjoyed the adulation of the film's fans. Newman reveled in the mass fantasy that the movie created among a generation of moviegoers—it was, as Hoberman contends, a founding document of the dream life of the 1960s.[33]

A veteran of an older American dream thought this younger generation was simply asleep. The playwright and screenwriter John Howard Lawson (one of the blacklisted Hollywood Ten whom Crowther had defended) found it offensive that the cinematic Barrow gang had camped Depression-era values. Here was a crime much worse than gratuitous violence. The film transformed class warfare into a fashion statement. Social concerns were of no concern at all, and worse, given the opportunity to popularize rebellion against a repressive society, the film played as one long inside joke among a generation that had no need for any other generation. Lawson's view echoed Parker Tyler's critique of *The Chelsea Girls*—elevating *Bonnie and Clyde* to new cultural heights wasn't heroic, it was merely childish. "We can have compassion for them if we look upon them as pitiful victims," Lawson contended. "They are not rebels, for they accept all the false values of their society. Even their love of their mothers, which is touching, expresses their dependence, the inability to become adults."[34]

But what about Pauline Kael? Was her enthusiasm no better than Jonas Mekas's unqualified support of the underground? It seems to me that Kael's treatise in defense of *Bonnie and Clyde* was inspired in part by her desire, once and for all, to supplant the critic who had been her professional opposite, Bosley Crowther. Before coming to the *New Yorker*, Kael worked in relative obscurity in San Francisco, writing reviews for small journals and reading many more on a public radio show. Crowther, of course, wrote for the largest daily newspaper in the country, in the nation's largest city, on the coast that mattered. He offered a middle-class, middle-aged, middle-of-the-road, male liberalism that grated against Kael's biting Berkeley feminist bohemianism. But the feature that most acutely distinguished the two critics was what they expected from moviegoers. Both expected a great deal from the audience, but in different ways. The interesting thing is that they arrived at these different positions from similar assumptions. Both thought daily reviewing was important to establishing a critical perspective — they did not reject such work as beneath them. Both refused to play cheerleader for Hollywood. Both relished deflating pretentious attitudes among the audience. And both believed that unreasonable expectations placed on American films had made it difficult for them to get at the kind of truth a popular art could reveal.

In November 1967, the *New York Times* put an end to this debate. It published a brief, one-column article explaining that Crowther, as of 1 January 1968, would step down from his regular reviewing duties. Renata Adler, a much younger and more "with it" critic than the sixty-two-year-old Crowther, took his place. Adler had written pieces for the *New Yorker* and was clearly the intellectual match of any movie critic in New York, especially the newest, hottest voice in town, Pauline Kael. Kael's review of *Bonnie and Clyde* earned her a home at the cosmopolitan *New Yorker* for the next thirty-three years. Crowther's review of the same movie hastened the end of his career at the *Times*, which had spanned twenty-seven years. There was, though, something a bit unseemly about these twin developments. I do not mean to suggest that Kael didn't earn her new job or that Crowther was not due to retire from his, but there was something less than noble in the way that both critics were treated by their home institutions. The *New Yorker* rewarded Kael as much for being on the right side of a debate as for writing a landmark review. On the other side, the *Times* used Crowther's anachronistic opinion to move him out of the way while it chased the new youth market. *Bonnie and Clyde* certainly marked a cultural moment for a generation, but it was a fleeting experience. To me, the best thing about that movie was Kael's review.[35]

Perhaps tellingly, letters in response to the announcement of Crowther's retirement filled almost an entire page in the *New York Times* — dwarfing the room given to the initial announcement. Under the title "A Critic for All Seasons," the paper ran letters from Arthur Mayer and Lillian Gerard, both of whom wrote to remind readers of Crowther's stance during the *Miracle* case. Mayer had been Joseph Burstyn's business partner and an importer of foreign films for most of the postwar period. He hoped to place Crowther's recent problems in some context. "Far-out film fans, prepared to loathe any critic who has not promptly and vociferously greeted experimental avant-garde productions from Godard to Andy Warhol, may not recognize the services of Bosley Crowther to the motion picture medium." But "those with longer memories are better equipped to appreciate the memorable and courageous battles he has conducted over the past 25 years." Gerard echoed such sentiments, especially since as manager of the Paris Theater she had been directly affected by New York State's ban of *The Miracle*. Crowther had been an important ally in that battle and, she noted, in the more general fight to improve movie culture. Through his support for foreign films and his opposition to censoring bodies, Crowther had been a strong advocate for "the freedom of the screen." She concluded: "We have on record a critic who served, a critic who worked, more often right than wrong, more faithful to the medium than interested in personal aggrandizement." Mayer put what Crowther represented succinctly: "His integrity and dedication to the film medium have been a bulwark of strength to moviemakers and movie lovers for a quarter of a century."[36]

Crowther exchanged many replies with those who wrote to express similar sentiments, including one to his longtime friend Thomas Pryor, whose decision to leave the *Times* in the 1940s opened up a spot for Crowther to begin his duties as the paper's regular reviewer. He told Pryor that his stepping down had been in the works for "over a year" and was seen by the editors and publisher as part of the "whole program of 'rejuvenation' that is going on at the *Times*." He dispelled the rumors that directors he had panned, such as Arthur Penn and Otto Preminger, had had something to do with the move. The *Times* had been considering, even trying out, a number of people to replace him, including some well-known critics who had failed to impress people at the paper. "They didn't want Stanley Kauffmann," Crowther noted. "And, thank God, they had no use for Judy Crist. This gal they've got, Renata Adler, from the *New Yorker*, is a big surprise to me. Although she's intelligent and writes well, I fear they're taking a big chance on her. Can she produce daily against deadlines? I can only say that I hope to God she can cut it, because this is a tremendously important job—a huge responsibility—in the present complex of films." He was right about those final two points: Adler left in a year, shaking her head at the mind-numbing business of maintaining a daily column about movies that she hated seeing and hated even more writing about. And Crowther was right, as he had been throughout his career, that being the first-string critic at the *New York Times* was an important job—although it was a position whose power was never again the same, in part because Crowther had left and because the culture that had bestowed authority upon him had disappeared.[37]

The day the *Times* announced Crowther's retirement, Richard Schickel wrote Crowther a letter. At the time, Schickel was a young film critic for *Life*, the most popular general periodical in the nation. He wrote in part to apologize for contributing to the vilification of Crowther. In a mixed review of *Bonnie and Clyde*, he had commented: "One reviewer, in an almost unprecedented display of overkill, issued three separate and distinct attacks—for historical inaccuracy, excessive violence, moral turpitude, and, I guess, bad breath." Trying to be diplomatic, Schickel "invited" all critics to join him in the middle ground. In his private note to Crowther, Schickel also tried to make peace. He told the retiring critic that he was sorry to see him moving away from daily reviews. "For the rest of us, who looked forward to testing our opinions against your [*sic*] every morning, things won't quite be the same." Schickel acknowledged that he didn't always agree with Crowther and had "even heard that you were upset by something of mine where I expressed that disagreement." But he also wanted to let Crowther know that he appreciated his critical integrity. "I think you have set a standard for sound moral judgment and personal probity that all of us who practice criticism must respect, admire and thank you for, since I believe that example has made all our lots a little easier."[38]

Near the close of his letter, Schickel acknowledged, much to Crowther's satisfaction, what the critic had been trying to do for years. "Since you did so much to bring the screen to its present state of freedom I feel strongly that you ought to stay around and actively help in the effort to see that that freedom is responsibly used." He then added, perhaps a bit sheepishly, "I hope our little clash over 'Bonnie and Clyde' does not make you think that I disagree with you generally and I certainly hope you found no personal malice in what I said about that film."[39]

Crowther wrote back a few days later: "It makes me feel very good to know that you perceived and respected what I have always tried to be and do." He told Schickel that the young critic was one of the few, "the very few," critics whom he admired, and that he was "distressed that so many special pleaders and personal poseurs have come along in recent years and generated a kind of film criticism that seems to be intended only for the elucidation and fortification of very limited and biased groups." When Crowther turned to the trouble over *Bonnie and Clyde*, he explained that he found nothing inherently wrong with the debate over the movie—"Critical disagreement and disputation has been fine." What had bothered him was "the bitter name-calling and the obvious attempts to use this controversy to discredit other critics, namely me!" That was why, Crowther added, he was "unhappy that you gave me a little person jab. . . . It was not that we disagreed, but that a critic of your intelligence and fairness should confuse the issue with a slap at me. However," Crowther quickly transitioned, "that is very minor." He closed expressing his sincere hope that he and Schickel, as the younger critic had suggested, would have more chances to meet and "continue our explorations in the realms of films."[40]

They did, according to Robert Steele of the *Catholic World*. Steele recounted a conversation he overheard between Crowther and Schickel regarding the critical flare-up over *Bonnie and Clyde*. Schickel argued that "a filmmaker has a right and a responsibility to reflect his times and that because our times are violent, there is no choice but to present violence in films." Not surprisingly, Crowther did not dispute that basic assumption but did suggest that the film went "beyond the bounds of good taste and judgment in the way it presented these killers. I don't want to sound like a Puritan, but I think it is our responsibility as critics to call the turn on of so many pictures that appear to be in a popular mood of liberated young people. They feel that the establishment has failed us and that they must be permitted to have their own values. Leadership and responsibility cannot be expected of very young critics. They are unaware of the wars we have gone through in order to liberate the screen, and . . . for the liberation of honest values. *Sound of Music* is like *Bonnie and Clyde* in being close to a kind of immorality. *Sound of Music* gives a romanticized, sugary, unreal notion of ideal behavior." Schickel concurred: *The Sound of Music* had to be damned. Crowther concluded: "Getting moral content into a picture is not the responsibility of the code or of censorship, but it is the responsibility of those who make pictures. And it is our responsibility to tell them when we think they are going wrong. The film critic is performing a function akin to a pastor. He is a counselor of a community about the values of a picture." Schickel refused to concede Crowther's fundamental point:

"The film critic has no business letting his morality shape his criticism. The critic should judge a film *vis a vis* other films of a comparable genre and not according to his moral preferences or prejudices."[41]

More than any other participant in New York City's movie culture, Crowther personified the central dilemma of the postcensor world. When Crowther was shouted down, told that he was irrelevant, his silence was profound. The fundamental problem of culture should be how to maintain and encourage debate. Crowther had built a career on the premise that intellectual exploration produced more intelligent discussion. He worked early in his career to free movie culture from conservative forces that wanted to shut down discussion on movies through a system of codes and censors. Late in his career he struggled against radical sensibilities that saw no point in discussing the implications of movie violence once the public had come "alive" to it. He played the middle, a place where most moviegoers reside. Yet Crowther failed to convince his audience that a vital center needed to persist in order for any debate to remain vibrant. His fate was to be disappointed by his audience's poor taste and juvenile attention spans.

In 1968, Crowther gave an address to the William Allen White Seminar at the University of Kansas. His remarks revealed a critic with sharp insight into the potential and nature of motion pictures, insight that was difficult to see in his daily reviews or even his longer Sunday pieces because, it seems to me, he wrote in an age during which film critics simply didn't assume that they had the right to ruminate. Reflecting on the controversy generated by *Bonnie and Clyde*, he had some advice for a generation that had grown to believe its own hype. "It is unwise and deluding to tackle movies with the idealistic thought that we can find in their commercial organization and production some ardent impulse to make them flow into forms that will have social purposes and values of an educational and soundly humanizing sort." Movies were made to entertain, engineered by people who wanted to make money. "Keeping the natives contented in their established environments has always been a function of merchants, as well as governments. And surely exercise of the privilege of seducing one's fellow man—or woman—with distracting enticements is respected in a free society."[42]

Crowther had never been an apologist for Hollywood, and he was not about to become one of the many critics who bought into the almost fanatical excitement generated by second-rate films. Historically, he noted with some consternation, what had been expected of movies was greatly out of proportion to what movies could or should ever deliver. "The movies have been candidly expected to be everything from a truant officer to an Art." But by the nature of the market in which movies existed, they could not escape the trap of becoming a reflection of what was perceived to be popular, rather than significant, in society. Movies traveled through an endless cycle—from producing magic to creating myths (mostly middle class) to ultimately being boring. "Caught between the fundamental cultural pressure of the mass audience for entertainment that is fashioned on myth and the constant demands of a galaxy of theaters for more and more product that they can merchandise, the never too intensely philosophical filmmakers have been prevented from exercising their skills on precisely true or bravely penetrating dramas. They have been pushed too often in the direction of mediocrity and thus eventual monotony."[43]

Crowther related his admiration for the ability of Ingmar Bergman's films to probe the darkness in humanity, whether sexual or violent. "If any one charge of malfeasance and culturally criminal negligence can be brought against the movies, it is that they have failed to present us and pervade us with realization of our true selves and of the world in which we live." Crowther liked Bergman's films because the Swedish filmmaker made audiences feel uncomfortable. When watching one of his films, moviegoers had to consider their own insecurities and faults in a way that was complicated and rarely trivial. Crowther did not object to scenes of sex and violence. What worried him was how audiences typically reveled in, and even found it heroic to praise, certain types of cinematic sex and violence. To Crowther, movies had remained an escape from the real pain that affected the world, even though the screen had grown more realistic. Unfortunately, near the end of his career, Crowther was the one being told to "get real."[44]

It was such logic he used to make a comparison of audience reactions to *Bonnie and Clyde* and *In Cold Blood*. The former, Crowther thought, had "two rollicking, fun-loving youngsters who just happen to rob banks and kill people," but who were "allowed to be part of the current myth of liberated and just possibly misguided youth. On the other hand, very few people will commit themselves—not even their

minds—to the ugly pair of dark, inexplicable murders that are represented so accurately and relentlessly in the film *In Cold Blood.*" The
difference in reception came from the difference in the art of each picture: *Bonnie and Clyde* was palatable myth; it made the audience feel
romantic and sentimental in a way that revealed little of the darkness
that would need to exist in order for someone to commit a murder. *In
Cold Blood* was similar to Bergman films, Crowther believed, in the
way it revealed the worst aspects of human nature and therefore made
the audience feel uncomfortable by forcing it to imagine what lurked
beneath the surface of any one individual watching the movie or on the
streets outside the theater.[45]

But what did Crowther think of his own stance against *Bonnie and
Clyde?* At the conclusion of his talk, Crowther revealed a side of himself that few critics, apparently, had recognized. Crowther recounted
how he had gone to see *Bonnie and Clyde* for what he believed was the
third time and was again dismayed by audience reaction. Some young
men around him began "stomping their feet and squealing gleefully
when the policemen were shot in the ambush scene and . . . when
Bonnie and Clyde were mowed down." Poking fun at himself, he offered: "Perhaps, I am like the husband of the lady" who went to see
the sexy *And God Created Woman* and was shocked by it—"absolutely
shocked. Indeed, he was not only shocked the first time he saw it, but
he was shocked the second time, too!" It was, despite the nasty little
fight over it, only a movie.[46]

8

The Failure of Porno Chic

IN 1965, BOSLEY Crowther had observed that the category of obscenity was the last frontier that the movies could not venture into. When they did, it was up to judges, rather than the old moral guardians and official censors, to impose standards of taste. At the time, that seemed like progress. "The difference is," Crowther pointed out, "that now the charges of offense must be aired in open court and the public is given some inkling of what it is being protected from." But he also knew that simply breaching these new boundaries had consequences. Thus, he wondered: "Is it merely the depiction of actions that violate sensibilities? . . . Or is it some real and positive projection of corruption and degeneracy that imperils the health of individuals and the welfare of society?"[1]

In the absence of censors, the courts practiced cultural criticism and, in effect, presided over the criminalization of culture. When it came to pornography many commentators and judges agreed that they "knew it when they saw it," but of course that was not a legally useful definition. Thus, the U.S. Supreme Court attempted in *Roth v. United States* (1957) to rebuild cultural standards. Justice William Brennan, writing for the majority in the 6 to 3 decision, defined as illegal material that was "utterly without redeeming social importance." The test to determine if something met that definition was "whether to the average person, applying contemporary community standards, the dominant theme of the material taken as a whole appeals to prurient interests." Ambiguous at best, the notion of community standards quite often became a target of derision by those who rejected it because such a thing was difficult to identify and by those who believed that such a notion was precisely what art was made to transgress. And yet with each new case that tested the ambiguous boundary between offensive and obscene culture it became apparent that defending something controversial was often a less than honorable venture. Thus, as Crowther intimated, it was not entirely clear which side had more to lose—society or its culture. That irony, however, was lost in a movie culture that made it "chic" to take a stand in defense of dubious art.[2]

The case that began this unfortunate ruse was a Swedish film, *I Am Curious—Yellow*. In late 1966, U.S. customs officials in New York confiscated a print of the film that had been imported by its American distributor, Grove Press—a publishing house that had become notorious for distributing sexualized novels and magazines. The trial that ensued became a cause célèbre in New York's movie culture, for it not only involved many of the issues that tested the limits of the new era of screen freedom, it was defended in court by many of the city's intellectuals and film critics. Because this was the beginning of the postcensor era, Grove Press was allowed to introduce expert testimony in its defense, a tactic that up until that point had been nearly impossible. The courts needed help distinguishing artistic obscenity from inartistic obscenity. If this situation sounds a bit ridiculous, it was. When courts must determine taste and culture, something has gone seriously wrong with taste and culture.

Curious (as it was known) was ostensibly a story about contemporary youth challenging social, political, and sexual conventions—but it was also a foreign film rather than merely a naughty nudie-cutie from sexploitation filmmakers such as Radley Metzger and Russ Meyer. The film's content, though, went well beyond a few shots of naked breasts and buttocks. It contained unusually graphic sex scenes between the heroine and her patronizing boyfriend. However, the actors did not look like porn stars; nor did the sound track include the usual heavy breathing and expressions of unbridled ecstasy that moviegoers would in years hence expect as part of the necessary atmosphere to "heighten" the enjoyment of the film. Rather, *Curious* posed a curious problem: it struck many as a very serious film, with content that might also be seen as a little smutty. The very serious film critic and defense expert John Simon characterized the story as "a young girl's search for identity in contemporary Sweden, in the course of which she rummages around in all accepted values: political, social, and sexual." As for those scenes that were certain to draw audiences, he thought that this quest to find herself was "supplemented with her quest for a good sex life, [which was] handled with frankness and also with wit and style. The sexual problems are shown as relating to the other ones in the process of self-discovery."[3]

The trial was something of a circus. Over the course of four days in the historic month of May 1968, both sides paraded "experts" who testified by either praising or condemning the social significance of the movie. The prosecution, represented by federal attorneys Robert M. Morgenthau, the future district attorney of New York County, and Lawrence W. Schilling, called only one witness, the Reverend Dan M. Potter, executive director of the Protestant Council of New York City and an emerging leader of an antiporn campaign in the city. Attorneys for the defense, Edward De Grazia and Richard T. Gallen, veterans of legal battles against obscenity statutes, raised the profile of their case by calling some fairly prominent New Yorkers, including novelist Norman Mailer; film critics Stanley Kauffmann, John Simon, Hollis Alpert, and Paul Zimmerman; the Reverend Dr. Howard Moody of the Judson Memorial Church in New York City; and an assortment of faculty from psychology and sociology departments.

The testimonies achieved an entertaining quality as quite prominent and accomplished men discussed the finer points of naked Swedes engaging in floppy, flabby sex. One has to keep in mind that this was an era before the massive proliferation of cinematic pornography made every sex film seem basically the same. *Curious* played as a radical film that appeared to push the limits of cinematic sex for political reasons, not simply to make an easy buck. Norman Mailer told the court that he had "thought a lot about the problem of sexuality in movies." In fact, he admitted that he was "obsessed with the problem and concerned with the problem and devoted to the problem in one way or another for twenty years of writing novels." He was, therefore, worried that *Curious* would have the effect of moving society closer to filming actual sexual intercourse, which would, if defended as art, lead to the "debasement of the sexual act." But somewhat to his surprise, Mailer was "moved" by *Curious*. And while he thought "the picture moved into terribly dangerous ground," he concluded that it was "a profoundly moral movie. I felt it was one of the most important motion pictures I have ever seen in my life because it attempts to deal with the nature of modern reality, the extraordinary complexity of modern reality."[4]

The Reverend Potter could not find much complexity in the depiction of sexual intercourse on the balustrade of Sweden's royal palace, with one of the king's guards looking on. When asked whether the sex in that scene could be considered "sanctified," Potter responded: "It is the most ridiculous thing I ever heard of. . . . I can't imagine throwing a girl down, out on a street someplace, or, as in this instance, in front of a building, and virtually equivalent [sic] to raping her, being considered sanctified."[5]

But was it defensible as art? Stanley Kauffmann contended the woman's sexual behavior "rings perfectly true to me for the character shown." Those notorious scenes, Kauffmann argued, had to be provocative if they were "to be equally consistent and bow no more to convention on the sexual scale than [the director] does on any other, either of cinematic technique or political-social approach." Here at long last was a movie in which the sex actually played a role in the film, rather than operating as an awkward interlude or as eye candy. Hollis Alpert believed that the sexual honesty of the film was "of very great importance" and was "one of the reasons why [he] was [in court] to talk about it." He explained that he had been "concerned . . . with dishonesty in the portrayal of sex and sexual relationships over a great many years." Like Mailer, he also seemed to have been ruminating on the topic for a while. "I think this is one of the very few [films] which has dealt with the theme and the subject with great candor and honesty, and, to a certain extent, artistry." For these reasons, he told the court that he found the film "very important." Kauffmann explained to the jury that what director Vilgot Sjöman wanted was to blur "the line between what is fact and what is fiction. What used to be thought of as a clear dividing line, an iron barrier between art and life," Kauffmann explained, "should go or can go or has gone, and we are not really aware of it yet."[6]

The problem for the jury, however, was that it was charged with holding that line. So there the jurors sat, trying to determine whether it was obscene when a woman kissed the genitalia of a man (even if it was in the branches of Sweden's oldest tree), or whether the depictions of oral sex were socially significant because the director attempted to relate them to "oral" protests and "oral" psychological fixations. On 24 May, the jury gave its answer, finding that the film met the legal definition of obscenity. The "people" had spoken.

But not definitively. A little over a half year later, *Curious* won a major victory when the jury decision was overturned by a federal court of appeals. In a piece published in the *New York Times*, John Simon characterized the fight as one between sophistication and philistinism. Simon dismissed the jury because, he argued, it included everybody but a panel of the filmmaker's peers. Not one person who sat in judgment of the film was of that most precious of ages—between twenty-one and thirty-two—and few had any intellectual connection to larger questions of art and morality, other than they were residents of the New York area. He noted that a history professor from Columbia was dismissed by the prosecution, thus leaving an editor from *Reader's Digest* as the lone "intellectual" on the jury. "A film and its maker that have artistic and intellectual pretensions are thus entitled to be pronounced upon by a panel of artists and intellectuals," Simon contended. "So I would argue that neither the said jury nor the three circuit judges are the proper choice of arbiters." He also made the dangerous assertion that if "it is all up to the average man [to decide such cases], then it is precisely the large masses that must decide, and 12 men and women . . . are *not* the large masses." Here was the ultimate corruption of the democratic option—let the market figure out what the masses want. Frustrated by any attempt to protect the public through the work of "higher authorities," whether they be judges or a rating system, Simon placed his trust in that most alluring of arbiters, the will of the people.[7]

Critics Vincent Canby and Rex Reed speculated on what that was. In parallel columns, the critics took shots at each other and hinted at the larger significance of this case. For Canby, the experience of being able to see *Curious* illustrated a hypocrisy in American culture. Americans publicly declared their objections to sexualized society all the while lining up to see it and—here was the kicker—never admitting their lust. He called the film a "wise, serious, sometimes deadpannedly funny movie about the politics of life—and of moviemaking." And he explained that even though the movie was *not* his favorite kind because it did not appeal to him "on all levels," he felt compelled to defend it.[8]

In his defense of the film, Canby offered some dubious rationalizations. He argued that using sex in this movie to sell it was no different from using singing parts in *The Sound of Music*. Furthermore, he concluded that the moral opponents of *Curious* had to be "right-wing moviegoer[s]" who had deluded themselves by buying the sugarcoated world of old Hollywood. Thus, just as Bosley Crowther had been labeled a new censor for voicing objections to *Bonnie and Clyde,* a person who was on the "wrong" side of the debate over *Curious* could get labeled a conservative. Canby also observed, more astutely, that *Curious,* though not a landmark film in the same way as Warhol's *The Chelsea Girls,* most likely marked yet another stage in "a revolution in movie mores of really stunning rapidity and effect." He observed that the sex scenes were real enough to make one wonder what it was like for the actors to perform them, and to imagine—without much trouble—that in the future these new conventions would most likely be broken. How right he was.[9]

Rex Reed had evidently grown tired of too many cocktail party defenses of *Curious.* He was in no mood to stand on the barricades for what he considered part of the "trash explosion" or for a movie that was at the "bottom of the garbage dump." There are few things more pleasurable in movie culture than watching a critic pan a film; and Reed did not disappoint. He unleashed a critical barrage: "This genuinely vile and disgusting Swedish meatball is pseudo-pornography at its ugliest and least titillating, and pseudo-sociology at its lowest point of technical ineptitude." What most "distressed" Reed was the popular reaction to *Curious*—the movie was a hit. People lined up to see it; they even asked the driver of a cab he was in for directions to the art theater that was running it.[10]

Yet he found it criminally boring. "I don't think it should be seen by any people of *any* age with I.Q.'s of 25 or over," Reed roared. It wasn't that he supported censorship or couldn't appreciate porn, he just hated the pretentious posturing that went along with defending porn as social comment. The audience was duped and was allowing itself to be duped, Reed charged, by an ad campaign and a controversy that made a bad, dirty movie better and more sexy than it was. He pointed out that theaters in the city that were showing it were even taking advance orders for tickets and charging as much as $4.50 a seat. Shaking with frustration at the exposure the film was receiving, Reed thundered that it was smut that audiences wanted, but what they would get in *Curious* was such a "simpleminded, badly photographed, crudely directed textbook sociology with pretentious overtones of seriousness that they could easily stay home and make the same movie themselves." It was the worst form of hybrid moviemaking—a sex film that pretended to be something else. "All this pretentious, revolting, cheapjack Grove Press sideshow proves . . . is that there are as many stupid and provincial no-talents trying to make a fast buck in Sweden as there are in every other part of the world. They're just more devious about it in Sweden; they call it art there."[11]

Reed recalled seeing a preview of the film with other critics. Several "talked loudly back to the screen, moaned, and made other gratifying noises. Some even dozed off." All, according to Reed, were happy to walk out of the theater when the ordeal was over, even Canby. How-ever, the abuse was not over; the projectionist had discovered a mis-placed reel. The critics were ushered back into the room and shown what Reed described as sequences that seemed impossible or simply unnecessary to place in the film as a whole—none of it made sense anyway. Reed warned that the director had included "Yellow" in the title as a reference to the Swedish flag; thus, there was another film, *I A`m Curious—Blue*, which was "somewhere, in some outhouse . . . waiting to be unleashed on us all." He would make it a point to miss the next color-coded Swedish film.[12]

Letters poured in to the *Times*. One self-professed "old lady" was happy with Canby's positive review of a movie she thought put "good old-fashioned sex back in its proper niche." Another praised Reed for revealing what she thought was "out and out pornography covered up with a little artistic photography." Another, from rural Massachusetts, confirmed what the rest of the country probably thought about New York: "We country folk, of whom America is really made, will not stand in line to see pictures made by neurotic Swedes. The only places where people flock to these voyeuristic savagings of sex are, it seems, cities full of savage, sick, neurotic people who no longer regard sex as anything human and personal." Film historian Bernard Dick wrote to critique both reviews. He claimed that each "critic has told his special audi-ence exactly what it wanted to hear." What both missed, Dick wrote, was that most halfway sophisticated moviegoers found the film hollow and soulless. It was "worse than pornographic," he concluded, "it is a frighteningly loveless film."[13]

And that was why the disturbing aspect of the movie was how its box office appeal determined its defense. It made a ton of money. *News-week* reported that the line to buy tickets outside the Cinema 57 Ren-dezvous started to form at 10:00 in the morning, with "well-dressed, healthy-looking people" willing to pay $3 a ticket to see the sexiest art film in the city. In its first week it broke all records for an art film—if in fact it could be categorized as one—by grossing $79,101. The Cinema Rendezvous had prestigious neighbors; it was near Carnegie Hall, and even though it sat only 587 people, it outgrossed the film playing at 6,200-seat Radio City Music Hall for two days in a row. Such success in New York City attracted other suitors. A film distributor in Texas told the magazine he wanted the film because he could make $2 million just in that state alone. "This can no longer be called a film—it's a social phenomenon," said another distributor.[14]

That phenomenon was far more than simply commercial, though, in New York City. The city's movie culture seemed like a culture trapped in its own sophistication, unable to distinguish art from porn. Writers in *Newsweek* suggested that this dilemma was "a matter of national concern. . . . The floodgates have opened one by one and the inundation is now a matter of fact, in the hinterlands as well as the big cities." Yet all the examples that made this situation notable came from New York, from magazines such as *Screw* and the *New York Review of Sex* to serious works of art such as Philip Roth's novel *Portnoy's Complaint*. Perhaps American culture was becoming New York–ized. If that was the case, the country had to grapple with a bewildering development—the intellectualization of porn.[15]

In 1970, *Screw* magazine and promoter Ken Gaul launched the short-lived New York Erotic Film Festival. It began on Friday, 5 November, running through 12 December in Greenwich Village theaters, including the Cine Malibu, Agee I and II, and the Cinema Village. With more than fifty international movies at a price of $3 a person—all nonprofit—the event played upon the name and the elevation of movies made possible by the growing significance of the New York Film Festival. The organizers had managed to convince the likes of Gore Vidal, Betty Dodson (an erotic painter), Andy Warhol, Al Goldstein, Karen Sperling, and WPLJ disc jockey Alex Bennett to be judges. The *New York Post* reported that the youngish Gaul had been a onetime managing editor at *Screw* and was interested in establishing "erotic film as a valid art form free from the money-loving embraces of exploitive theaters." Festival organizers considered more than 125 films, a detail that a few reporters thought illustrated a similarity between Gaul's sex fest and what was happening uptown at Lincoln Center. The opening gala was held at the Village Gate and attended by celebrities such as Anthony Perkins and Candy Darling. Topless dancers and loops of pornographic films set the mood, while a flasher wandered through the crowd "exposing himself while the freak chic tried not to notice."[16]

Of course, the festival caused some controversy. New York City police officers raided a screening of Fred Baker's *Room Service* at the Cine Malibu and Downtown Village. The organizers and some filmmakers disagreed over whose responsibility it was to defend the right to exhibit such fare. And a women's liberation group picketed the Agee I and II house on Broadway, though, according to *Variety*, the picketers didn't seem to know exactly what they were against. Even with such resistance, audiences poured out the first week, registering 10,900 paid admissions for $32,700 at the box office. Advertising for the event was widespread, even though, *Variety* noted, "the *Daily News* balked at the word 'erotic' but finally went with it, eliminating the photo of the copulating couple. The *Post* removed the man figure from the photo leaving the woman looking rather lonely [but] the *Times* offered no resistance."[17]

Variety concluded: "At the very least, the festival proves that a number of young filmmakers are turning their talents to something other than the usual tales of their first affairs at New York University." Moreover, the judges took their work to heart. Vidal saw every movie and called his jury together to discuss the entries. Jonas Mekas didn't think much of the festival but added: "an Erotic movie is an arty porno movie intended to be shown at film festivals. That's about it, that does it." I find it revealing that Mekas passed up an opportunity to explain how his battle over *Flaming Creatures* was either different from or had been corrupted by Gaul's film festival. Perhaps he thought the differences were obvious enough, though. Mekas concluded: "The only change I'd consider making in this concise definition, is perhaps replacing the word 'arty' with the word 'artsy.'"[18]

What made the New York Erotic Film Festival significant was the aura of intellectual legitimacy that seemed to envelop this issue of obscenity. Bernard Weinraub summed up this odd situation in a brief editorial entitled "Obscenity or Art? A Stubborn Issue." A stubborn issue? Really? Was it really that hard to tell the difference between obscenity and art? In New York in the late 1960s and early 1970s, it had become completely unclear what the laws were and, more disturbingly, what constituted art. "What standards does New York apply," Weinraub asked, "to deal with the delicate and proliferating phenomenon of erotic films and books, sexually oriented newspapers and stage presentations that shock some and delight others?" He had hinted at the central problem: how would a city evaluate expressions in the public realm without stepping on personal standards of taste? It was a conundrum of democratic culture, but only if the idea of democratic participation merely entailed giving every individual the privilege to veto any attempt to propose a set of community standards. In this sense, New York City was the ultimate spoiler of any scheme to determine legal or artistic obscenity. The city and by extension the country seemed destined to replay the same debate over what constituted obscenity, art, and taste, as if these questions had never been raised before. Weniraub reported that even though the police had begun to crack down on the most explicit examples of smut in the city, the city's chief of police had to admit that even he was unsure exactly how and when to take action.[19]

Into this ambiguous breach strode Andy Warhol yet again. In August 1969, New York City criminal court judge Arthur Goldberg authorized the arrest of the staff of the Garrick Theater on Bleeker Street in the Village for exhibiting Andy Warhol's *Blue Movie*. In their report, the arresting officers listed the depiction of "separate sex acts" as the reason for police action. The following weekend, *New York Times* critic Vincent Canby asked why anyone was surprised that Warhol, "that bored, pale pace-setter," showed actual sexual intercourse in "the kind of cold, clinical detail that has heretofore been the exclusive subject matter of stag movies." Based on the precedent set by *Curious*, Canby was pretty sure that if *Blue Movie* reached the federal appeals level it, too, would set a precedent that would make it difficult to take action against other films like it. "Everything that Warhol does—even his being bored—seems somehow relevant and inevitable." Canby mused, "He is the manifestation of a society, or, at least, a portion of a society, that is going to hell in a handcar and determined to do it with a certain Pop style and élan."[20]

In *Blue Movie*, Viva and costar Louis Waldron engage in passionless sex while having a conversation. The dialogue in the film, Canby suggested, seemed designed to capture the distinction that made *Curious* legal. The film included a program note that declared it was "a film about Vietnam and what we can do about it." Canby called Warhol's movie "a cheerful stag film, rather prettily photographed in a greenish-blue color, in which the performers actually do what has only been simulated in more conventional films." As had happened many times in the past, the theater employees, rather than the filmmakers, were arrested for showing the film, as if the ticket takers had commissioned the work from Warhol. When faced with the problem of whom to bust for peddling smut, the artist and the audience were somehow protected by their impregnable defense of taste (or tastelessness), leaving the lowest-level middlemen open to prosecution. For this reason, Canby stated that he couldn't "take the arrest very seriously . . . if it is designed to protect the morals of the adult public. It's impossible to walk very far in any direction in this city and not feel that the city, if not the country, is collapsing in mindless second-rateness." He also concluded that while he couldn't take Warhol's film seriously—he didn't find much redeeming social value in it—in the context of the other trash available in midtown Manhattan, *Blue Movie* was a work of art. "In a society where tastelessness and vulgarity are inalienable rights, I'm not sure that prohibiting an adult's access to obscenity is not unconstitutional."[21]

In September, a three-judge panel heard the case against Warhol's movie, though it did not hear from the artist himself. Defense attorney Joel Weinberg was allowed to introduce expert testimony. He called on Parker Tyler to explain what the sex in *Blue Movie* meant—in case it was not clear to the judges. Tyler offered that the film showed "attitudes of the cool world toward sex . . . an indifference to emotions, everything in a cool way." Though the film did appeal to prurient interests, it was too cool to care—it was an ironic wink at the commercialization of sex. So where was the crime in that? The judges didn't care, either, finding the film obscene and dismissing the expert testimony as useless because it failed to persuade them that what they had seen was anything but sex between a man and a woman. Joel Weinberg dismissed the experts who sat on the bench. As the attorney for other noble causes, such as those of the theaters around Times Square that exhibited such fine films as *Hot Erotic Dreams* and *Baby, Light My Fire*, he took what he must have figured was an irreproachable stand against the authority of the judges. In this Warhol moment, he argued, "people see in motion pictures what they want to see, nobody's an expert." Why bother with courts, laws, codes, and critics? Fair enough. But what were the implications of such a stance when considered in the context of a mass art?[22]

Andrew Sarris found the whole messy debate over sexualized movies to be a pathetic distraction from serious movie culture. Sarris was a self-proclaimed auteur critic, meaning that he was a close watcher of films—he cataloged them as a botanist keeps records of the minute differences in tulips. In this way, Sarris had begun a revolution of his own. He was the man who popularized the idea that directors were artists and that they controlled the destiny of films as writers dictated texts. Sarris was an adept student of film history, having watched hundreds of films in order to highlight cinematic masters.

In a column for *Sight and Sound*, Sarris attempted to make sense of the state of movie culture in his beloved city. "Apart from the rhetorical reflex of defending the artist against society on every possible occasion, it is difficult to become concerned, much less inspired, by the issues involved in *Blue Movie, I am Curious—Yellow* and all the other cheerlessly carnal exercises in film-making." Because Sarris was such a purist, he was the perfect critic to pop the bubble of pretentious explanations surrounding obscene movies. He understood movies as art, and found most of the sex films of the late 1960s and early 1970s to be absolutely awful. "The evolution of the sexploitation movie in America deserves a separate chapter heading, though mainly sociological and only marginally aesthetic," he wrote. One can almost imagine him arguing with his fellow critics who had denounced the policing of sex films as if the fate of the free world depended on it. Sarris was unable to get very excited by either the issues involved or the material included in these films. He asked: "What has this to do with Art or Truth or even Realism? Not very much thus far." Sarris suggested: "By any reasonably objective standard, the movie fare of 1939 is, in retrospect, more interesting and more exciting than that of 1969." One could almost hear his colleagues groan; after all, he revealed a preference for films made at the height of censorship.[23]

Sarris suggested that the new openness of film would not make the medium more socially significant or intellectually honest. It would, though, make it more difficult for "performers lacking ideal proportions" to find consistent work and stardom. In fact, truth and honesty were nowhere to be found on the free screen:

> What has happened instead is that one set of fantasies has been replaced by another. And the change is *less political than com-*

mercial. In this context, the increasing frankness of the screen implies a social malaise it is under no obligation to explore. We are back again to [Michelangelo] Antonioni's commercially convenient diagnosis of eroticism as the disease of our age. Of course, we are all sick, and our society is sick, and our system is sick, and we can't wait to take off all our clothes, and cross-copulate and wife-swap and engage in polymorphous perverse diversions. But contrary to the expectations of optimistic liberals that the public would soon tire of libidinous license, audiences continue to prefer Antonioni's explicit disease to his implicit cure.[24]

Sarris had explained the tragedy of postwar movie culture: in the rush to free itself from restrictions, it also became free of thought. All along moviegoers and critics thought the censors were the enemies, when in fact it was the audience—or, rather, its taste—that was the ultimate problem. Movies were not an abstraction, and neither was the act of seeing them. The old regimes of taste and control had operated under an assumption that public culture was not a zone for complete freedom—commercial, political, or cultural. Yet making the notion of freedom—simplistically drawn—an end in itself was ultimately a naive act. Because of that, Sarris smartly concluded, "the censors allowed us nothing when we asked for so little, and so now it is only fitting that we allow the censors nothing no matter how base the screen becomes. There can be no compromise with censorship even when there is regret for some of the lost charm of repression and innocence."[25]

So in the absence of censorship, what happened? The greatest casualty was that the ability to speak in subtle tones, to be ironic in a genuine sense, had been replaced by the desire to be both outrageous and outraged. It was in an atmosphere of reactionary culture that *Deep Throat* emerged.

In the early 1970s, the New York Police Department began using hidden cameras to bust theaters, peep shows, sex shows, massage parlors, and prostitutes. New York's mayor, John V. Lindsay, ordered such sweeps after his attempt to run "Fun City" as a cosmopolitan experiment, hoping that the flowering of many cultural expressions would illustrate the richness of life in the Big Apple, had failed. As Lindsay's biographer Vincent Cannato explains, "During the late 1960s and early 1970s, many New Yorkers felt their city was spiraling into hopeless-ness and decay." Many residents blamed Lindsay for his lax approach to law and order, which seemed to encourage the exploitation of the city's freedoms. The mayor attempted to regain some control by ap-pointing the Times Square Enforcement Coordination Committee in 1972. It was one of many such organizations emerging from Lindsay's administration that were supposed to enforce the law without necessar-ily appearing too heavy-handed.[26]

In August 1972, in a sweep of the Times Square area, police con-fiscated a print of a film and advertising paraphernalia from the World Theater. Murray Schumach of the *Times* reported that the raid was "something new in Broadway matinees, a form of street theater that drew an audience that would have overflowed any Broadway the-ater. Wooden barricades had to be set up to hold back the crowd that watched the police climbing ladders to rip down the signs with ham-mers, hooks, pliers and iron claws." The movie that caused all the com-motion was *Deep Throat*.[27]

The trial over *Deep Throat* would not begin until December 1972, six months after the film premiered in New York and six months into its run as a commercial phenomenon. Al Goldstein of *Screw* told an interviewer that he "felt like a prophet" when he predicted that *Deep Throat* would be a hit. He made his prediction in his magazine in a review entitled "Gulp." In June 1972, *Variety* reported that prerelease publicity "was hot enough to pack the lunch-time show on opening day at N.Y.'s World Theatre. While 'Deep Throat' doesn't quite live up to its advance reputation as the 'Ben-Hur' of porno-pix, it is a supe-rior piece which stands a head above the current competition." Mort Sheinman of the *Christian Science Monitor* ran a playful review in which he speculated that the movie was "a bold thrust forward in the history of contemporary cinema, plunging deeply into areas seldom, if ever, explored on screen." Talk of the movie appeared in a disparate array of outlets, from *Harper's Bazaar* and *Women's Wear Daily* to *Play-boy* and *Screw*. Writing for the *Village Voice*, Blair Sobol explained that she "*had* to go," especially because she had never seen a pornographic film. "It was part of my higher education," she insisted. "Besides, I al-ready knew of one consciousness raising group formed by women who had seen the movie and were so taken by Linda's technique that they now meet twice a week and discuss the movie in detail." The star—or

victim—of the movie (depending on the political stance one took) was
Linda Lovelace, whose signature sex act gave the film its title and, according to Sobol, its social relevance. Archer Winsten, writing from his
vantage point at the New York Post, offered a belated review of the film
because "public curiosity, not to say demand, has forced the issue."
No stranger to controversial films, Winsten found that Deep Throat
delivered what one might expect but did so with such repetition that it
became an outright bore. "Even as shock it wears off, leaving behind
a sense of wonder that the human animal has this capacity for experimentation and the documentation of it."[28]

The New York Times recorded the details of the trial. Ralph Blumenthal and Paul Montgomery reported on the arguments advanced
to determine whether Deep Throat was obscene according to New York
City law. The trial was unique because a lone judge was to decide
whether the defendant, Mature Enterprises, Inc., was guilty of profit-
ing from illegal smut. At first, charges had been brought against the
usual suspects, the cashier and the manager of the theater. But the city
changed its strategy and decided to go after the corporation instead.
Not only did that bring the prospect of a bigger fine, it avoided the
necessity for a jury. Former New York City license commissioner Joel
J. Tyler, a Manhattan criminal court judge, heard the case.[29]

Like the trial involving Curious, this one, too, provided entertaining
moments, as the serious space of American law turned into a hearing
on porn. Paul Montgomery attended a screening of the film, this time
sanctioned by the court, in a room provided by the Loews Corporation
on Fifth Avenue. Members of the press watched as Judge Tyler and the
attorneys took notes on a film that, by Montgomery's count, contained
"15 acts of sexual intercourse, including seven of fellatio and four of
cunnilingus." The defense hoped the court would understand that the
film was merely "a satire on contemporary sexual mores." One might
have said the same thing of the screening as well.[30]

The courtroom in which the case was heard was a converted store-
room off a "noisy corridor frequented by prostitutes and others being
arraigned." Herbert Kassner represented Mature Entertainment as
one of the city's foremost defenders of obscenity. He and his partner
Seymour Detsky had faced off against the city's officials throughout
the late 1960s and early 1970s. Assistant District Attorney William O.
Purcell tried the case for the city. In a thirty-one-page brief, Kassner

made clear his strategy, arguing that all judges and all juries needed to hear expert testify about obscenity. He told Judge Tyler that he needed "expert help . . . to determine whether material is pornographic." Tyler allowed it.[31]

The court heard from five "experts" over the course of the ten-day trial. As with the experts who testified in the trial involving *Curious*, nothing of much significance emerged from their statements, and, not surprisingly, the testimonies had little effect on Judge Tyler's eventual ruling.[32]

Novelist Larry McMurty offered perhaps the most incisive testimony, in the pages of *New York* magazine. On a Sunday afternoon in 1973, he strolled over to Times Square to catch a screening of *Deep Throat*. He noted that the audience was mostly middle-aged couples, well dressed and seemingly unfazed by the high price of admission. "It was to an unusual degree an audience without a sense of shame," he observed. "Unusual because the atmosphere in skin flicks or smut films is usually thick with guilt and frustration, even in these liberated days." Censors and sensibilities no longer posed a challenge to the cynical minds of moviegoers. McMurty joked that rather than shame he found "a group apathy of a weight I had previously only experienced in certain classrooms. . . . To this audience, at least, *Throat* choked, and many, like myself, left long before it was over, $5 or no."[33]

When the trial of *Deep Throat* came to an inglorious end on 3 January 1973, Judge Tyler told reporters that it was the longest case he had heard in his four years as a criminal court judge. On 1 March 1973, Tyler handed down a decision that many observers had anticipated. He declared: "Deep Throat—a nadir of decadence—is indisputably obscene by any legal measurement, and particularly violative of Penal Law Section 235.05. . . . Its dominant theme, and in fact, its only theme is to appeal to prurience in sex. It is hard-core pornography with a vengeance. It is neither redeemed nor redeemable. It does, in fact, demean and pervert the sexual experience, and insults it, shamelessly, without tenderness and without understanding of its role as a concomitant of the human condition." Then, with the flare that he had shown during the ten-day trial over the exhibition of what had become the most famous pornographic movie of all time, he concluded: "This is one throat that deserves to be cut. I readily perform the operation in finding the defendant guilty as charged." Defendant Robert Sumner responded in kind. The marquee of the theater announced in large red letters: "Judge Cuts Throat; World Mourns."[34]

In the appendix to his decision, Tyler sought to reach beyond the somewhat petty legal issues of the case and make a statement about culture itself. He smartly chose to echo an argument made by First Amendment attorney Morris Ernst, thus allying himself with the side normally opposed to restricting culture. Ernst declared to a reporter that he would "not choose to live in a society without limits to freedom. The fact that legally enforceable standards of public decency have been interpreted away by the courts almost to the point of no return does not absolve artists, producers or publishers from all responsibility or restraint in pandering to the lowest possible public taste in quest of the largest possible monetary reward." To Tyler, Ernst's comments had illustrated that "these fundamental issues do not require nor have they resulted in the positioning of civil libertarians on the one side and the alinement [sic] of the philosophical conservatives on the other." Rather, what was at stake was a sense of community that supported an idea of culture that, while perhaps too romanticized for contemporary America, still had value as an intellectual structure. What Tyler feared (and what he warned against) was the complete dismantling of that idea. "As a society we have come upon the crossroads," he wrote, "but we have not as yet crossed the road." "To find 'Deep Throat,' and the rest of its genre, legally viable, will not only cross the road, but will help obliterate it as well. The law, common sense and the history of experience, tell us that this is not in society's best interest, nor do present community standards, whether National or State, demand it."[35]

But even Tyler could not appreciate the sad irony of a court deciding cultural issues. New York City, the cultural and intellectual capital of the postwar world, had to resort to a criminal court judge to decide value in culture. Ralph Blumenthal captured the irony of that situation, albeit unwittingly.

In January 1973, shortly after Tyler had retired to deliberate on the *Deep Throat* case, Blumenthal wrote a substantial article in the venerable *New York Times* meant to capture the cultural moment. The title of the essay was "Porno Chic," a play on journalist Tom Wolfe's pithy phrase "The Radical Chic." Like Wolfe, Blumenthal attempted to take stock of a trend in popular culture that seemed to define (and defy) social assumptions, though he did so without any of the biting satire that

Wolfe had brought to his subject. Instead, Blumenthal adopted a tone and treated the case in a way that suggested that he saw Sumner's exhibition of *Deep Throat* as a legitimate enterprise that deserved, at least, a legal defense. Why? The movie was, after all, financially successful and relatively popular, even if its popularity was notoriety.[36]

Thus, the feature that seemed to make *Deep Throat* important was the money it made—its box office return indicated that it was popular. Blumenthal reported that for an initial investment of around $25,000, the film had grossed more than $700,000 at the New Mature World Theater since it opened on 12 June 1972. The film would go on to gross an estimated $3.2 million in seventy theaters throughout the country. Business at Robert Sumner's theater had soared in part because the film had become a target of police and then court action. It was the most popular "bad" movie to see in the city.[37]

The theater drew an average of five thousand people weekly, including, Blumenthal noted, "celebrities, diplomats, critics, businessmen, women alone and dating couples, few of whom, it might be presumed, would previously have gone to see a film of sexual intercourse, fellatio and cunnilingus." While *Deep Throat* was hardly unique—"one need only walk down 42nd Street these days for an unmistakable vista of sexploitation gone berserk"—its audience was. Among the film's noteworthy patrons were Johnny Carson, Mike Nichols, Sandy Dennis, Ben Gazzara, and Jack Nicholson. Diplomats from the French United Nations delegation saw the film alongside off-duty cops who "became the objects of searches in the theater by fellow officers." Even writers from the news staff at the *Times* and their colleagues from the *Book Review* went to see the film, though not together. On a tip from Mike Nichols, curator of chic, Truman Capote went one night "with a bunch of people from Elaine's [a trendy Manhattan restaurant]," later warning *Newsweek* critic Shana Alexander that she should see the film only at her own "peril." The film even received a number of reviews and notices from most of the respectable critics in the city. Most found the film trashy, but they had at least expended energy and print to pan it. Sumner's attorney, Herbert Kassner, told Blumenthal, "It's a fad. You know how these things catch on in New York." Even those who busted the film found themselves caught up in the chicness of the moment. One cop, much to his surprise, found himself humming the theme music on his way home. And David Vandor, an official in

Mayor Lindsay's administration charged with finding a way to clear midtown of porn, thought it "better than most situation comedies or grade C comedies."[38]

Blumenthal suggested that *Deep Throat* had run awry of the law precisely because of its popularity. Its financial windfall had attracted federal investigators looking into possible mob ties, making the theater a prime target for Mayor Lindsay's campaign to clean up midtown Manhattan. The *Times* reporter wondered if all the publicity generated by the mayor's efforts to do something about porn in midtown hadn't heightened the effect of films like *Deep Throat.* Blumenthal concluded that porn "nevertheless seems to be meeting a substantial public demand."[39]

Yet there was a fundamental problem with Blumenthal's term "porno chic." He intended it to describe the cultural moment that made *Deep Throat* significant—pornography represented an authentic challenge to authority; the commercial success of *Deep Throat* made it a symbol of clashing forces. But the fact that *Deep Throat* went on to make millions of dollars across the country made its success crass, not cool. Ellen Willis curtly concluded in the highbrow *New York Review of Books* that porn like *Deep Throat* was "hard to swallow." She dismissed *Throat*, porno chic, Al Goldstein, and the rest of the "die-hard porn liberationists" as "embarrassments to what is left of the hip subculture that spawned them. . . . As an ideology the fuck-it-and-suck-it phase of the sexual revolution may be passé," but "as a mentality it is nonetheless big business." Indeed, the popularity of *Deep Throat* and other porn films made sense only as a phenomenon of consumption, not, as Blumenthal seemed to suggest, as part of some struggle over culture.[40]

Andrew Sarris also caught a glimpse of this convoluted debate as a member of the audience for a panel discussion at the A. J. Liebling Counter-Convention sponsored by *More* magazine. The discussants included Molly Haskel; Larry Parish, the federal prosecutor who prosecuted *Deep Throat* star Harry Reams; constitutional lawyer Charles Rembar; Brendan Gill of the *New Yorker,* who moderated the panel; the infamous Al Goldstein of *Screw; Hustler* owner Larry Flynt; Ernest van den Haag, the NYU professor who had testified in the *Deep Throat* case; and Gay Talese, a New York–based writer. Sarris watched as Gill "adroitly transformed the occasion into an appellate hearing for the libertarian cause by authorizing Charles Rembar to define the issues involved." Rembar proceeded to characterize Flynt and Goldstein as First Amendment heroes like James Joyce and Ralph Ginzburg. Talese defended porn theaters and massage parlors as working-class venues, making his defense an exercise in egalitarian equivocation. The evening, Sarris felt, displayed the typical sympathies for free speech and its new martyrs. And yet he had trouble working up any concern for the plight of porn's defenders. In the end, when the evening's righteous defenses of Reams and *Deep Throat* were over, Sarris could only shrug: "Do these activities have to *look* so sordid and unseemly? I have been a Times Square buff from way back, but the area these days seems more menacing than liberating."[41]

A year after the trial over *Deep Throat*, the U.S. Supreme Court effectively obliterated the future of a common culture in *Miller v. California* (1973). Chief Justice Warren Burger, writing for a slim five-member majority, rejected the idea that courts and communities that wanted to restrict hard-core pornography had to abide by a national standard of taste. "It is," Burger declared, "neither realistic nor constitutionally sound to read the First Amendment as requiring that the people of Maine or Mississippi accept public depiction of conduct found tolerable in Las Vegas, or New York City. . . . People in different States vary in their tastes and attitudes," he continued, pointing out the obvious, "and this diversity is not to be strangled by the absolutism of imposed uniformity." So in *Miller v. California*, the Court decided that a jury needed to apply the standards only of its own community. Here was a way to resist the influence of the culture of Times Square and dismiss the influence of any other authority. The decision rejected the obligation to create a common culture in favor of an odd sort of cultural federalism. Yet the controversies covered in this book were far more than the sum of their legal precedents. In short, how did we go from a culture that defended *The Bicycle Thief* to one that defended *Deep Throat* in nearly the same terms?[42]

Walter Berns had an explanation. In the spring of 1973, Berns, a professor of political science at the University of Toronto, wrote an article for *Harper's* that sharply critiqued the intellectualization of pornography. *Harper's* introduced this article with an illustration of a large animated newspaper—meant to look like the *New York Times*—protecting a group of cowering buildings by jousting with an enormous pair of breasts across the New York skyline. The cartoon suggested that the *New York Times* had taken up some sort of fight against porn. Berns contended that the reality was quite different. "So great a change in public opinion cannot have been wrought by the 'porno dealers' and their customers, and it is time to cease blaming them," he argued. "So great a change in what is held to be respectable can have been wrought only by those who are themselves held to be respectable—by the opinion leaders, as they are sometimes called. The conclusion is obvious: the editors [of the *New York Times*] must look beyond Times Square, *or to another part of Times Square*, in order to understand the cause of what has happened there. In fact, they have only to look at the *New York Times*."[43]

According to Berns, the paper's editors and writers had become "a metaphor for the kind of cultural pretension that has been so fashionable in New York during the past few years. It was from the *Times* that we learned we need not be ashamed to patronize the Times Square arts." For "if there is nothing shameful about enjoying *Curious . . .* there is then absolutely no reason to be ashamed to be seen enjoying the same thing in Times Square."[44]

Berns fairly accurately described the conundrum the *Times* had created for itself. In editorials from 1969 and 1972, the paper had roundly condemned what it called the "utter degradation of taste in pursuit of the dollar." The editors had been justifiably outraged by "artists, producers, and publishers . . . pandering to the lowest possible public taste in quest of the largest possible monetary reward." It was, they concluded, a "continuous saga of what makes the Times Square area a boulevard of filth instead of a Great White Way."[45]

Yet the *Times* was also complicit in the rise and proliferation of a new attitude toward cultural authority. Berns noted: "What it denounces as filth on its editorial pages it praises as art or serious social comment on the film and drama pages, and that is absurd to the extent to which it is not hypocritical." He pointed to the editors' periodic denunciations of the sex businesses and theaters that had infiltrated Times Square, their neighborhood. He contrasted those righteous sermons with the apologias for cultural expressions such as *I Am Curious—Yellow*. "By tolerating critics Canby, [Clive] Barnes, and the others, the *Times* has made it possible for vice to take on the likeness of decency." The *Times* and its critics had forfeited their role as cultural curators.[46]

What made that development especially troubling to Berns was not that anyone liked pornography or even that it was legal, but that it was made to seem normal and given access to a broader public culture under the guise of intellectual sophistication. It had become common for pornography to be "display[ed] . . . openly in the marketplace, so to speak, whereas in the past it had been confined by the laws to the back alleys, or to the underworld, where its sales were limited not by a weakness of potential demand but rather by the comparative inaccessibility of the market." The new attitude toward pornography had made it "a growth industry by giving it license to operate in the accessible and legitimate market." And many intellectuals and critics seemed unmoved by what this development had done to popular taste. Berns intimated that critics who actively shaped popular taste and operated in the public realm—especially film critics—had an obligation to consider what their praise and endorsements of certain types of culture might mean. Such a responsibility was out of step with the prevailing view that cultural authority was itself obsolete. Berns wondered if the preferred alternatives, an open market and an impotent court system, were really the most appropriate arenas for determining popular taste.[47]

In the rush to topple censorship, critics had come to the conclusion that almost any limits were either too difficult to define or harmful to artistic genius. "Thus, having begun by exempting the work of art from the censorship laws," Berns noted, "we have effectively arrived at the civil libertarian's destination: the case where the Supreme Court throws up its hand and concludes that there is no such thing as obscenity." This, he concluded with obvious frustration, was done in the name of progress. The elevation of art to a realm untouchable by politics had the concurrent effect, he believed, of reducing taste to a level that knew "no shame." Yet, without shame, could there be controversy in culture? Would it matter if anyone felt offended ever again? Had the failure of porno chic revealed a deeper, far more troubling prospect—that controversial culture had become irrelevant?[48]

Conclusion

The Irrelevance of Controversial Culture

WE NEED CONTROVERSY in culture. Offensive art that transgresses cultural boundaries plays a vital role in preserving—not merely challenging—aesthetic and moral traditions. For how will we know what matters to us otherwise? However, we still need to retain some way to distinguish constructive transgression from that which is destructive. In other words, we need to be able to recognize and dismiss gratuitous controversy that shocks the public without asking much from it other than to be shocked.[1]

In her 1996 book, *The Repeal of Reticence*, cultural critic Rochelle Gurstein laments what she observes as a growing inability to appreciate controversial culture. The problem, she argues, is the disappearance of shame. "With the defeat . . . of reticence in the twentieth century, the faculties of taste and judgment—along with the sense of the sacred and the shameful—have become utterly vacant; yet, without them, it is now clear that disputes about the character of our common world can only be trivial, if not altogether meaningless." After all, what is the point of transgressive culture if there are few or no boundaries to transgress?[2]

Yet certainly people continue to get offended by culture, right? True, but such offense has become woefully ahistorical. We function as a public that thrives on controversy of a different kind—the kind that affirms inherently hostile assumptions held by rigid, almost mechanistic, ideological constituencies. Oppositional ideas that have relevance or at least resonance beyond our microcommunities and our own time have effectively disappeared. We are left with a culture of consumption in which controversy is manufactured and consumed in almost hedonistic delight. It seems to me that the dynamics that emerged out of porno chic gave rise to our present predicament of a regenerating cycle of senseless controversy. The intellectual richness that made controversial culture significant before porno chic gradually gave way to an ideological simplicity—the organizing principle of transgression became the goal as well. Not that pornography as a form is to blame for the contemporary cultural confusion, but the sensibility that made it chic to defend the popularity of porn illustrated a dangerous drift in American culture.[3]

An assessment of the damage done by the cycle of hollow controversy appeared in a 2005 essay by *New York Times* writer Barry Gewen. Gewen ruminates specifically about the decline of art criticism and how it has created an art world without direction—critics are powerless to answer the most direct and profound question: what is art? For artists, Gewen points out, this world offers a great deal of freedom. They can retreat into a "privileged zone" where their actions are protected by appeals to free speech and the piety of art. Yet the lack of cultural gravity, Gewen contends, has ultimately trained artists "to behave like unsocialized children." Of course, such immaturity comes in part from fending off philistines—reverends as well as representatives—who search out art that they can condemn as a way to score quick political points with their constituents. Lost in this fight, though, is the conversation that great art—and controversial art—can inspire within the public. "Today, after decades of narcissistic and exhibitionistic spectacles . . . we can see," Gewen concludes, "that . . . art was not only a space for the individual to realize himself in knowing himself, but also a space to enable others to know themselves, as well as a space to evoke the bonds that exist between artist and spectator in their common self-awareness, which is to say in the common humanity. It's a definition that understands art is necessarily a social interaction, communication between people, dialogue, not merely unfettered expression of the boundless ego as has been the case with so much work over the past few decades."[4]

Not surprisingly, Gewen blames artists for acting as if their obligation to their audience were to shock them. Yet why should we expect artists to act otherwise when it seems the only currency worth having is notoriety—when the relationship between the artist and the audience is one mediated through mutual recognition that judgment is irrelevant but shock sells? We can't simply blame the artists. Indeed, shouldn't popular artists—especially those who make movies—simply give the public what it wants? That approach might sound crass, but it also explains the rather dismal attempts by artists to be provocative. Controversy sells tickets just as readily as sex, explosions, and stars. Every generation encounters its ensemble of controversial impresarios, and neither censorship nor free speech will improve our ability to deal with them.

Yet, whereas popular culture, at its core, is a commercial venture, provocative culture, even when it aims to make money, must speak beyond itself and the constituencies that it hopes to please and anger. In other words, there must be a way for us to transcend the hostile extremes that so often dictate public debate and encounter each other in greater debate over a vast middle ground of culture. We in the audience, though, seem to find it imperative to live within an environment that rewards artists and critics who play to those extremes, for only then will they seem relevant to us. In this way, perhaps it is the audience rather than the specter of censorship that has a more chilling effect on the one aspect of culture that the audience has control over—criticism. Amid the flourishing of postcensor culture in the early 1970s, there were signs of this impending crisis.[5]

Andy Warhol had made art out of transgressing mainstream culture, and yet, in a world of porno chic, he sensed that even he could do little that would offend anybody. In 1974, Warhol confessed (with a wink) to a writer for the *Times* that he would simply do what he had always done: "just give the people what they want." But Andy Warhol wasn't a follower, was he? He coyly suggested to Paul Gardner that his success had always been predicated on pleasing the audience. While far from true, Warhol's explanation clearly rationalized the fact that his output in the 1970s became decidedly derivative. Gardner noted that since "today's moviegoers can see all the hardcore fare they want at the so-called skinflicks, [they] prefer their sex spiked with horror, and humor." To accommodate this taste, Warhol and his filmmaking partner Paul Morrissey offered the public *Frankenstein*. In an attempt to remain relevant, Warhol made a movie showing that "the hour had come to move from private parts to cold cuts." This X-rated *Franken-*

stein had nudity and sex but also severed body parts, impalements, and, Gardner wrote, "wriggly purple scar tissue disfiguring naked torsos—all captured in blood-red 3-D." And the public loved it. The film pulled in over $1 million in two months playing in a few major cities and was projected to gross over $10 million by the end of its run.[6]

In the past, Warhol had been relevant—radically so—by exposing popular preferences for things that had previously been simply notorious. His success with *The Chelsea Girls* was significant because it was predicated on his ability to subvert the demands of more traditional box office success. With *Frankenstein*, he sold out. In order for *him*—Andy Warhol, trendsetter—to remain relevant he needed to remain notorious, not significant, transgressive, or good. The audience demanded a certain kind of Andy Warhol and Andy Warhol had to deliver or suffer the ultimate indignity of irrelevance.

What were the implications for radical culture if Warhol could not find a way to be controversial? Susan Sontag and Pauline Kael offered suggestions that were strikingly uncharacteristic of their previous work and therefore all the more important as harbingers of a growing crisis in criticism. In early 1972, a movie premiered that practically compelled condemnation because of its conflation of excessive violence and sex. The film was Stanley Kubrick's *A Clockwork Orange*, and one New York critic bemoaned not merely the film's content but the depressing realization that critics were powerless to do much about it.

There seems to be the assumption that if you're offended by movie brutality, you are somehow playing into the hands of the people who want censorship. But this would deny those of us who don't believe in censorship the use of the only counterbalance: the freedom of the press to say that there's anything conceivably damaging in these films—the freedom to analyze their implications. If we don't use this critical freedom, we are implicitly saying that no brutality is too much for us—that only squares and people who believe in censorship are primarily concerned with brutality. . . . Yet surely, when night after night atrocities are served up to us as entertainment, it's worth some anxiety. We become clockwork oranges if we accept all this pop culture without asking what's in it. How can people go on talking about the dazzling brilliance of

movies and not notice that the directors are sucking up to the
thugs in the audience?[7]

From 1945 through 1968, the most obvious author of this passage
would have been Bosley Crowther. Yet it wasn't Crowther who wrote
it but his most persistent critic, Pauline Kael. While Kael rejected the
political implications that Crowther might have gleaned from such a
film—Crowther was a more linear liberal thinker than Kael—even
she felt the sting of the postcensor paradox that had undone Crowther.
The alternative to censorship was not acceptance of popular culture
but critical judgment of popular culture. But exercising such power
proved difficult because it seemed to smack of elitism, even though
it was out of a sense of decency that she had responded. And so Kael
was in a somewhat awkward position: even though she sensed that *A
Clockwork Orange* pandered to a kind of pop sadism in the audience
(the same kind of thing Crowther had identified in *Bonnie and Clyde*),
she wanted to avoid being lumped in with either apologists for movie
brutality or simpletons who shunned any cinematic violence.

Susan Sontag, though, accepted the label of elitist. As early as 1974
she began recanting many of the ideas that had made her famous. "Art
that seemed eminently worth defending ten years ago as a minority or
adversary taste, no longer seems defensible today, because the ethical
and cultural issues it raises have become serious, even dangerous, in a
way they were not then. The hard truth is that what may be acceptable
in elite culture may not be acceptable in mass culture, that tastes which
pose only innocuous ethical issues as the property of a minority become
corrupting when they become more established." Contemporary critic
Craig Seligman finds Sontag's turnabout to be, at best, an expression of
intellectual authority and, at worst, a kind of cultural fascism. Seligman
contends that Sontag's staunchly elitist attitude toward the public was
her worst aspect as a critic—it revealed her antidemocratic view of culture and exposed her dismally low opinion of "the people." In his book
Sontag and Kael: Opposites Attract Me, he contrasts Sontag's opinion
with Kael's much more democratic embrace of "Yahoo" culture and re-
joices that Kael was "from another psychic planet. She is not puritanical;
she is not ascetic; she is not *guilty.*" Thus, when Kael took issue with the
audience, she did so without necessarily wanting to distance herself from
it. Sontag, Seligman suggests, wished the rabble would just go away.[8]

I agree with Seligman that Kael treated moviegoers with an admirable amount of respect, or at least she considered the audience worthy enough to be corrected. But I think Seligman is a bit too hard on Sontag. We need not necessarily like her dismissive attitude to be attentive to her warnings. Hadn't Sontag identified a concern voiced by other critics—including Crowther and Kael—that it had become increasingly difficult to defend culture that mattered from culture that did not? Of course, Sontag's solution might have sounded like a neo–Legion of Decency—a Legion of Taste. But it seems that Seligman misses the crisis and the environment to which Sontag attempted to respond. Indeed, wasn't it significant that people as diverse as Crowther, Kael, Sontag—and even Warhol—all seemed caught in a similar bind?

The arc of postwar movie culture suggested that things would improve once censorship and a provincial view of movies receded. Many of the figures discussed in this book worked to refute a tradition that underestimated the public's ability to appreciate controversial movies because the practitioners of that tradition feared the idea of controversy itself. Ironically, though, we seem to be hopelessly awash in cultural controversies that we can neither appreciate nor differentiate. I have suggested that perhaps it was a bit naive to think that once cultural authority became more democratic and decentered, something better would organically appear to mediate future controversies. Well, we now know what that something was: a fractured culture composed of groups that each have their own cultural custodians guarding narrowly defined interests. Even though censors treated the entire public shabbily, at least the entire public had something on which to focus its ire. That is why it seems to me that Bosley Crowther's career has significance—in retrospect, he was not merely a person other critics loved to hate, but a symbol for an age that had yet to feel the effects of its own naïveté.[9]

Andrew Sarris provided insight into Crowther's legacy in an essay he wrote when Crowther died in 1981. Sarris concluded that there really had not been a successor to Crowther. Crowther had belonged to no one, including the movie industry, and thus allowed all readers to feel that he belonged to them. Unlike Pauline Kael, whose style attracted many admirers but was far from comforting to readers, or Sarris himself, who won over many converts to the auteur theory, Crowther was warmly liberal. He was not a fan of any film theory. He did not bow to Hollywood, nor did he vilify it. Thus, Sarris suggested, Crowther might have been the last reviewer to approach his job with an admirable level of objectivity. Crowther's readers, Sarris noted, "could talk a good game of *nouvelle vague* or *politique de auteures* or *mis en scene* or even Genre at cocktail parties, but in the pit of their beings they still yearned for that warm glow that lit up their hearts when they were brought face to face on the screen with a sentimental restatement of a humanist homily."[10]

While that was clearly meant as an insult, Sarris had, perhaps inadvertently, touched on a significant part of Crowther's success as a critic. "Crowther and his readers agreed that some subjects were more 'significant' than others. . . . He was perhaps too much a gentleman to speculate on the power of eros in the cinema. He was too much of a good citizen to accept the rising tide of violence on the screen." The implication here, of course, was that Crowther and his audience were simply too decent to embrace that which was once considered the vanguard. And although Sarris noted that "we could have profited in that crucial period between 1940 and 1960 from a more adventurous and more playful *Times* reviewer," he also suggested that "it is doubtful that any other reviewer of the time or of *The Times* could have read the mood of the public any more astutely than did Bosley Crowther." Crowther did not pander to the public nor cultivate a constituency within it—he merely responded to it.[11]

I did not set out to rehabilitate Crowther's reputation (perhaps I have not). But after reflecting on the concerns that Crowther had for both sides of the screen, for audiences as well as the movies they watched, I have come to the conclusion that his socially oriented criticism comprised a moment that was all too fleeting. For the era in which his criticism was most effective illustrates that between the abstractions of moralists and free speech absolutists there is a realm for social critics (not merely Crowther) who care about art and community in equal parts and for a public that cares about that criticism. While these critics tend to be labeled humane, liberal, staid, even boring, we as their audience profit from our arguments with them at least as much as we profit from our experience with the art they critique and the controversy they mediate. It is unfortunate, therefore, that we seem incapable of appreciating the significance of such criticism because it refuses to be polemical.

Notes

Introduction

1. See the Web site designed for the documentary film, *Inside Deep Throat*, under the heading "Production Notes," at http://www.insidedeepthroatmovie. com/. See also Laura M. Holson, "The Long View on *Deep Throat*," *New York Times*, 5 September 2004.

2. "Production Notes." For the argument that porn is progress, see Heins, *Sex, Sin, and Blasphemy*, 137–64; Williams, *Hard Core*, 229–64; Lewis, *Hollywood v. Hard Core*.

3. Anthony Lane, "Oral Values," *New Yorker*, 28 February 2005, 97.

4. Lewis, *Hollywood v. Hard Core*, 192.

5. For a concise illustration of this position, see Heins, *Sex, Sin, and Blasphemy*, 1–14. The quote regarding *Natural Born Killers* is from Jesse Walker, "Bringing Art to Court: The New Censors," *Reason* (August–September 1999) accessed at http://www.reason.com/news/show/31098.html. The opinion about *Brokeback Mountain* is quoted in John Leland, "New Cultural Approach for Conservative Christians: Reviews, Not Protests," *New York Times*, 26 December 2005.

6. Gurstein, *The Repeal of Reticence*, 3, 307; Fish, *There's No Such Thing as Free Speech*, 102–15.

7. For an overview of the topic see Black, *Hollywood Censored*; Brisbin, "Censorship, Ratings, and Rights"; Carmen, *Movies, Censorship, and the Law*; De Grazia, *Girls Lean Back Everywhere*; Giglio, "The Decade of the Miracle"; Westin, *The "Miracle" Case*; Wittern-Keller, "Freedom of the Screen."

8. For a sense of New York City's movie market, see Gomery, *Shared Pleasures*; Magliozzi, "Witnessing the Development of Independent Film Culture in New York"; MacDonald, *Cinema 16*; Wilinsky, *Sure Seaters*; Giovacchini, "'Hollywood Is a State of Mind.'" The literature on film censorship is extensive. Among the most relevant to this study are Lewis, *Hollywood v. Hardcore*; Friedman, *Prurient Interests*; Leff and Simmons, *The Dame in the Kimono*; Bernstein, "A Tale of Three Cities"; Wittern-Keller, "Freedom of the Screen"; Walsh, *Sin and Censorship*; Black, *The Catholic Crusade*.

9. Brooks Atkinson, "Censorship," *New York Times*, 2 March 1947, sec. 2, p. 1.

10. Ibid. On the elevation of movies to art, see Haberski, *It's Only a Movie*;

Taylor, *Artists in the Audience*; Wasson, *Museum Movies*; Decherney, *Hollywood and the Cultural Elite*.

11. Interview with Martin Quigley, 1958, *Popular Arts*, 20.

12. Seldes, *The Seven Lively Arts*, 293–94; Seldes, *The Great Audience*, 3, 4.

13. See also Rosenberg and White, *Mass Culture*; Rosenberg, "Pop Culture"; Macdonald, "Masscult and Midcult." See also Kammen, *The Lively Arts*, 322–28.

14. Seldes, *The Great Audience*, 14.

15. Sontag, "One Culture and the New Sensibility."

16. Seligman, *Sontag and Kael*, 22; Sontag, "Notes on Camp," 275–76.

17. Sontag, "Notes on Camp," 276; Seligman, *Sontag and Kael*, 57.

18. Kramer, *The Twilight of the Intellectuals*, 229; Seligman, *Sontag and Kael*, 62. On the influence of New York City, see Bender, *The Unfinished City*, 59–68, 133–48; Dickstein, *Leopards in the Temple*, 11–16.

19. Sontag, "The Pornographic Imagination," 45.

20. Ibid., 46.

21. Gurstein, *The Repeal of Reticence*, 280–81.

1. The Web of Control

1. Black, *The Catholic Crusade*, 85.

2. "The Bicycle Thief," *New York Times Magazine*, 4 December 1949, 24–25; "The Screen: Fathers and Sons," *Commonweal*, 23 December 1949, 319; John Mason Brown, "Struggle for Survival," *Saturday Review of Literature*, 7 January 1950, 30, 32.

3. Leff and Simmons, *The Dame in the Kimono*, 150. See also Gardner, *The Censorship Papers*, 174–75.

4. *New York Times*, 17 November 1950, 32; 12 May 1950, 33; 26 May 1950, 19.

5. *The Bicycle Thief*, Motion Picture Division, file 53819; Leff and Simmons, *The Dame in the Kimono*, 154–55; Skinner, *The Cross and the Cinema*, 93.

6. "Senator Proposes U.S. Film Control," *New York Times*, 15 March 1950, 33; *New York Times*, 28 May 1950, sec. 2, p. 3.

7. Fred Niblo to Joseph Breen, as quoted in Leff and Simmons, *The Dame in the Kimono*, 155; see also 146, 161. That suspicion was a bit misplaced. Three out of five MPAA theater chains did end up booking *The Bicycle Thief* without the seal, the first time such a thing had happened since 1934, the year Breen had taken over as director of the PCA. And, as historians Leff and Simmons suggest, "Breen's exaggerated fears no longer seemed exaggerated. The circuit bookings for *The Bicycle Thief* represented the first serious 'chink in the Code's armor.' It meant that the exhibitors' pledge—the fundamental link in the movies' system of voluntary Code compliance—had finally been broken" (161).

8. Schatz, *The Genius of the System*, 12.

9. Jowett, *Film*, 473.

10. Balio, *The American Film Industry*, 254.

11. Reprinted in Jowett, *Film*, 468–72.

12. Balio, "Retrenchment, Reappraisal, and Reorganization, 1948–Present," in Balio, *The American Film Industry*, 406.

13. "Public Is Blamed for Poor Movies," *New York Times,* 17 November 1946.

14. Eric Hodgins, "What's with the Movies?" *Life,* 16 May 1949, 97, 106.

15. "Free Advice to Hollywood," *New York Times,* 12 January 1947, sec. 2, p. 6.

16. "Of Quality and Taste in Films," *New York Times,* 19 January 1947, sec. 2, p. 7; "Glancing over the Week's Mail," *New York Times,* 7 September 1947, sec. 2, p. 3. See also Herman G. Weinberg, "The European Film in America," *Theatre Arts,* October 1948, 48–49.

17. "Glancing over the Week's Mail."

18. Gilbert Seldes, "Are the Foreign Films Better?" *Atlantic Monthly,* September 1949, 52.

19. Black, *The Catholic Crusade,* 22.

20. Ibid., 25.

21. Ibid., 27; "Legend of Decency Pledge," *Sign,* October 1945, 25; "Pledge of the Legion of Decency," *Ecclesiastical Review* 113 (1945): 306.

22. Black, *The Catholic Crusade,* 27.

23. W. A. Barrett to IFCA, 10 March 1926; note on "Radio Address by Mary Looram," 15 June 1934, note dated 19 June 1934, National Board of Review of Motion Pictures Collection, box 30.

24. Elmer Rice, press release, 4 June 1948, National Board of Review of Motion Pictures Collection, box 30, National Council on Freedom from Censorship folder.

25. "Catholic Influence," *Ave Maria,* 30 December 1944, 418; "The Code under Fire," *Sign,* October 1945, 41.

26. Cadegan, "Guardians of Democracy or Cultural Storm Troopers?" 256, 272.

27. Joe Breig, "'Objectionable in Part' for Whom?" *Ave Maria,* 7 January 1956, 7.

28. *Ave Maria,* 15 June 1946, 742; Francis J. Connell, "How Should Priests Direct People regarding the Movies?" *Ecclesiastical Review* 114 (1946): 253; "Renewing the Decency Pledge," *Commonweal,* 20 December 1946, 245.

29. Jowett, *Film,* 113.

30. *Universal Film Manufacturing Co. v. George H. Bell.*

31. See *Hughes Tool Company v. Benjamin Fielding.*

32. Wittern-Keller, "Freedom of the Screen," 7–8, 14. See also Timothy Lyne to Ward Bowen, 21 November 1947; Bowen to Lyne, 24 November 1947; Watkins to Bowen, 31 December 1948; Flick to Betty Sibley, 24 May 1949, Motion Picture Division, Sub-agency History Record, NYSV86-A1565.

33. *Law, Rules, and Regulations for Review and Licensing of Motion Pictures,* 1 November 1948, Motion Picture Division (emphasis in the original); *Illegal Wives,* Motion Picture Division, file 48213.

34. *La mulata de Cordoba,* Motion Picture Division, file 48973. See also the French film *Sirocco* (file 48676).

35. Otis L. Guernsy Jr., "Film Censor's Dilemma," *New York Herald Tribune Magazine,* 27 February 1955, 16, 18.

36. Ibid., 18.

37. Herbert Mitgang, "The TransAtlantic 'Miracle' Man," *Park East,* August 1952, 34.

38. Ibid.

39. Ibid., 33, 36.

40. "By Way of Report," *New York Times*, 24 August 1947, sec. 2, p. 3; Thomas M. Pryor, "Foreign Films Become Big Business," *New York Times*, 8 February 1948, sec. 2, p. 5; "Sexacious Selling Best B.O. Slant for Foreign Language Films in U.S.," *Variety*, 9 June 1948, 2.

41. Wilinsky, *Sure Seaters*, 38–39, 76; Mayer, *Merely Colossal*, 224, 233.

42. Bosley Crowther, "Hollywood versus New York," *New York Times Magazine*, 3 August 1947, 17, 18.

2. *The Miracle* and Bosley Crowther

1. Booton Herndon to Crowther, 8 January 1951; Crowther to Herndon, 23 January 1951, Crowther Collection, MSS 1491, box 7, folder 1.

2. Bosley Crowther, "Ways of Love," *New York Times*, 13 December 1950, 50; Crowther, "Short-Story Movie," *New York Times*, 17 December 1950, sec. 2, p. 1; Crowther, "The Strange Case of the Miracle," *Atlantic Monthly*, April 1951, 35.

3. By far the best work on the legal case surrounding *The Miracle* is Wittern-Keller's manuscript "Freedom of the Screen." The "*Miracle* case," as it came to be known, has been a well-researched topic, yet Bosley Crowther's role in it and the effect it had on his career have remained largely overlooked. Other studies include Draper, "'Controversy Has Probably Destroyed Forever the Context'"; Jowett, "'A Significant Medium for the Communication of Ideas'"; Randall, "Censorship."

4. Lillian Gerard, "Withdraw the Picture! the Commissioner Ordered," *American Film*, June 1977, 28, 29.

5. Richard Parke, *New York Times*, 24 December 1950 and 25 December 1950. In the second of his two articles, Parke reprinted part of the letter sent by McCaffrey.

6. Interview with Bosley Crowther, 1958, *Popular Arts*, 2.

7. Bosley Crowther, "The Censors Again," *New York Times*, 13 January 1946; *New York Times*, 27 December 1950.

8. *Joseph Burstyn, Inc. v. Edward T. McCaffrey*; Wittern-Keller, "Freedom of the Screen," 177.

9. Spellman's comments were reprinted in *New York Times*, 8 January 1951, 1, 14.

10. Wittern-Keller, "Freedom of the Screen," 186.

11. Leonard Hacker to the *New York Times*, 27 December 1950; postcards to Crowther; Barbara Berman to Crowther, 24 December 1950; J. B. T. Fisher to Crowther, 24 December 1950, Crowther Collection, "The *Miracle* Case," MSS 1491, box 7, folder 1.

12. Bosley Crowther, "For a Free Screen," *New York Times*, 14 January 1951, sec. 2, p. 1.

13. *New York Times*, 21 January 1951; Crowther to Thomas J. Joseph, 31 January 1951, Crowther Collection, "The *Miracle* Case," MSS 1491, box 7, folder 1.

14. Salvatore Cantatore to Crowther, 5 January 1951, Crowther Collection, "The *Miracle* Case," MSS 1491, box 7, folder 1.

15. Crowther to Cantatore, 31 January 1951, in ibid.

16. Patricia Mitchell to Crowther, 23 January 1951; Crowther to Mitchell, 29 January 1951, in ibid.

17. Marion Malara to Crowther, 14 January 1951; Crowther to Malara, 23 January 1951; Crowther to F. J. Urbanowicz, 23 January 1951, in ibid.

18. *New York Times*, 21 January 1951, 28 January 1951. See also Gerard, "*The Miracle* in Court," 26–28; Wittern-Keller, "Freedom of the Screen," 187.

19. *New York Times*, 23 January 1951; Gerard, "*The Miracle* in Court," 29.

20. Mr. and Mrs. R. F. Holzman to Crowther, 23 January 1951; Crowther to the Holzmans, 29 January 1951, Crowther Collection, "The *Miracle* Case," MSS 1491, box 7, folders 1 and 2.

21. Mrs. C. R. Passatino to Crowther, 14 January 1951; John Biehl to Crowther, 14 January 1951; Rev. Elbert M. Conover to Crowther, 11 January 1951; Dewitt Hornor to Crowther, 22 January 1951, in ibid.

22. Letter from Crowther, 19 January 1951; Crowther to Patrick F. Scanlon, 29 January 1951, in ibid.

23. Gilbert Seldes, "Pressures and Pictures: II," *Nation*, 10 February 1951, 132.

24. Crowther, "The Strange Case of the Miracle," 35–39.

25. Robert Sherrill to the editors of the *Atlantic Monthly*, 30 July 1951; Walter A. Stay to the editors of the *Atlantic Monthly*, 24 March 1951; Marguerite M. Steffens to the editors of the *Atlantic Monthly*, 4 April 1951, Crowther Collection, "Letters to the Editor of the *Atlantic Monthly*, re: 'The Strange Case of the Miracle,'" MSS 1491, box 18, folder 4.

26. Editors of the *Atlantic Monthly*, reply to letters, in ibid.

27. William P. Clancy, "The Catholic as Philistine," *Commonweal*, 16 March 1951, 569. There were many contemporary articles regarding the *Miracle* case, but see Alfred H. Barr Jr., "Letters to the Editor," *Magazine of Art*, May 1951, 194, for a succinct view of conflicting reports about the case. Also see Draper, "'Controversy Has Probably Destroyed Forever the Context,'" and especially Wittern-Keller, "Freedom of the Screen," 178–85.

28. *Sign*, May 1951, 37.

29. Clancy, "The Catholic as Philistine," 568–69. For a similar view, see Otto L. Spaeth, "Fogged Screen," *Magazine of Art*, February 1951, 44. For discussions about Catholic intellectual debates in the mid-twentieth century, see Cadegan, "Guardians of Democracy or Cultural Storm Troopers?"; McGreevy, "Thinking on One's Own."

30. William P. Clancy, "Freedom of the Screen," *Commonweal*, 19 February 1954, 501, 502.

31. Bosley Crowther, *New York Times*, 9 April 1952.

32. William P. Clancy to Crowther, 16 April 1952, Crowther Collection, MSS 1491, box 7, folder 3.

33. *Joseph Burstyn, Inc. v. Lewis A. Wilson; Burstyn v. Wilson*.

34. *Burstyn v. Wilson*.

35. Ibid.

36. Wittern-Keller, "Freedom of the Screen," 217–22.

37. Bosley Crowther, "Burstyn's Funeral," Crowther Collection, box 18, folder 1; Herbert Mitgang, "The TransAtlantic 'Miracle' Man," *Park East*, August 1952, 36; Bosley Crowther, *New York Times*, 10 February 1952, sec. 2, p. 1.

38. Frank E. Beaver, author of a book on Crowther's criticism, interviewed the critic before his death in 1981. Beaver characterizes Crowther's career as running on two tracks: Crowther campaigned for a "more mature, honest, and tasteful use of the medium" and, as a consequence of that proposition, argued that filmmakers had an "artistic responsibility" to the material they filmed and to the audience that watched it. See Beaver, *Bosley Crowther*, 18.

39. Bosley Crowther, *New York Times*, 1 June 1952, sec. 2, p. 1; Bosley Crowther, *New York Times*, 24 January 1954, sec. 2, p. 1.

40. For a study that characterizes movies as a democratic art, see Jowett, *Film*.

41. Bosley Crowther, *New York Times*, 2 December 1959; Beaver, *Bosley Crowther*, 68.

3. *Baby Doll* and *Commonweal* Criticism

1. Meyer Berger, "A Red-Blonde Beauty with 75-Foot Legs? Why, It's Baby Doll of Times Square," *New York Times*, 22 October 1956, 23; Ciment, *Kazan on Kazan*, 80. See also Brook, "Courting Controversy," 355–56.

2. Ciment, *Kazan on Kazan*, 80.

3. *New York Herald-Tribune*, 17 December 1956. See also Brook, "Courting Controversy."

4. Among the most the vocal critics of the Catholic Church was Paul Blanchard, who wrote two influential and widely discussed books in the 1950s that suggested the effects of a Catholic fascism in American life. See McGreevy, "Thinking on One's Own."

5. Cadegan, "Guardians of Democracy or Cultural Storm Troopers?" 272, 276.

6. Among the many excellent works on the Catholic Church and the movies, these are the best: Black, *The Catholic Crusade*; Walsh, *Sin and Censorship*; Skinner, *The Cross and the Cinema*; McLaughlin, "A Study of the National Catholic Office for Motion Pictures."

7. "The Commonweal Approach: An Editorial," *Commonweal*, 30 October 1959, 115–16.

8. Walter Kerr, "Where the Author Meets the Critics," *Commonweal*, 7 April 1950, 671, 672.

9. Ibid., 673.

10. Van Allen, *The "Commonweal" and American Catholicism*, 190, 191.

11. *Commonweal*, 15 November 1974, 126; Bredeck, *Imperfect Apostles*, 138, 214–15.

12. "The Critics and the Guardians," *Commonweal*, 19 December 1952, 271; Walter Kerr, "Catholics and Hollywood," *Commonweal*, 19 December 1952, 276.

13. Kerr, "Catholics and Hollywood," 276–77.

14. Gerald Vann, "Morals Makyth Movies," *Commonweal*, 29 May 1953, 204.

15. Kerr, *Criticism and Censorship*, 3.

16. Ibid., 14–15.

17. Ibid., 85–86.

18. Wittern-Keller, "Freedom of the Screen," 265, 266, 274.

19. Emmet Lavery, "Is Decency Enough?" *Commonweal*, 19 December 1952, 278–79.

20. Ibid.

21. Martin Quigley, *Commonweal*, 22 January 1954, 392; *Catholic World*, March 1954, 404; *American Ecclesiastical Review* (1955): 276; William P. Clancy, "Freedom of the Screen," *Commonweal*, 19 February 1954, 500–502.

22. Clancy, "Freedom of the Screen," 501.

23. Ibid., 502.

24. Ibid.

25. Martin H. Work, "Freedom of the Screen," *Commonweal*, 12 March 1954, 578–79.

26. "Catholics and the Movies," *Commonweal*, 3 June 1955, 219–20.

27. Walsh, *Sin and Censorship*, 258, 260, 261.

28. Ibid., 281–85.

29. John Courtney Murray, "Literature and Censorship," *Books on Trial*, June–July 1956, 393–95, 444–46.

30. Ibid., 394, 444.

31. Ibid., 444–45.

32. Ibid., 445–46.

33. "To B or Not to B," *Brooklyn Tablet*, 8 December 1956.

34. Ibid.

35. William H. Mooring, "About 'Art' and 'Truth' in Movies," *Brooklyn Tablet*, 8 December 1956, 29.

36. "*Baby Doll* Condemned," *Columbia*, January 1957, 22.

37. *Baby Doll* (1956) file, clippings files, Billy Rose Theater Collection; Rev. Timothy J. Flynn, director of Radio and Television Communications of the Archdiocese of New York, to Francis Cardinal Spellman, 24 January 1957, Galeazzi Collection.

38. *Baby Doll* (1956) file, clippings files, Billy Rose Theater Collection.

39. Press release from NCWC News Service, re: *Variety* statement on *Baby Doll*, 6 May 1957, Galeazzi Collection; Willam H. A. Carr and Malcolm Logan, "*Baby Doll* in New Row," *New York Post*, 17 December 1956, Galeazzi Collection.

40. "Catholics in at Least Ten Dioceses Warned by Bishops to Keep Away from *Baby Doll*," press release, 31 December 1956, Galeazzi Collection; press release from NCWC New Service, 25 March 1957, Galeazzi Collection; newspaper clippings, Galeazzi Collection, box 328, folder 12.

41. "Public Opinion Can Be Effective," *America*, 18 May 1957, 222–23; "The Fate of *Baby Doll*," *Ave Maria*, 1 June 1957, 6.

42. "*Baby's Doll's* Failure," *America*, 1 June 1957, 273.

43. *"Baby Doll," Commonweal*, 11 January 1957, 371–72.

44. Ibid.

45. Martin Quigley to Francis Cardinal Spellman, 25 January 1957; Spellman to Galeazzi, 26 January 1957, Galeazzi Collection; newspaper clippings, Galeazzi Collection, box 328, folder 12; *Life*, 7 January 1957, in *Baby Doll* (1956) file, clippings files, Billy Rose Theater Collection.

46. John Cogley, "The *Baby Doll* Controversy," *Commonweal*, 11 January 1957, 381.

47. Ibid.

48. John Cogley, "More on *Baby Doll," Commonweal*, 1 February 1957, 465.

49. Ibid.

50. Black, *The Catholic Crusade*, 177; *Miranda Prorsus (On Entertainment and Media): Encyclical Letter of His Holiness Pius XII*, reprinted in English in *Catholic Mind*, November–December 1957, 539–70; "The Legion's Code," *Commonweal*, 19 December 1958, 304.

51. Walsh, *Sin and Censorship*, 301–2.

52. McLaughlin, "A Study of the National Catholic Office for Motion Pictures," 54, 87, 92.

53. As quoted in Black, *The Catholic Crusade*, 220.

54. Cadegan, "Guardians of Democracy or Cultural Storm Troopers?" 281; McLaughlin, "A Study of the National Catholic Office for Motion Pictures," 88.

55. McLaughlin, "A Study of the National Catholic Office for Motion Pictures," 90–91.

56. Moira Walsh, "A Right Conscience about Films I," *America*, 9 May 1964, 658; Moira Walsh, "A Right Conscience about Films II," *America*, 16 May 1964, 684, 685, 686.

4. Amos Vogel and Confrontational Cinema

1. Amos Vogel to Kenneth Anger, 23 April 1953, in MacDonald, *Cinema 16*, 195–96.

2. Scott MacDonald interview with Amos Vogel, February and March 1983, in MacDonald, *Cinema 16*, 45; MacDonald interview with Marcia Vogel, January 1985, in MacDonald, *Cinema 16*, 65.

3. Program announcement, Fall 1951, in MacDonald, *Cinema 16*, 167–68.

4. Parker Tyler, program notes for *Fireworks*, April 1952, in MacDonald, *Cinema 16*, 174–75.

5. Anger to Vogel, 20 November 1947, in MacDonald, *Cinema 16*, 90; Vogel to Anger, 17 December 1947, in MacDonald, *Cinema 16*, 98.

6. MacDonald interview with Amos Vogel, February and March 1983, 41; see also MacDonald, "Introduction," *Cinema 16*, 4.

7. MacDonald interview with Amos Vogel, February and March 1983, 42.

8. Ibid., 47.

9. MacDonald, "Introduction," 1; MacDonald interview with Amos Vogel, September 1995, in MacDonald, *Cinema 16*, 56.

10. MacDonald interview with Robert Kelly, 19 December 2000, in MacDonald, *Cinema 16*, 218.

11. Dobi, "Cinema 16," 258, 255, 239.

12. MacDonald, "Introduction," 25; MacDonald interview with Cecile Starr, December 2000, in MacDonald, *Cinema 16*, 82, 83.

13. MacDonald interview with Starr, 58.

14. MacDonald interview with Amos Vogel, February and March 1983, 45; MacDonald interview with Jack Goelman, February 1985, in MacDonald, *Cinema 16*, 74.

15. MacDonald interview with Amos Vogel, February and March 1983, 45.

16. Siegfried Kracauer, "Program Notes for Fritz Hippler's *The Eternal Jew*, Shown at Cinema 16 in November 1958," in MacDonald, *Cinema 16*, 352.

17. MacDonald interview with Ed Emshwiller, 4 January 1985, in MacDonald, *Cinema 16*, 368.

18. Dobi, "Cinema 16," 202; MacDonald interview with Marcia Vogel, in MacDonald, *Cinema 16*, 65.

19. On Iris Barry and the founding of the film library, see Haberski, *It's Only a Movie*, 81–101; Wasson, *Museum Movies*.

20. Richard Griffith, "A Report on the Film Library, 1941–1956," *Museum of Modern Art Bulletin*, Fall 1956, 8, 24.

21. Magliozzi, "Witnessing the Development of Independent Film Culture in New York," 78; letters to the editor, *New York Times*, 2, 9, 23 February 1947; Andrew Sarris, "MOMA & the Movies," clippings file, Department of Film, Museum of Modern Art, New York.

22. Frank Stauffacher to Vogel, 20 September 1947, in MacDonald, *Cinema 16*, 80; Amos Vogel, "Film Do's and Don'ts," *Saturday Review*, 20 August 1949, in MacDonald, *Cinema 16*, 131; Cecile Starr, "Ideas on Film," *Saturday Review*, 8 March 1952, 64.

23. Griffith, "A Report on the Film Library," 12.

24. Ibid.

25. Sarris, "MOMA & the Movies."

26. "Illustration 4," in MacDonald, *Cinema 16*, 15.

27. "Response to Survey of Cinema 16 Membership," Fall 1953, in MacDonald, *Cinema 16*, 213–14.

28. Ibid., 214–15.

29. MacDonald interview with Goelman, 76; MacDonald interview with Carmen D'Avino, February 1985, in MacDonald, *Cinema 16*, 278.

30. MacDonald interview with P. Adams Sitney, 20 May 2000, in MacDonald, *Cinema 16*, 405; Al Hine, "Cinema 16," *Holiday*, March 1954, 27, 30.

31. "Response to Survey of Cinema 16 Membership," 215–17.

32. Robert McG. Thomas Jr., "Obituary for Archer Winsten," *New York Times*, 23 February 1997; Archer Winsten, "Cinema 16's Project Starts Auspiciously," *New York Post*, 6 November 1947; Archer Winsten, "Cinema 16's Fast Start Continues for 2nd Bill," *New York Post*, 4 December 1947; Archer Winsten, "Rages and Outrages," *New York Post*, 2 March 1959. All three Winsten articles can also be found in MacDonald, *Cinema 16*.

33. James Agee, *Nation*, 3 July 1948, in *Agee on Film*, 308.

34. Ibid., 308, 309.

35. Dwight Macdonald, "Some Animadversions on the Art Film," *Esquire*, April 1962, in MacDonald, *Cinema 16*, 395, 396.

36. Amos Vogel, "Riposte from Cinema 16," *Esquire*, September 1962, in MacDonald, *Cinema 16*, 402.

37. Macdonald's reply to Vogel, in MacDonald, *Cinema 16*, 402.

38. Ernest Callenbach, "Cinema 16 vs. Macdonald," *Film Quarterly*, Summer 1962, 2.

39. Dwight Macdonald, "Cinema 16," *Film Quarterly*, Winter 1962–63, 61, 62.

40. Macdonald, "Some Animadversions on the Art Film," 398–99.

41. MacDonald, *Cinema 16*, 25.

42. Hy Hollinger, "Talbot's Offbeat Policy Uphill," *Variety*, 27 April 1960, 3.

43. "Daily Box Office Reports—1960," Talbot Papers, MCHC74-024; *Variety*, Daniel Talbot clippings file, Billy Rose Theater Collection.

44. Ibid.; James Monaco, "An Interview with Dan Talbot," *Take One*, in Talbot Papers.

45. Roger Greenspun, "The New Yorker Theatre: In Memoriam," *Film Comment*, May–June 1974, 20.

46. Talbot Papers, book 1, box 1..

47. Talbot Papers, book 15, box 1.

48. Talbot Papers, book 9, box 1; Talbot Papers, book 1, box 4.

49. Talbot Papers, book 2, box 1.

50. Talbot Papers, book 9, box 4.

51. MacDonald, "Introduction," 19, 24.

52. MacDonald interview with Amos Vogel, September 1995, in *Cinema 16*, 55; MacDonald interview with Jonas Mekas, May 1985, in *Cinema 16*.

53. MacDonald interview with Sitney, 404.

5. The "Flaming" Freedom of Jonas Mekas

1. "Report," submitted by Detective Arthur Welsh to Criminal Court of the City of New York, County of New York, 4 March 1964, censorship files, Anthology Film Archives.

2. Dickstein, *Leopards in the Temple*, 16–20.

3. James, *To Free the Cinema*, 4.

4. Tom Gunning, "'Loved Him, Hated It': An Interview with Andrew Sarris," 10 March 1990, in James, *To Free the Cinema*, 64–66, 68. See also Andrew Sarris, "Independent Cinema," in Battock, *The New American Cinema*, 51–57.

5. Jonas Mekas, "The Experimental Film in America," *Film Culture*, May–June 1955, in Sitney, *Film Culture Reader*, 21–26; Peter Carter, "American Cinemas and Visionary Films," *CinemaScope*, transcript of a symposium on *Film Culture*, Columbia University, 3 March 2001; James, *To Free the Cinema*, 8.

6. Jonas Mekas, "Film Journal," *Village Voice*, 12 November 1958, 6; letters to the editor, *Village Voice*, 25 February 1959.

7. Jonas Mekas, "A Call for a New Generation of Film Makers," *Film Culture*, no. 19 (1959): 2.

8. Carney, *Cassavetes on Cassavetes*, 79, 80.

9. Ibid., 83. An interesting additional reason for Mekas's anger, Carney explains, was that Mekas intended to give the first Independent Film Award to Cassavetes at a $10-a-ticket benefit at the Waldorf Astoria in January 1959. That was before Cassavetes told Mekas that he couldn't show the film and was intending to recut it. "Mekas was placed," Carney writes, "in the uncomfortable position not only of having to cancel his ceremony and refund the ticket purchases, but of having publicly championed a film which the filmmaker had renounced." Carney argues that Cassevetes was affected by Mekas's attack and even allowed the first version to be screened at the 92nd St. Y Film Center in mid-January 1960. Thus Mekas's accusations have some truth: Cassevetes did tell his cast that he had a big production deal in the works and needed it to return to New York City to reshoot scenes that, once added to the movie, would make them all rich and famous.

10. J. Hoberman, "Forest and *The Trees*," in James, *To Free the Cinema*, 100; Mekas, "A Call for a New Generation of Film Makers," 2.

11. Mekas, "A Call for a New Generation of Film Makers," 2.

12. Jonas Mekas, "New York Letter," *Sight and Sound*, Summer–Autumn 1959, 119.

13. Scott MacDonald interview with Stan Brakhage, 30 November 1996, in MacDonald, *Cinema 16*, 298; MacDonald interview with Jonas Mekas, 24 May 1985, in MacDonald, *Cinema 16*, 416.

14. Jonas Mekas, "The First Statement of the New American Cinema Group," *Film Culture*, Summer 1961, reprinted in Sitney, *Film Culture Reader*, 81, 83.

15. Mekas, *Movie Journal*, 7, 64, 80, 82.

16. Hoberman and Rosenbaum, *Midnight Movies*, 40, 42, 43.

17. Ibid., 49.

18. Marshall Lewis to Mekas, "New American Cinema File," Anthology Film Archives.

19. Mekas, *Movie Journal*, 85.

20. Ibid., 83, 84–85, 86.

21. Pete Hamill, "Explosion in the Movie Underground," *Saturday Evening Post*, 28 September 1963, 83, 84; "Cinema Underground," *New Yorker*, 13 July 1963, 16, 17.

22. Arthur Knight, "New American Cinema," *Saturday Review of Literature*, 2 November 1963, 41.

23. Jonas Mekas, "Fifth Independent Film Award," *Film Culture*, Summer 1964, 2.

24. Ken Kelman, "Smith Myth," *Film Culture*, Summer 1963, 4.

25. Mekas, *Movie Journal*, 88, 93, 94.

26. Ibid., 103.

27. *Flaming Creatures*, clippings files, Billy Rose Theater Collection.

28. Ibid.

29. Elliott Stein, "Fog at Knokke," *Sight and Sound*, Spring 1964, 89.

30. Mekas, *Movie Journal*, 111–15.

31. *Flaming Creatures,* clippings files, Billy Rose Theater Collection.

32. Ibid.

33. Hoberman, *On Jack Smith's "Flaming Creatures,"* 43; Jonas Mekas, "Film Journal," *Village Voice,* 19 March 1964.

34. *Flaming Creatures,* clippings files, Billy Rose Theater Collection.

35. Mekas, *Movie Journal,* 173–75; Jonas Mekas, editorial, *Film Culture,* Spring 1964, 3.

36. "Filmmakers Co-operative," clippings files, Billy Rose Theater Collection; Jonas Mekas, notice for "Film-Makers' Cooperative Anti-Censorship Fund," *Film Culture,* Spring 1964, 2.

37. Joseph Peter Carbone to Mekas, 15 March 1964, censorship files, Anthology Film Archives; Robert W. Richards to Mekas, 8 March 1964, censorship files, Anthology Film Archives.

38. Gordon Hitchens to Mekas, 26 March 1964; Randolfe Wicker to Mekas, 12 April 1964, censorship files, Anthology Film Archives.

39. Mekas to Frank Hogan, District Attorney, N.Y. County, 25 March 1964, "New American Cinema File," Anthology Film Archives.

40. Handwritten notes and typed lists referring to cases involving *Flaming Creatures* and *Un chant d'amour,* in censorship files, Anthology Film Archives.

41. Amos Vogel, "Flaming Creatures Cannot Carry Freedom's Torch," *Village Voice,* 7 May 1964, 9.

42. Ibid., 18.

43. Letters to the editor, *Village Voice,* 14 May 1964; Mel Garfinkel to *Village Voice,* 7 May 1964, censorship files, Anthology Film Archives.

44. Mekas, *Movie Journal,* 137–38.

45. "Flaming Censorship," *Nation,* 30 March 1964, 311.

46. Sontag, "A Feast for Open Eyes," 208, 212.

47. Susan Sontag, "Jack Smith's *Flaming Creatures,*" in Battock, *The New American Cinema,* 204–10; Sontag, "Notes on Camp," 287.

48. Film-Makers' Cooperative Anti-Censorship Fund, "Statement," *Village Voice,* 9 April 1964, and *Variety,* 18 March 1964, censorship files, Anthology Film Archives.

49. *Village Voice,* 3 June 1958; 28 October 1959.

50. Flim-Makers' Cooperative, flier on legal trouble, censorship files, Anthology Film Archives.

51. "Spellman Assails Court Rulings on Pornography," *New York Times,* 7 August 1964.

52. *Village Voice,* 29 August 1963.

53. Stephanie Gervis Harrington, "City Puts Bomb under Off-Beat Culture Scene," *Village Voice,* 26 March 1964; Harrington, *Village Voice,* 9 April 1964.

54. Wakefield, *New York in the 1950s,* 116–59.

55. *Village Voice,* 16 July 1964; "'Villagers' Hold a Town Meeting," *New York Times,* 29 July 1964.

56. "City's License Chief," *New York Times,* 28 March 1964; "DeSapio Proposes More Housing as Part of His 'Village' Program," *New York Times,* 20 May 1964; "'Village' Assured of Added Police," *New York Times,* 7 October 1964. For

contemporary Village views of homosexuality, see two articles published in the *Village Voice*: Seymour Krim, "Revolt of the Homosexual," 18 March 1959, 12, 16, and "The Gay Underground—A Reply to Mr. Krim," 25 March 1959.

57. New York City League for Sexual Freedom, flier; Committee for Freedom of the Arts, "We Are Walking for Freedom Now," censorship files, Anthology Film Archives.

58. The Committee for Freedom of the Arts, "We Are Walking for Freedom Now"; Michael Smith, *Village Voice*, 30 April 1964.

59. Mekas, editorial; Jonas Mekas, *Village Voice*, 21 May 1964.

60. Paul Hoffman, *New York Post*, 3 June 1964; Stephanie Gervis Harrington, "Pornography Is Unidentified at Film-Critic Mekas Trial," *Village Voice*, 18 June 1964.

61. Jonas Mekas, "On the Misery of Community Standards," *Village Voice*, 18 June 1964. Incidentally, many commentators noted that Anger had been awarded a Ford Foundation fellowship that same week. J. Hoberman, "Ali Baba Is Coming!" *Village Voice*, 3 February 1972, in which he announces that *Flaming Creatures* will be shown at Manhattan's Film Forum and the Anthology Film Archives after seven and one-half years of legal limbo; Noral Sayre in the *New York Times* of 21 February 1975 reported that *Flaming Creatures* would be shown as part of a three-film series at the First Avenue Screening Room on 61st Street; and Vincent Canby, Bosley Crowther's long-term replacement at the *Times*, informed readers that the 1991 New York Film Festival would screen *Flaming Creatures* as part of a series entitled Avant-Garde Visions (1 October 1991).

62. Jack Smith, "'Pink Flamingo' Formula in Focus," *Village Voice*, 19 July 1973; "Uncle Fishook and the Sacred Baby Poo Poo of Art: An Interview with Jack Smith," *Semiotext(e)* 3, no. 2 (1978): 193.

63. Jack Smith, "Journal Notes on the Uses of Pornography," in Hoberman and Leffingwell, *Wait for Me at the Bottom of the Pool*, 78.

64. Mekas, *Movie Journal*, 175; J. Hoberman, "The Big Heat," *Village Voice*, 12 November 1991.

65. Paul Krassner, *Cavalier*, 1967, in Jonas Mekas, clippings files, Billy Rose Theater Collection. Dwight Macdonald had a similar interaction with Mekas; see Macdonald, "Objections to the New American Cinema," in Battock, *The New American Cinema*, 198.

6. The End of New York Movie Culture

1. "Film Censorship Is Upset by Court," *New York Times*, 11 June 1965; Lewis, *Hollywood v. Hard Core*, 143.

2. Anthony Lewis, "Sex . . . and the Supreme Court," *Esquire*, June 1963, 82.

3. Ibid., 83, 143.

4. "The New Pornography," *Time*, 16 April 1965, 28.

5. Ibid., 29.

6. "The Obscenity Cases," *New York Times*, 24 March 1966.

7. Russell Baker, *New York Times*, 24 March 1966.

8. Vincent Canby, *New York Times*, 13 April 1966.

9. *New York Times*, 17 November 1966; Vincent Canby, *New York Times*, 5 January 1967.

10. *The Chelsea Girls*, clippings files, Billy Rose Theater Collection.

11. Koch, *Stargazer*, 100.

12. Elenore Lester, "So He Stopped Painting Brillo Boxes and Bought a Movie Camera," *New York Times*, 11 December 1966.

13. Hoberman and Rosenbaum, *Midnight Movies*, 73; Watson, *Factory Made*, 306, 308; Warhol and Hackett, *POPism*, 184, 202. Discussion of *The Chelsea Girls* is copious and basically focuses on Watson's general point that it was a turning point in the history of New York's underground cinema. See Koch, *Stargazer*, 89–99; Staiger, *Perverse Spectators*, 144–48; Hoberman and Rosenbaum, *Midnight Movies*, 71–73; Suarez, *Biker Boys, Drag Queens, and Superstars*, 225, 232.

14. "FDC Report on 2-Week Limited Engagement of Andy Warhol's *The Chelsea Girls* at the Cinema Rendezvous—Dec. 1 thru Dec. 14, 1966," Film-Makers' Distribution Center, 15 December 1966, in Clarke Papers, MSS 145 AN, box 11, folder 3; Vincent Canby, "Chelsea Girls in Midtown Test," *New York Times*, 1 December 1966.

15. Jonas Mekas, "On *The Chelsea Girls*," *Village Voice*, 29 September 1966, reprinted in *Movie Journal*, 254, 256.

16. Ibid., 257.

17. Calvin Tomkins, "All Pockets Open," *New Yorker*, 6 January 1973, 42.

18. Jonas Mekas, "On Andy Warhol," *Village Voice*, 19 September 1963, reprinted in *Movie Journal*, 97; Jonas Mekas, "Warhol Shoots *Empire*," *Village Voice*, 30 July 1964, reprinted in *Movie Journal*, 150.

19. Hoberman and Rosenbaum, *Midnight Movies*, 61, 70–72; see also "Film-Makers Cinematheque," clippings files, Billy Rose Theater Collection.

20. John Gruen, "Pop Scene: Warhol's *Chelsea Girls* Adds a New Dimension," *New York World Journal Tribune*, 25 November 1966, clippings files, Billy Rose Theater Collection; Archer Winsten, "Warhol Pops Up with *Chelsea Girls*," *New York Post*, 21 October 1966, clippings files, Billy Rose Theater Collection; Jack Kroll, "Underground in Hell," *Newsweek*, 14 November 1966, 109; Jack Kroll, "Up from Underground," *Newsweek*, 13 February 1967, 117; Lawrence Witchel and Ernest Leogrande, "The Gamey Tastemakers," *Daily News*, 11 June 1967, clippings files, Billy Rose Theater Collection.

21. Rosalyn Regelson, "Where Are 'the Chelsea Girls' Taking Us?" *New York Times*, 24 September 1967.

22. Richard Roud, "The Underground Surfaces," *Sight and Sound*, Winter 1967–68, 19.

23. Tomkins, "All Pockets Open," 45.

24. Koch, *Stargazer*, 99, 100.

25. Bosley Crowther, *New York Times*, 13 April 1966; Crowther, "The Underground Rising," *New York Times*, 8 May 1966.

26. Bosley Crowther, "The Underground Overflows," *New York Times*, 11 December 1966.

27. Amos Vogel to Schuyler Chapin, memo re: 16mm Equipment at Philharmonic Hall, 26 April 1966), Programming Film Festival, 1964–66, Mazzola Papers, box 3. See also "Independent Cinema: Special Events Program," Fourth New York Film Festival, 1966, Mazzola Papers, box 2.

28. Interview transcript, *Sandy Lesberg Show*, WOR Radio, 12 August 1966, Fourth New York Film Festival, Mazzola Papers, box 2.

29. "What Are the New Critics Saying?" *Film Culture*, Fall 1966, 77.

30. Ibid., 79, 81–82.

31. Ibid., 82.

32. Ibid., 85–86.

33. Amos Vogel, "Thirteen Confusions," *Evergreen Review*, June 1967, reprinted in MacDonald, *Cinema 16*, 428, 429.

34. Ibid., 430–31.

35. Ibid., 431–35.

36. "The New American Cinema: Five Replies to Amos Vogel," *Evergreen Review*, August 1967, 54.

37. Ibid., 55.

38. Ibid., 55, 56.

39. Mekas, *Movie Journal*, 362–64; Tyler, *Underground Film*, 24.

40. Taylor, *Artists in the Audience*, 153.

41. Ibid., 116.

42. Tyler, *Underground Film*, 25, 42, 50.

43. Ibid., 234–35.

7. Did *Bonnie and Clyde* Kill Bosley Crowther?

1. Bosley Crowther, "Around in Circles," *New York Times*, 13 August 1961.

2. Bosley Crowther, "Choice of Words," *New York Times*, 11 February 1962; Crowther, "All for the Kids," *New York Times*, 3 March 1957; Crowther, "Victory for Ideas," *New York Times*, 5 July 1959.

3. *America*, 16 May 1959, 325; Bosley Crowther, *New York Times*, 4 March 1962.

4. Bosley Crowther, "Cumulative Violence," *New York Times*, 15 May 1955.

5. Bosley Crowther, "Not for the Children," *New York Times*, 16 April 1961.

6. Bosley Crowther, review of *Blackboard Jungle*, *New York Times*, 21 March 1955.

7. Dore Schary to Crowther, 6 April 1955; Crowther to Schary, undated, Crowther Collection, box 7, folder 4.

8. Bosley Crowther, *New York Times*, 4 September 1955.

9. Interview with Bosley Crowther, 1958, *Popular Arts*, 17, 18, 19–20.

10. Bosley Crowther, "Movies and Censorship," *Public Affairs Pamphlet*, no. 322 (New York: Public Affairs Committee, 1962), reprinted in McClure, *The Movies*, 376, 380.

11. Bosley Crowther, "Socially Hurtful," *New York Times*, 21 June 1964, sec. 2, p. 1; Bosley Crowther, "Moral Brinkmanship," *New York Times*, 13 December 1964, sec. 2, p. 3. See also Beaver, *Bosley Crowther*, 143; Steven Alan Carr, "From

'Fucking Cops' to "Fucking Media': *Bonnie and Clyde* for a Sixties America," in Friedman, *Arthur Penn's "Bonnie and Clyde,"* 70–96.

12. Bosley Crowther, "The Heat Is on Films," *New York Times,* 17 January 1965, sec. 2, p. 1.

13. Ibid.

14. Bosley Crowther, "Movies to Kill People By," *New York Times,* 9 July 1967, 65.

15. Bosley Crowther, "Another Smash at Violence," *New York Times,* 30 July 1967, 59. See also a very different take on Crowther in Hoberman, *Dream Life,* 163–69.

16. "Where Will the Violence End?" *New York Times,* 13 August 1967, 98; "Still the Talk Is of Violence," *New York Times,* 3 September 1967, 76.

17. Bosley Crowther, "Shoot-Em-Up Film Opens World Fete," *New York Times,* 7 August 1967.

18. Bosley Crowther, "*Bonnie and Clyde* Arrives," *New York Times,* 14 August 1967.

19. Vincent Canby, "Arthur Penn: Does His *Bonnie and Clyde* Glorify Crime?" *New York Times,* 17 September 1967.

20. Jean-Louis Comolli and Andre S. Labarthe, "An Interview with Arthur Penn," *Evergreen Review,* June 1968, reprinted in Cawelti, *Focus on "Bonnie and Clyde,"* 18.

21. "*Bonnie and Clyde*—Facts? Meaning? Art?" *New York Times,* 17 September 1967; Crowther, "Shoot-Em-Up Film"; Crowther, "*Bonnie and Clyde* Arrives"; Crowther, "Run, Bonnie and Clyde," *New York Times,* 3 September 1967.

22. Richard Bennett to Crowther, 23 September 1967; Renee D. Pennington, high school senior from Elmhurst, to Crowther, 3 September 1967; Joyce Mack to Crowther, 3 August 1967; Orson Bean to Crowther, 4 September 1967; Robert Downing to Crowther, 3 September 1967, Crowther Collection, box 13, folder 3.

23. Roger Ebert, *Los Angles Times,* 1 October 1967, Crowther Collection, box 13, folder 3.

24. Charles T. Samuels, "The American Scene: *Bonnie and Clyde,*" *Hudson Review,* Spring 1968, 10–22, reprinted in Cawelti, *Focus on "Bonnie and Clyde,"* 91; J. Hoberman, *Dream Life,* 169. For contemporary accounts that argue along the lines of Hoberman, see "Anything Goes: The Permissive Society," *Newsweek,* 13 November 1967, 74, 75, 76; Stefan Kanfer, "The New Cinema: Violence . . . Sex . . . Art," *Time,* 8 December 1967, 67. See also Friedman, *Bonnie and Clyde,* 33–38.

25. Penelope Gilliat and Andrew Sarris quoted in Samuels, "The American Scene," 91; Moira Walsh, "Bonnie and Clyde," *America,* 2 September 1967, 227.

26. Samuels, "The American Scene," 87, 90.

27. Hoberman, *Dream Life,* 174; Charles Moskowitz, *Village Voice,* December 1967, quoted in Hoberman, *Dream Life,* 173.

28. Pauline Kael, "Bonnie and Clyde," *New Yorker,* 21 October 1967, reprinted in Kael, *For Keeps,* 141–50.

29. Joseph Morgenstern, "Ugly" and "The Thin Red Line," in Schickel and Simon, *Film 67/68,* 25–29.

30. Kael, "Bonnie and Clyde," 142.

31. Ibid., 144.

32. Peter Collier, "The Barrow Gang: An Aftertaste," *Ramparts*, May 1968, 16–22, reprinted in Cawelti, *Focus on "Bonnie and Clyde,"* 29–31.

33. Mikael Colville-Andersen interview with David Newman, 1 October 1998, http://zakka.dk/euroscreenwriters/interviews/david_newman_536.htm; Hoberman, *Dream Life*, 169.

34. John Howard Lawson, "Our Film and Theirs: *Grapes of Wrath* and *Bonnie and Clyde*," *American Dialog* 5 (Winter 1968–69): 30–33, reprinted in Cawelti, *Focus on "Bonnie and Clyde,"* 113. See also Hoberman, *Dream Life*, 169, 174.

35. *New York Times*, 20 November 1967, 60.

36. "A Critic for All Seasons," *New York Times*, 10 December 1967, 176.

37. Crowther to Thomas Pryor, 18 November 1967, Crowther Collection, MSS 1491, box 16, folder 1. See also Crowther Collection, MSS 1491, box 13, folder 3; box 15, folder 6 (interoffice memos).

38. Richard Schickel, "Flaws in a Savage Satire," *Life*, 13 October 1967, 16, reprinted in Cawelti, *Focus on "Bonnie and Clyde,"* 25; Richard Schickel to Crowther, 20 November 1967, Crowther Collection, MSS 1491, box 13, folder 5.

39. Schickel to Crowther.

40. Crowther to Richard Schickel, 26 November 1967, Crowther Collection, MSS 1491, box 13, folder 5.

41. Robert Steele, "The Good-Bad and Bad-Good in Movies: *Bonnie and Clyde* and *In Cold Blood*," *Catholic World*, May 1968, 76–79, in Cawelti, *Focus on "Bonnie and Clyde,"* 115–16.

42. Bosley Crowther, "Magic, Myth, and Monotony: Movies in a Free Society," *Television Quarterly*, Fall 1968, 51, 52.

43. Ibid., 57, 59.

44. Ibid., 60–63.

45. Ibid., 64.

46. Ibid., 60–65.

8. The Failure of Porno Chic

1. Bosley Crowther, "Obscenity Is a Dirty Word," *New York Times*, 5 December 1965, sec. 2, p. 1.

2. *Roth v. United States*.

3. John Simon, "Getting Furious over *Curious*," *New York Times*, 9 February 1969.

4. Sjöman, *I Am Curious—Yellow*, 232–33.

5. Ibid., 245, 248.

6. Ibid., 194, 203.

7. Simon, "Getting Furious over *Curious*."

8. Vincent Canby, "*I Am Curious* (Yes)," *New York Times*, 23 March 1969.

9. Ibid.

10. Rex Reed, *"I Am Curious* (No)," *New York Times,* 23 March 1969.

11. Ibid.

12. Ibid.

13. *"Curious* (In All Colors)," *New York Times,* 6 April 1969.

14. "Sex and the Arts: Explosive Scene," *Newsweek,* 14 April 1969, 67. See also Allyn, *Make Love, Not War,* 130–32.

15. "Sex and the Arts: Explosive Scene," 68–70.

16. New York Erotic Film Festival, clippings files, Billy Rose Theater Collection.

17. Ibid.

18. Ibid.

19. Bernard Weinraub, "Obscenity or Art? A Stubborn Issue," *New York Times,* 7 July 1969.

20. Vincent Canby, "Warhol's Red Hot and 'Blue' Movie," *New York Times,* 10 August 1969.

21. Ibid.

22. *New York Times,* 17 September 1969; *New York Times,* 18 September 1969; Howard Thompson, *New York Times,* 22 October 1969.

23. Andrew Sarris, "A View from New York," *Sight and Sound,* Autumn 1969, 203.

24. Ibid.; emphasis added.

25. Ibid., 219.

26. Cannato, *The Ungovernable City,* 525, 532, 538.

27. Murray Schumach, "Three Times Square Theaters Raided in Obscenity Drive," *New York Times,* 30 August 1972; *New York Times,* 20 August 1972. See also *New York Times,* 12 March 1971; *New York Times,* 28 July 1971; Murray Schumach, "Nine Peep Shows Are Raided in Times Square Area," *New York Times,* 11 August 1971; Dale Burg and Abby Hirsch, "Adventures in the Skin-Flick Trade," *Village Voice,* 12 August 1971, 45; "Behind the Façade," *New York Times,* 5 September 1972.

28. Al Goldstein, "Gulp," *Screw,* reprinted in Smith, *Getting into "Deep Throat,"* 33–34; *Variety,* 28 June 1972; Mort Sheinman, *Christian Science Monitor,* 1 September 1972, clippings collection, Films Study Center, MoMA; Blair Sobol, "The Only Girl in the World Seeing *Deep Throat," Village Voice,* 14 September 1972, 75; Archer Winsten, *New York Post,* 27 November 1972, *Deep Throat* clippings file, Billy Rose Theater Collection. See also Turan and Zito, *Sinema,* 143; Lewis, *Hollywood v. Hard Core,* 208–10.

29. Ralph Blumenthal, "Is Film *Deep Throat* Obscene? Trial in Manhattan Opens Today," *New York Times,* 18 December 1972.

30. Paul Montgomery, "Court Officers See *Deep Throat* in Unusual Fifth Avenue Setting," *New York Times,* 19 December 1972.

31. *"Throat* Lawyer Calls for Expert," *New York Times,* 20 December 1972.

32. Smith, *Getting into "Deep Throat."*

33. Larry McMurty, *New York,* 5 February 1973, *Deep Throat* clippings files, Billy Rose Theater Collection.

34. Opinion of Judge Joel J. Tyler Jr., reprinted in *The "Deep Throat" Papers,* 175–90; Paul Montgomery, *"Throat* Obscene, Judge Rules Here," *New York Times,* 2 March 1973.

35. Opinion of Judge Tyler, appendix.

36. Ralph Blumenthal, "Porno Chic," *New York Times Magazine,* 21 January 1973, 28+. Brendan Gill, a longtime contributor to the *New Yorker,* dismissed the chicness of porn but still defended it as legitimate culture, if not exactly art. See Brendan Gill, "Blue Notes," *Film Comment,* January 1973, reprinted in Lopate, *American Movie Critics,* 476–84.

37. Blumenthal, "Porno Chic," 28.

38. Ibid.

39. Ibid.

40. Ellen Willis, "Hard to Swallow," *New York Review of Books,* 25 January 1973, 22.

41. Andrew Sarris, "Pundits Ponder the Perils of Porn," *Village Voice,* 6 December 1976, 67.

42. Chief Justice Warren Burger, majority opinion in *Miller v. California.*

43. Walter Berns, "Absurdity at the *New York Times:* The Confusion between Art and Self-Righteousness," *Harper's,* May 1973, 40.

44. Ibid.

45. "Beyond the (Garbage) Pale," *New York Times,* 1 April 1969; "Behind the Façade," *New York Times,* 5 September 1972.

46. Berns, "Absurdity at the *New York Times,*" 35, 36, 39.

47. Ibid., 36, 39.

48. Ibid., 39.

Conclusion

1. Among the many books on this topic, one struck me as particularly useful: see Julius, *Transgressions.*

2. Gurstein, *The Repeal of Reticence,* 7.

3. Gablik, *Has Modernism Failed?* 32, 37–38, 74–77.

4. Barry Gewen, "State of the Art," *New York Times Book Review,* 11 December 2005.

5. Gablik, *Has Modernism Failed?* 122.

6. Paul Gardner, "Warhol—from Kinky Sex to Creep Gothic," *New York Times,* 14 July 1974, 105.

7. Pauline Kael, "Stanley Strangelove," *New Yorker,* 1 January 1972, reprinted in Kael, *For Keeps,* 418. See also Kolker, *A Cinema of Loneliness,* 150–51.

8. Seligman, *Sontag and Kael,* 62, 63–65.

9. Steigerwald, *Culture's Vanities,* 18–21; Lyons, *The New Censors,* 183–92.

10. Andrew Sarris, "Not to Praise Bosley Crowther, but Not to Bury Him Either," *Film Comment,* May–June 1981, 70.

11. Ibid.

Bibliography

Archival Sources

Anthology Film Archives, New York.

Billy Rose Theater Collection. New York Public Library, Lincoln Center for the Performing Arts, New York.

Clarke, Shirley, Papers. Wisconsin Center for Film and Theater Research, Wisconsin State Historical Society, Madison.

Clippings Collection, Film Study Center, Museum of Modern Art, New York.

Crowther, Bosley, Collection. L. Tom Perry Special Collections Library, Harold B. Lee Library, Brigham Young University, Provo, Utah.

Galeazzi, Count Enrico Pietro, Collection. Knights of Columbus Archive, Hartford, Conn.

Mazzola, John, Papers. Archives, Lincoln Center for the Performing Arts, New York.

Motion Picture Division. Department of Education, New York State Archives, Albany.

National Board of Review of Motion Pictures Collection. Manuscript and Archive Division, New York Public Library, New York.

Popular Arts. Oral History Project. Columbia University, Rare Book and Manuscript Collection, New York.

Talbot, Daniel, Papers. Wisconsin Center for Film and Theater Research, Wisconsin State Historical Society, Madison.

Legal Cases

Burstyn v. Wilson. 522, Supreme Court of the United States, 343 U.S. 495 (1952).

Hughes Tool Company v. Benjamin Fielding (commissioner of licenses of the City of New York). Supreme Court of New York, Special Term, New York County, 188 Misc. 947; 73 N.Y.S. 2d 98 (3 April 1947).

Joseph Burstyn, Inc. v. Edward T. McCaffrey, as Commissioner of Licenses of the City of New York. Supreme Court of New York, 198 Misc.; 101 N.Y.S. 2d 8921 (1951).

Joseph Burstyn, Inc. v. Lewis A. Wilson as Commissioner of Education of the State of New York, et al. Supreme Court of New York, Appellate Division Third Department, 278 A.D. 253; 104 N.Y.S. 2d 740 (1951).
Miller v. California. 70–73, Supreme Court of the United States, 413 U.S. 15 (21 June 1973).
Opinion of Judge Joel J. Tyler Jr. In *The People of the State of New York v. Mature Enterprises, Inc.* Criminal Court of the City of New York, New York County, 73 Misc. 2d 749; 343 N.Y.S. 2d 911 (1 March 1973).
Roth v. United States. Supreme Court of the United States, 354 U.S. 476 (1957).
Universal Film Manufacturing Co. v. George H. Bell, Commissioner of Licenses of the City of New York. Supreme Court of New York, Special Term, New York County, 100 Misc. 281; 167 N.Y.S. 124 (June 1917).

Secondary Literature

Agee, James. *Agee on Film: Review and Comments by James Agee.* New York: Beacon, 1966.
Allyn, David. *Make Love, Not War: The Sexual Revolution and Unfettered History.* Boston: Little, Brown, 2000.
Altschuler, Glenn C. *All Shook Up: How Rock 'n' Roll Changed America.* New York: Oxford University Press, 2003.
Balio, Tino, ed. *The American Film Industry.* Madison: University of Wisconsin Press, 1985.
Battock, Gregory. *The New American Cinema: A Critical Anthology.* New York: Dutton, 1967.
Beaver, Frank E. *Bosley Crowther: Social Critic of the Film, 1940–1967.* New York: Arno, 1974.
Bender, Thomas. *The Unfinished City: New York and the Metropolitan Idea.* New York: New Press, 2002.
Bernstein, Matthew. "A Tale of Three Cities: The Banning of *Scarlet Street.*" In *Controlling Hollywood: Censorship and Regulation in the Studio Era*, edited by Matthew Bernstein, 157–85. New Brunswick, N.J.: Rutgers University Press, 1999.
Biskind, Peter. *Seeing Is Believing: How Hollywood Taught Us to Stop Worrying and Love the Movies.* New York: Pantheon, 1983.
Black, Gregory. *The Catholic Crusade against the Movies, 1940–1975.* Cambridge: Cambridge University Press, 1997.
———. *Hollywood Censored: Morality Codes, Catholics, and the Movies.* Cambridge: Cambridge University Press, 1994.
Blake, Richard A. *Street Smart: The New York of Lumet, Allen, Scorsese, and Lee.* Lexington: University Press of Kentucky, 2005.
Blanchard, Paul. *American Freedom and Catholic Power.* Boston: Beacon, 1949.
Bredeck, Martin J. *Imperfect Apostles: The "Commonweal" and the American Catholic Laity, 1924–1976.* New York: Garland, 1988.

Brisbin, Richard A., Jr. "Censorship, Ratings, and Rights: Political Order and Sexual Portrayals in American Movies." *Studies in American Political Development* 16 (Spring 2002): 1–27.

Brook, Vincent. "Courting Controversy: The Making and Selling of *Baby Doll* and the Demise of the Production Code." *Quarterly Review of Film and Video* 184, no. 4 (2001), 347–61.

Cadegan, Una M. "Guardians of Democracy or Cultural Storm Troopers? American Catholics and the Control of Popular Media, 1934–1966." *Catholic Historical Review* 87 (April 2001): 252–82.

Cannato, Vincent J. *The Ungovernable City: John Lindsay and His Struggle to Save New York.* New York: Basic, 2001.

Carmen, Ira. *Movies, Censorship, and the Law.* Ann Arbor: University of Michigan Press, 1966.

Carney, Ray. *Cassavetes on Cassavetes.* London: Faber and Faber, 2001.

Carroll, Noel. "Art and Ethical Criticism: An Overview of Recent Directions of Research." *Ethics* 110 (January 2000): 350–87.

Cawelti, John G., ed. *Focus on "Bonnie and Clyde."* Englewood Cliffs, N.J.: Prentice-Hall, 1973.

Ciment, Michel. *Kazan on Kazan.* New York: Viking, 1974.

Coates, Paul. *Film at the Intersection of High and Mass Culture.* New York: Cambridge University Press, 1994.

Cogley, John. *Report on Blacklisting: Movies.* New York: Fund for the Republic, 1956.

Cook, David A. *Lost Illusions: American Cinema in the Shadow of Watergate and Vietnam, 1970–1979.* Berkeley: University of California Press, 2000.

Couvares, Francis, ed. *Movie Censorship and American Culture.* Washington, D.C.: Smithsonian Institution Press, 1996.

Davis, Francis. *Afterglow: A Last Conversation with Pauline Kael.* Cambridge, Mass.: Da Capo, 2002.

Decherney, Peter. *Hollywood and the Cultural Elite: How the Movies Became American.* New York: Columbia University Press, 2005.

The "Deep Throat" Papers. New York: Manor, 1973.

De Grazia, Edward. *Girls Lean Back Everywhere: The Law of Obscenity and the Assault on Genius.* New York: Random House, 1992.

Dickstein, Morris. *Leopards in the Temple: The Transformation of American Fiction, 1945–1970.* Cambridge, Mass.: Harvard University Press, 1999.

Dobi, Stephen J. "Cinema 16: America's Largest Film Society." Ph.D. diss., New York University, 1984.

Draper, Ellen. "'Controversy Has Probably Destroyed Forever the Context': *The Miracle* and Movie Censorship in America in the 1950s." In *Controlling Hollywood: Censorship and Regulation in the Studio Era*, edited by Matthew Bernstein, 187–200. New Brunswick, N.J.: Rutgers University Press, 1999.

Fish, Stanley. *There's No Such Thing as Free Speech and It's a Good Thing, Too.* New York: Oxford University Press, 1994.

Freeland, Cynthia. *But Is It Art?* New York: Oxford University Press, 2001.

Friedman, Andrea. *Prurient Interests: Gender, Democracy, and Obscenity in New York City, 1909–1945.* New York: Columbia University Press, 1991.

Friedman, Lester D. *Arthur Penn's "Bonnie and Clyde."* Cambridge: Cambridge University Press, 2000.

———. *Bonnie and Clyde.* London: British Film Institute, 2000.

Gablik, Suzi. *Has Modernism Failed?* New York: Thames and Hudson, 1984.

Gardner, Gerald, ed. *The Censorship Papers: Movie Censorship Letters from the Hays Office, 1934 to 1968.* New York: Dodd, Mead, 1987.

Gerard, Lillian. "*The Miracle* in Court." *American Film* 2 (July–August 1977): 26–30.

Giglio, Ernest D. "The Decade of the Miracle, 1952–1962: A Study in Censorship of the American Motion Picture." Ph.D. diss., Syracuse University, 1964.

Giovacchini, Saverio. "'Hollywood Is a State of Mind': New York Film Culture and the Lure of Los Angeles from 1930 to the Present." In *New York and Los Angeles: Politics, Society, and Culture; A Comparative View,* edited by David Halle, 423–47. Chicago: University of Chicago Press, 2003.

Gomery, Douglas. *Shared Pleasures: A History of Movie Presentation in the United States.* Madison: University of Wisconsin Press, 1992.

Guilbaut, Serge. *How New York Stole the Idea of Modern Art: Abstract Expressionism, Freedom, and the Cold War.* Chicago: University of Chicago Press, 1983.

Gurstein, Rochelle. *The Repeal of Reticence: America's Cultural and Legal Struggles over Free Speech, Obscenity, Sexual Liberation, and Modern Art.* New York: Hill and Wang, 1996.

Haberski, Raymond J., Jr. *It's Only a Movie: Films and Critics in American Culture.* Lexington: University Press of Kentucky, 2001.

Heins, Marjorie. *Not in Front of the Children: "Indecency," Censorship, and the Innocence of Youth.* New York: Hill and Wang, 2001.

———. *Sex, Sin, and Blasphemy: A Guide to America's Censorship Wars.* New York: New Press, 1998.

Hentoff, Nat. *Free Speech for Me—but Not for Thee: How the American Left and Right Relentlessly Censor Each Other.* New York: HarperPerennial, 1993.

Hoberman, J., *Dream Life: Movies, Media, and the Mythology of the Sixties.* New York: New Press, 2003.

———. *On Jack Smith's "Flaming Creatures" and Other Secret-Flix of Cinemaroc.* New York: Granary/Hips Road, 2001.

Hoberman, J., and Edward Leffingwell. *Wait for Me at the Bottom of the Pool: The Writings of Jack Smith.* New York: High Risk, 1997.

Hoberman, J., and Jonathan Rosenbaum. *Midnight Movies.* New York: Harper and Row, 1983.

James, David E., ed. *To Free the Cinema: Jonas Mekas and the New York Underground.* Princeton, N.J.: Princeton University Press, 1992.

Jensen, Joli. *Is Art Good for Us? Beliefs about High Culture in American Life.* Lanham, Md.: Rowman and Littlefield, 2002.

Jowett, Garth. *Film: The Democratic Art.* Boston: Little, Brown, 1976.

―――. "'A Significant Medium for the Communication of Ideas': The *Miracle* Decision and the Decline of Motion Picture Censorship, 1952–1968." In *Movie Censorship and American Culture,* edited by Francis G. Couvares, 510–36. Washington, D.C.: Smithsonian Institution Press, 1996.

Julius, Anthony. *Transgressions: The Offences of Art.* Chicago: University of Chicago Press, 2002.

Jummonville, Neil. *Critical Crossings: The New York Intellectuals in Postwar America.* Berkeley: University of California Press, 1991.

Kael, Pauline. *For Keeps: 30 Years at the Movies.* 2nd ed. New York: Plume, 1996.

Kammen, Michael. *The Lively Arts: Gilbert Seldes and the Transformation of Cultural Criticism in the United States.* New York: Oxford University Press, 1996.

Kerr, Walter. *Criticism and Censorship.* Milwaukee: Bruce, 1954.

Koch, Stephen. *Stargazer: Andy Warhol's World and His Films.* New York: Marion Boyars, 1985. (Orig. pub. 1973.)

Kolker, Robert. *A Cinema of Loneliness: Penn, Stone, Kubrick, Scorsese, Spielberg, Altman.* New York: Oxford University Press, 2000.

Kramer, Hilton. *The Twilight of the Intellectuals: Culture and Politics in the Era of the Cold War.* Chicago: Ivan R. Dee, 1999.

Leff, Leonard J., and Jerold L. Simmons. *The Dame in the Kimono: Hollywood, Censorship, and the Production Code from the 1920s to the 1960s.* New York: Doubleday, 1990.

Lewis, Jon. *Hollywood v. Hard Core: How the Struggle over Censorship Saved the Modern Film Industry.* New York: New York University Press, 2000.

Lhamon, W. T., Jr. *Deliberate Speed: The Origins of a Cultural Style in the American 1950s.* 2nd ed. Cambridge: Harvard University Press, 2002.

Lopate, Phillip. *American Movie Critics: An Anthology from the Silents until Now.* New York: Library of America, 2006.

―――. *Totally, Tenderly, Tragically: Essays and Criticism from a Lifelong Love Affair with the Movies.* New York: Anchor, 1998.

Lyons, Charles. *The New Censors: Movies and the Culture Wars.* Philadelphia: Temple University Press, 1997.

Macdonald, Dwight. "Masscult and Midcult." In *Against the American Grain,* 3–75. New York: Random House, 1962.

MacDonald, Scott. *Cinema 16: Documents toward a History of the Film Society.* Philadelphia: Temple University Press, 2002.

Madoff, Steven Henry, ed. *Pop Art: A Critical History.* Berkeley: University of California Press, 1997.

Magliozzi, Ronald S. "Witnessing the Development of Independent Film Culture in New York: An Interview with Charles L. Turner." *Film History* 12 (2000): 72–96.

May, Lary. *The Big Tomorrow: Hollywood and the Politics of the American Way.* Chicago: University of Chicago Press, 2000.

Mayer, Arthur. *Merely Colossal: The Story of the Movies from the Long Chase to the Chaise Lounge*. New York: Simon and Schuster, 1953.

McClure, Arthur F., ed. *The Movies: An American Idiom*. Rutherford, N.J.: Farleigh Dickinson Press, 1971.

McGreevy, John T. "Thinking on One's Own: Catholicism in the American Intellectual Imagination, 1928–1960." *Journal of American History* 84 (June 1997): 97–131.

McLaughlin, Mary L. "A Study of the National Catholic Office for Motion Pictures." Ph.D. diss., University of Wisconsin, 1974.

Mekas, Jonas. *Movie Journal: The Rise of a New American Cinema, 1959–1971*. New York: Collier, 1972.

Miller, Frank. *Censored Hollywood: Sex, Sin, and Violence on Screen*. Atlanta: Turner, 1994.

O'Connell, Shaun. *Remarkable, Unspeakable New York: A Literary History*. Boston: Beacon, 1995.

Postman, Neil. *Amusing Ourselves to Death: Public Discourse in the Age of Show Business*. New York: Penguin, 1985.

Randall, Richard S. "Censorship: From *The Miracle* to *Deep Throat*." In *The American Film Industry*, edited by Tino Balio, 510–36. Madison: University of Wisconsin Press, 1985.

Rosenberg, Bernard, and David Manning White, eds. *Mass Culture: The Popular Arts in America*. Glencoe, Ill.: Free Press, 1957.

Rosenberg, Harold. "Pop Culture: Kitsch Criticism." In *The Tradition of the New*, 259–68. New York: McGraw Hill, 1965. (Orig. pub. 1959.)

Sayre, Wallace S., and Herbert Kaufman. *Governing New York City: Politics in the Metropolis*. New York: Norton, 1965.

Schatz, Thomas. *Boom and Bust: American Cinema in the 1940s*. Berkeley: University of California Press, 1999.

———. *The Genius of the System: Hollywood Filmmaking in the Studio Era*. New York: Henry Holt, 1988.

Schickel, Richard, and John Simon. *Film 67/68*. New York: Simon and Schuster, 1968.

Schumach, Murray. *The Face on the Cutting Room Floor: The Story of Movie and Television Censorship*. New York: William Morrow, 1964.

Seldes, Gilbert. *The Great Audience*. New York: Viking, 1950.

———. *The Seven Lively Arts*. New York: Viking, 1924.

Seligman, Craig. *Sontag and Kael: Opposites Attract Me*. New York: Counterpoint, 2004.

Sitney, P. Adams. *Film Culture Reader*. New York: Praeger, 1970.

———. *Visionary Film: The American Avant-Garde, 1943–2000*. 3rd ed. New York: Oxford University Press, 2002.

Sjöman, Vilgot. *I Am Curious—Yellow*. New York: Grove, 1968.

Skinner, James M. *The Cross and the Cinema: The Legion of Decency and the National Office of Motion Pictures, 1933–1970*. Westport, Conn.: Praeger, 1993.

Sklar, Robert. *Movie-Made America: A Cultural History of the Movies.* 2nd ed. New York: Vintage, 1994.

Sklar, Robert, and Charles Musser, eds. *Resisting Images: Essays on Cinema and History.* Philadelphia: Temple University Press, 1990.

Smith, Richard. *Getting into "Deep Throat."* New York: Playboy, 1973.

Sontag, Susan. "A Feast for Open Eyes." *Nation,* 13 April 1964. Reprinted in *Cinema Nation: The Best Writing on Film from the "Nation," 1913–2000,* edited by Carl Bromley, 207–14. New York: Thunder's Mouth, 2000.

———. "Notes on Camp." In *Against Interpretation,* 275–92. New York: Dell, 1966.

———. "One Culture and the New Sensibility." In *Against Interpretation,* 293–304. New York: Dell, 1966.

———. "The Pornographic Imagination." In *Styles of Radical Will,* 35–73. New York: Viking, 1994. (Orig. pub. 1969.)

Sova, Dawn B. *Forbidden Films: Censorship Histories of 125 Motion Pictures.* New York: Checkmark, 2001.

Staiger, Janet. *Perverse Spectators: The Practices of Film Reception.* New York: New York University Press, 2000.

Steigerwald, David. *Culture's Vanities: The Paradox of Cultural Diversity in a Globalized World.* Lanham, Md.: Rowman and Littlefield, 2004.

Suarez, Juan A. *Biker Boys, Drag Queens, and Superstars: Avant-Garde, Mass Culture, and Gay Identities in the 1960s Underground Cinema.* Bloomington: Indiana University Press, 1996.

Taylor, Greg. *Artists in the Audience: Cults, Camp, and American Film Criticism.* Princeton, N.J.: Princeton University Press, 1999.

Thompson, David, and Ian Christie, eds. *Scorsese on Scorsese.* London: Faber and Faber, 1989.

Turan, Kenneth, and Stephen Zito. *Sinema: American Pornographic Films and the People Who Make Them.* New York: Praeger, 1974.

Tyler, Parker. *Underground Film: A Critical History.* New York: Da Capo, 1995. (Orig. pub. 1969.)

Van Allen, Rodger. *The "Commonweal" and American Catholicism: The Magazine, the Movement, the Meaning.* Philadelphia: Fortress, 1974.

Wakefield, Dan. *New York in the 1950s.* Boston: Houghton and Mifflin, 1992.

Walsh, Frank. *Sin and Censorship: The Catholic Church and the Motion Picture Industry.* New Haven, Conn.: Yale University Press, 1996.

Warhol, Andy, and Pat Hackett. *POPism: The Warhol '60s.* New York: Harcourt, Brace, Jovanovich, 1980.

Warshow, Robert. *The Immediate Experience.* New York: Atheneum, 1975.

Wasson, Haidee. *Museum Movies: The Museum of Modern Art and the Birth of Art Cinema.* Berkeley: University of California Press, 2005.

Watson, Steve. *Factory Made: Warhol and the Sixties.* New York: Pantheon, 2003.

Weinberg, Herman G. *Saint Cinema: Writings on Film, 1929–1970.* 2nd ed. New York: Frederick Ungar, 1980.

Westin, Alan. *The "Miracle" Case: The Supreme Court and the Movies.* Tuscaloosa: University of Alabama Press, 1961.

Whitfield, Stephen J. *The Culture of the Cold War.* 2nd ed. Baltimore: Johns Hopkins University Press, 1996.

Wilinsky, Barbara. *Sure Seaters: The Emergence of Art House Cinema.* Minneapolis: University of Minnesota Press, 2001.

Williams, Linda. *Hard Core: Power, Pleasure, and the "Frenzy of the Visible."* Berkeley: University of California Press, 1999.

Wittern-Keller, Laura. "Freedom of the Screen: The Legal Challenges to State Film Censorship, 1915–1981." Ph.D. diss., University at Albany, State University of New York, 2003.

Wolfe, Tom. *The Kandy-Colored, Tangerine-Flake, Streamline Baby.* New York: Farrar, Straus and Giroux, 1965.

Index

Adler, Renata, 196
Agee, James, 40; critique of Cinema 16, 106–7
American Civil Liberties Union: and *The Bicycle Thief*, 16; and *The Miracle*, 44, 57
Anger, Kenneth, 90–92
art: controversial or transgressive, 1, 7, 10–11, 69–71, 74, 98, 212–14, 224–26. *See also* Mekas, Jonas; Sontag, Susan; Warhol, Andy
Atkinson, Brooks, 5, 44
avant-garde cinema, 96, 98; demise of, 173–75. *See also* Cinema 16; Mekas, Jonas; Tyler, Parker; Vogel, Amos; Warhol, Andy

Baby Doll (1956): billboard for, 61–62; Catholic protests against, 81–82; Catholic response to, 77–79; and John Cogley, 84–85; and Commonweal, 82–85; and Elia Kazan, 61–62; and Francis Cardinal Spellman, 62–64, 82–84; and Martin Quigley, 83–84; premiere of, 79; public reaction to, 79–80; and the waning of Catholic control over movies, 63–64; and William Mooring, 78
Baez, Joan, 115
Barry, Iris, 99–101, 103

Beatty, Warren, 189
Berns, Walter: on the intellectualization of pornography, 221–23. *See also* New York Times
Bicycle Thief, The (1949), 13–18; battle over distribution of, 14–15; reviews of, 13–14
Birth of a Nation, The (1915), 42, 81
Black, Gregory: on *The Bicycle Thief*, 13; on fall-out from *Baby Doll*, 86; on the Legion of Decency, 25–26
Bonnie and Clyde (1967): Bosley Crowther's critique of, 187–88; Pauline Kael's defense of, 191–93; popularity of, 188–89, 191
Blue Movie (1969), 211–12
Blumenthal, Ralph, 216; and "Porno Chic," 218–20. *See also* Deep Throat
Brakhage, Stan, 117–18
Breen, Joseph: and *The Bicycle Thief*, 14–17
Brooklyn Tablet, 25; and *Baby Doll*, 77–78
Burger, Warren, 221
Burstyn, Joseph, 34–36; and *The Bicycle Thief*, 14–18; and *The Miracle*, 44, 57–59
Burstyn v. Wilson, 35, 57–58

Cadegan, Una M., 27, 64, 88
Cahiers du cinema, 116
Callenbach, Ernest: and debate over Cinema 16, 108–9
camp, 118; Susan Sontag's idea of, 9–10
Canby, Vincent, 156; and *Blue Movie*, 211–12; and *I Am Curious—Yellow*, 206–7
Carney, Raymond: on *Shadows* controversy, 124
Catholic Action, 28
"Catholic as Philistine" (Clancy), 56–57
Catholic censorship. *See* Legion of Decency; Quigley, Martin; Spellman, Francis Cardinal. *See also specific movies*
Catholic cultural criticism, 64–66; and differences among Catholic journals, 28–30. *See also* Clancy, William; Cogley, John; *Commonweal*; Kerr, Walter
Catholic War Veterans, 45, 50
censorship: and American culture, 2–3, 12; and Joseph Breen, 14–17; and Joseph Burstyn, 15–17, 35; and the Legion of Decency, 24–30; and Martin Quigley, 6–7; and New York City, 5–6, 23, 152–53; New York City license commissioner, 30–31; New York Motion Picture Division, 31–34; and Production Code Administration, 19–21; as a web of control, 4–5, 16–18, 23–24, 34–35, 58. *See also specific court cases and movies*
Chapin, Schuyler, 166–67
Chaplin, Charlie: and patrons of the New Yorker Theater, 115

Chelsea Girls, The (1966), 156–66; and box-office success, 160; in cultural context, 157–58; and reception by New York film critics, 162–65
Christgua, Bob: on Jonas Mekas and *The Chelsea Girls*, 156–57
Cinema 16: audience survey, 104–5; and controversial films, 92; demise of, 118; membership, 96; origins of, 92–94; problems with, 106–10; and *Shadows*, 124–25; significance of, 95–96, 110; and avant-garde filmmakers, 95–96. *See also* MacDonald, Scott; Mekas, Jonas; Vogel, Amos; Vogel, Marcia
Clancy, William, 66; and Catholic cultural criticism, 72–73; and *The Miracle*, 55–57
Clockwork Orange, A (1972), 227–28
Cogley, John, 66, 67; and *Baby Doll*, 84–85
Collier, Peter: critique of *Bonnie and Clyde*, 193
Commonweal: and *Baby Doll*, 82–85; and Catholic cultural criticism, 64–66, 74; and *The Miracle*, 55–56; and New York City, 68; and the Second Vatican Council, 67. *See also* Clancy, William; Cogley, John; Kerr, Walter
confrontational cinema: and Amos Vogel's programming, 97, 103–5; and Jonas Mekas, 120
Crist, Judith, 196
Crowther, Bosley: Andrew Sarris's critique of, 229–30; argues for a free screen, 40, 41, 42, 49, 54–55, 59–60, 177–80; attacks

Bonnie and Clyde, 187–90,
    200–201; and Arthur Penn, 196;
    and *The Birth of a Nation*, 181;
    and *Blackboard Jungle*, 180–81;
    and *The Chelsea Girls*, 165;
    conflicted legacy of, 40–41, 54–
    55, 59–60, 229–30; criticized by
    readers, 186; defends *The Bicycle
    Thief*, 16; defends controversial
    films, 177–78; defends *The
    Miracle* as art, 41; defends *The
    Miracle* in the *Atlantic Monthly*,
    52–53; and democratic culture,
    42; derided by younger critics,
    167–69, 190–92; and *The Dirty
    Dozen*, 185–86; early years at
    the *New York Times*, 43–44;
    "free screen," campaign for,
    46–47; "Hollywood versus New
    York," 37–38; on *In Cold Blood*,
    200–201; and Joseph Burstyn, 59;
    letters to Crowther regarding *The
    Miracle*, 46–52; letters regarding
    article in the *Atlantic Monthly*,
    53–55; limits of a free screen,
    181–85, 198–201; and obscenity
    in films, 202; and the Paramount
    case, 20–21; retirement of,
    195–99; and Richard Schickel,
    197–99; as a social critic, 230; and
    violent movies, 185–87; William
    Allen White Seminar, 199–201

Deep Throat (1972): confiscation of,
    215; cultural context of, 1–2, 6,
    11; as a cultural event, 215–18;
    opinion of Judge Joel J. Tyler,
    217–18; and porno chic, 218–20;
    trial of, 216–18
democratic culture, 3–4, 6, 42,
    75–77, 221, 223, 228–29

Deren, Maya, 92
Dirty Dozen, The (1967), 185–86
Dobi, Stephen J., 95

Emshwiller, Ed, 98
Ernst, Morris, 218
Eternal Jew, The (1940), 97–98
Everhart, Robert, 61–62

Film-Makers' Cinematheque, 157;
    and *The Chelsea Girls*, 160
Film-Makers' Cooperative, 127.
    See also Mekas, Jonas; New
    American Cinema
Film-Makers' Distribution Center,
    157
Fireworks (1947), 90–92
Flaming Creatures (1963), 119–20;
    and Amos Vogel, 139–41; Arthur
    Knight's review of, 131; initial
    controversy over, 133–36; Jonas
    Mekas's reviews of, 128–31; Ken
    Kelman's reviews of, 132; the
    Nation's support for, 141–42;
    public premiere, 129; and Susan
    Sontag, 143–44; trial of, 138–39,
    148–50. *See also* Mekas, Jonas
Flick, Hugh, 33–34. *See also* New
    York State Motion Picture
    Division
foreign films, 36–37
free screen, 40, 46, 54, 59–60, 177–
    80. *See also* Crowther, Bosley
free speech, 3–4

Galeazzi, Enrico Pietro, 84
Gaul, Ken, 209
Gerard, Lillian, 42–43, 49–50, 196
Gewen, Barry, 225–26
Gilliat, Penelope, 190
Ginsberg, Allen, 146–47

Ginzburg, Ralph: obscenity case,
    154–55
Goldstein, Al, 114, 215, 220
Grazer, Brian, 1–2
Greenwich Village: as a culture
    of controversy, 145–48; and
    harassment by New York City
    officials, 143–44
Griffith, Richard, 99–102
Gruen, John, 162
Gurstein, Rochelle: on Susan
    Sontag, 12, 224

"Have the Movies Failed Us?" (radio
    forum), 21
Hoberman, Jim: on Bonnie and
    Clyde, 190, 191; on Shadows
    controversy, 125–26
Hodgins, Eric, 22
Hollywood: and audience
    dissatisfaction, 21–23; economic
    dominance of, 18–19. See also
    Paramount case; Production
    Code Administration

I Am Curious—Yellow (1966), 203–9
Image in the Snow (1952), 104
Inside Deep Throat (2005), 1–2
irony: and aesthetics, 1, 12; as
    cultural criticism, 12; and
    cultural extremes, 1, 4; decline
    of, 214

Jacobs, Lewis, 91
Johnston, Eric, 23–24

Kael, Pauline: attacks movie
    brutality, 226–27; contrasted with
    Bosley Crowther, 40, 194–95;
    criticism of Bosley Crowther,
    192, 194–95; defense of Bonnie

and Clyde, 191–93; and "Yahoo"
    culture, 228
Kauffmann, Stanley, 196; testifies
    in trial of I Am Curious—Yellow,
    205
Kazan, Elia, 61, 62, 96
Kelly, Robert, 94–95
Kerr, Walter: and Catholic cultural
    criticism, 66–67, 69–71; "Catholics
    and Hollywood," 68–69
Knights of Columbus, 45, 78–79
Knokke-le-Zoute film festival
    (Belgium): and Flaming
    Creatures, 133–34
Koch, Edward, 145–47
Koch, Stephen: critique of Andy
    Warhol's movies, 164–65
Kracauer, Siegfried, 97–98
Kramer, Hilton: critique of Susan
    Sontag, 10
Kroll, Jack, 162

Lady in a Cage (1964), 183
Lane, Anthony: review of Inside
    Deep Throat, 2
La Ronde (1950), 60
Lavery, Emmett: "Is Decency
    Enough?" 71–72
Lawson, John Howard: critique of
    Bonnie and Clyde, 194
Legion of Decency, 64, 68–69, 71,
    152; and classification of movies,
    25, 72, 87; and collusion with
    Production Code Administration,
    27–28; legacy of, 88–89; and
    pledge, 26, 42, 87; pressure to
    change, 75, 83, 85–88; and the
    web of control, 5, 17, 23, 24–30.
    See also Baby Doll; The Miracle;
    Quigley, Martin; Spellman,
    Francis Cardinal

Lewis, Anthony: and demise of censorship laws, 153
Lewis, Jon: on introduction of MPAA rating system, 152; on pornography and democracy, 2–3
Lindsay, John V., 145, 214–15, 220
Little, Thomas F., 87
Lolita (1962 film), 86
Looram, Mary, 25, 27, 88

Maas, Willard, 104, 118
Macdonald, Dwight: critique of Cinema 16, 107–10; critique of Jonas Mekas, 109
MacDonald, Scott: significance of Cinema 16, 94
Mailer, Norman: and the Village Voice, 123; testifies in I Am Curious—Yellow case, 204
Markopoulos, Gregory, 172
Mayer, Arthur: on Bosley Crowther, 195–96; and Joseph Burstyn 34, 37
McCaffrey, Edward T., 42–43, 45–47. See also New York City license commissioner
McLaughlin, Mary, 87, 88
Mekas, Jonas, 98, 110; and Amos Vogel, 127–28, 141, 170–71; and Andy Warhol, 160–62; arrest of, 119; background of, 121–22; and censorship, 132; critique of Cinema 16, 117, 127; breaking with traditions, 120–21, 126–28, 130, 132–33, 137; early criticism for the Village Voice, 123–24; and Film Culture, 122–23; and Film-Makers' Cooperative, 127; and Flaming Creatures, 119–20, 128; frustration with, 150–51, 157; Knokke-le-Zoute

film festival, 133–34; and New American Cinema, 126–28; and New York City movie culture, 120–23; and New York Erotic Film Festival, 210; and police harassment, 132, 135–37, 143; and pornography, 151; and protests for free expression, 147–48; preparations for trial over Flaming Creatures, 138–39; responds to Parker Tyler's criticism, 173; and Shadows, 124–25; and trial of Flaming Creatures, 148–50
Miller v. California (1973), 221
Miracle, The (1950), 35, 41–42; Catholic boycott of, 49–50, 53; controversial premiere of, 42–44; New York State hearing for, 45; popular reaction to controversy, 46–50, 53–54. See also Burstyn, Joseph; Crowther, Bosley; Gerard, Lillian; Legion of Decency
Miranda Prorus, 86
Montgomery, Paul, 216
Mooring, William, 78
Motion Picture Association of America (MPAA), 16
mulata de Cordoba, La (1946), 32–33
Murray, John Courtney: "Literature and Censorship," 75–77
Museum of Modern Art (New York), 98–103
Mussman, Toby, 167–69
Mutual v. Ohio, 35
My Son John (1952), 57

Nation: support for Flaming Creatures, 141–42

National Board of Review, 26–27
National Catholic Office for Motion
    Pictures, 88
National Catholic Welfare
    Conference, 75, 81
National Council on Freedom from
    Censorship, 27
Nevins, Sheila, 2
New American Cinema: Amos
    Vogel's critique of, 170–73; and
    difference from Cinema 16, 116–
    17, 127–28. See also Flaming
    Creatures; Mekas, Jonas
Newman, David: encounter with
    Bosley Crowther, 193–94
New York City license
    commissioner, 5, 44, 46, 156
New York City movie culture: and
    Bosley Crowther, 39–41; and
    Catholics, 63–64; and Cinema
    16, 94; decline of censorship,
    152–53; diversity of, 34, 102,
    110; and end of, as an idea, 158,
    171–72, 175, 177; and Jonas
    Mekas, 121–22; and Museum of
    Modern Art, 98–100; and New
    American Cinema, 127–28; and
    New Yorker Theater, 111–12; and
    obscene movies, 209; and Parker
    Tyler, 173; significance of, 4–5
New York Erotic Film Festival,
    209–11
New Yorker Theater, 110–16; record
    of audience reactions, 113–16.
    See also Talbot, Daniel
New York Film Critics Circle, 44, 50
New York Film Festival (1966),
    166–69
New York Post: and Spellman's
    condemnation of Baby Doll, 80
New York State Board of Regents, 45

New York State Motion Picture
    Division (censors), 5, 15–16,
    31–34. See also Miracle, The
New York Times: coverage of Deep
    Throat, 216, 218–20; and
    obscenity as art, 221–23; and
    obscenity cases, 154–55; and
    retirement of Bosley Crowther,
    195
Niblo, Fred, 17

obscene films: legal distinction, 202–
    3, 209, 221. See also Blue Movie;
    Chelsea Girls, The; Deep Throat;
    I Am Curious—Yellow; New York
    Erotic Film Festival; Weinraub,
    Bernard
Office catholique international du
    cinéma, 86

Paramount case, 20
Paris Theater: and controversy over
    The Miracle, 45, 49–50
Penn, Arthur, 196; and Bonnie and
    Clyde, 189–90; Mickey One, 184
Phillips, William, 154
Pike, James A., 84
porno chic, 218–21
pornography: and cultural criticism,
    11–12; as cultural rebellion,
    153–55; intellectualization of,
    218–23, 224–25
Production Code Administration:
    and Baby Doll, 63, 71–72,
    77–78; and The Bicycle Thief,
    14–17; demise of, 152; as part of
    the web of control, 5, 19–24, 59
Pryor, Thomas, 196

Quigley, Martin, 6, 24, 72, 86;
    and Baby Doll, 83–84; and

controversy over *The Miracle*, 50, 53

Reed, Rex, 115; and reaction to *I Am Curious—Yellow*, 207–8
Regelson, Rosalyn, 163–64
Renan, Sheldon, 168–69
Rossellini, Roberto, 36, 39
Roth v. United States, 202
Roud, Richard, 164

Samuels, Charles: on critical battle over *Bonnie and Clyde*, 190
Samuelson, Harold, 168–69
Sarris, Andrew: criticizes Bosley Crowther, 190, 229–30; critique of MoMA, 102; critique of sexualized cinema, 213–14, 220–21
Scanlon, Patrick F., 52
Schary, Dore: and Bosley Crowther, 180
Schatz, Thomas: and Hollywood's "special genius," 17
Schickel, Richard: and Bosley Crowther, 197–99
Schuman, Robert, 114
Seldes, Gilbert, 7–9, 23–24; and *The Miracle*, 52
Seligman, Craig: on Susan Sontag, 9–10, 228–29
Shadows (1959): controversy over, 124–27
Sica, Vittorio de, 13
Simon, John: defends *I Am Curious—Yellow* as art, 203–4, 206
Sitney, P. Adams: and Cinema 16, 105, 114, 117–18; and "What Are the New Critics Saying?" 168–69
Skillin, Edward S., 68
Smith, Jack, 119, 128, 132; and Jonas Mekas, 150–51. *See also Flaming Creatures*
Sontag, Susan, 7, 9–11, 227, 228–29; and *Flaming Creatures*, 142–43; and New Yorker Theater, 115; and *The Pornographic Imagination*, 10–11
Spellman, Francis Cardinal: and *Baby Doll*, 62–64, 82–84; and *The Miracle*, 45, 50–51; and moral degradation of New York City, 144–45
Starr, Cecile, 96, 100–101
Stauffacher, Frank, 100
Steele, Robert, 95
Steuer, Aron, 44
Supreme Court of the United States, 42, 57–59, 153, 202, 221

Talbot, Daniel, 110–13, 172. *See also* New Yorker Theater
Taylor, Greg: on Parker Tyler's vanguard criticism, 173–74
"Thirteen Confusions" (1966), 169–72; and responses to Amos Vogel, 172–73
Times Square Enforcement Coordination Committee, 215
Tomkins, Calvin, 164
Turner, Charles, 100
Tyler, Joel J.: and Andy Warhol, 156; opinion in *Deep Throat* case, 218; and trial over *Deep Throat*, 215–18
Tyler, Parker: and *Blue Movie*, 212; and the demise of avant-garde cinema, 173–75; introducing *Fireworks* at Cinema 16, 91–92; and New American Cinema, 172–73; and 1966 New York Film Festival, 168–69

Un chant d'amour (1950), 136–37
underground filmmakers. *See*
  avant-garde cinema; Cinema
  16; Mekas, Jonas; 1966 New
  York Film Festival; Tyler, Parker;
  Vogel, Amos; Warhol, Andy

Vann, Gerald, 69
Vogel, Amos: and avant-garde
  cinema, 90, 94–96, 98, 105,
  166; cataloging films, 96–97;
  and censors, 93–94; and *The
  Chelsea Girls*, 166, 170–71;
  and confrontational cinema,
  97–99, 103, 105–6; and Dwight
  Macdonald's criticism, 108; and
  Flaming Creatures, 139–41; as
  a gatekeeper of cinema, 103;
  ideology of, 93–94; and "invisible
  filmmakers," 92; and Jonas
  Mekas, 117, 127–28, 140–41,
  170–71; and programming
  underground films for the New
  York Film Festival, 166–67; and
  origins of Cinema 16, 92–93;
  and *Shadows*, 125; "Thirteen
  Confusions," 169–72. *See also*
  Cinema 16
Vogel, Marcia, 96, 99

Walsh, Frank, 74–75
Walsh, Moira, 88–89, 190
Warhol, Andy: and *Blue Movie*,
  211–12; and *The Chelsea Girls*,
  159–60, 227; and cinema as
  transgressive art, 155–56, 226;
  and *Frankenstein*, 226–27; and
  Jonas Mekas, 156, 160–62; and
  My Hustler, 156; and New York
  Erotic Film Festival, 209
Warshow, Robert, 40

Watson, Steve: on *The Chelsea Girls*,
  159–60
Ways of Love, The (1950), 39, 50. *See
  also Miracle, The*
"What Are the New Critics Saying?"
  (New York Film Festival),
  167–69
Weinberg, Joel, 212
Weinraub, Bernard: "Obscenity or
  Art?" 210–11
Wilinsky, Barbara, 37
Willis, Ellen, 220
Winsten, Archer: and *The Chelsea
  Girls*, 162; and Cinema 16, 106;
  and *Deep Throat*, 216
Wittern-Keller, Laura, 31–32, 44, 45
Work, Martin, 73–74,
World Theater, 12, 13